DIMENSIONS

and The Holograms

Facebook **facebook.com/idwpublishing**
Twitter **@idwpublishing**
YouTube **youtube.com/idwpublishing**
Tumblr **tumblr.idwpublishing.com**
Instagram **instagram.com/idwpublishing**

COLLECTION COVER BY
DEREK CHARM

LETTERS/DESIGN BY
SHAWN LEE

SERIES ASSISTANT EDITOR
CHASE MAROTZ

SERIES EDITOR
SARAH GAYDOS

COLLECTION EDITS BY
JUSTIN EISINGER
& ALONZO SIMON

PUBLISHER
GREG GOLDSTEIN

Licensed By:

ISBN: 978-1-68405-242-4   21 20 19 18   1 2 3 4

JEM AND THE HOLOGRAMS: DIMENSIONS. JUNE 2018. FIRST
PRINTING. HASBRO and its logo, JEM & THE HOLOGRAMS, and all
related characters are trademarks of Hasbro and are used with
permission. © 2018 Hasbro. All Rights Reserved. The IDW logo is
registered in the U.S. Patent and Trademark Office. IDW
Publishing, a division of Idea and Design Works, LLC. Editorial
offices: 2765 Truxtun Road, San Diego, CA 92106. Any similarities
to persons living or dead are purely coincidental. With the
exception of artwork used for review purposes, none of the
contents of this publication may be reprinted without the
permission of Idea and Design Works, LLC. Printed in Korea. IDW
Publishing does not read or accept unsolicited submissions of
ideas, stories, or artwork.

Originally published as JEM AND THE HOLOGRAMS: DIMENSIONS
issues #1–4.

Special thanks to John Barber; Hasbro's Andrea Hopelain,
Elizabeth Malkin, Ed Lane, Beth Artale, and Michael Kelly for their
invaluable assistance.

Greg Goldstein, President & Publisher
Robbie Robbins, EVP & Sr. Art Director
Matthew Ruzicka, CPA, Chief Financial Officer
David Hedgecock, Associate Publisher
Laurie Windrow, Sr. VP of Sales & Marketing
Lorelei Bunjes, VP of Digital Services
Jerry Bennington, VP of New Product Development
Eric Moss, Sr. Director, Licensing & Business Development

Ted Adams, Founder & CEO of IDW Media Holdings

ART BY **SOPHIE CAMPBELL**

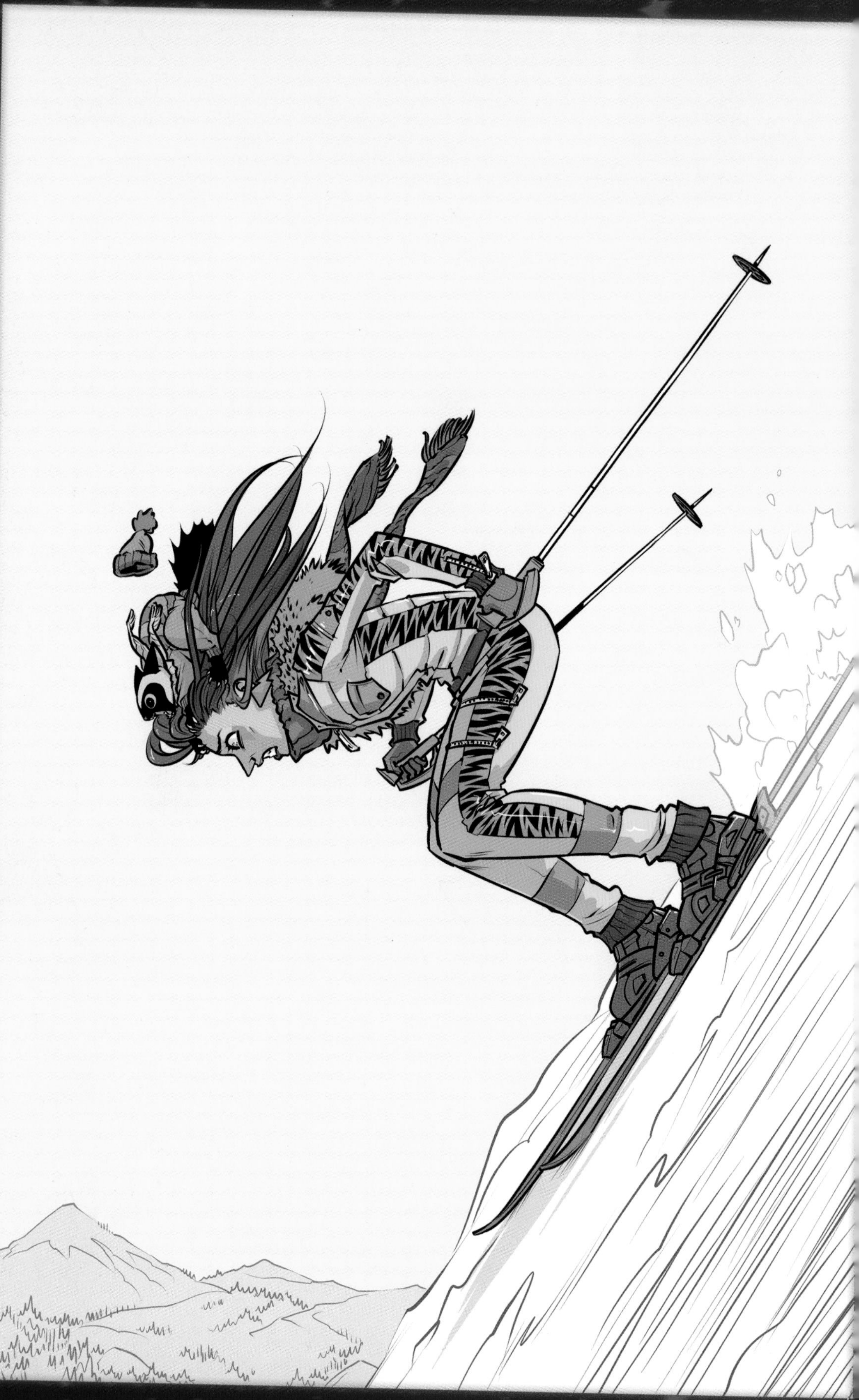

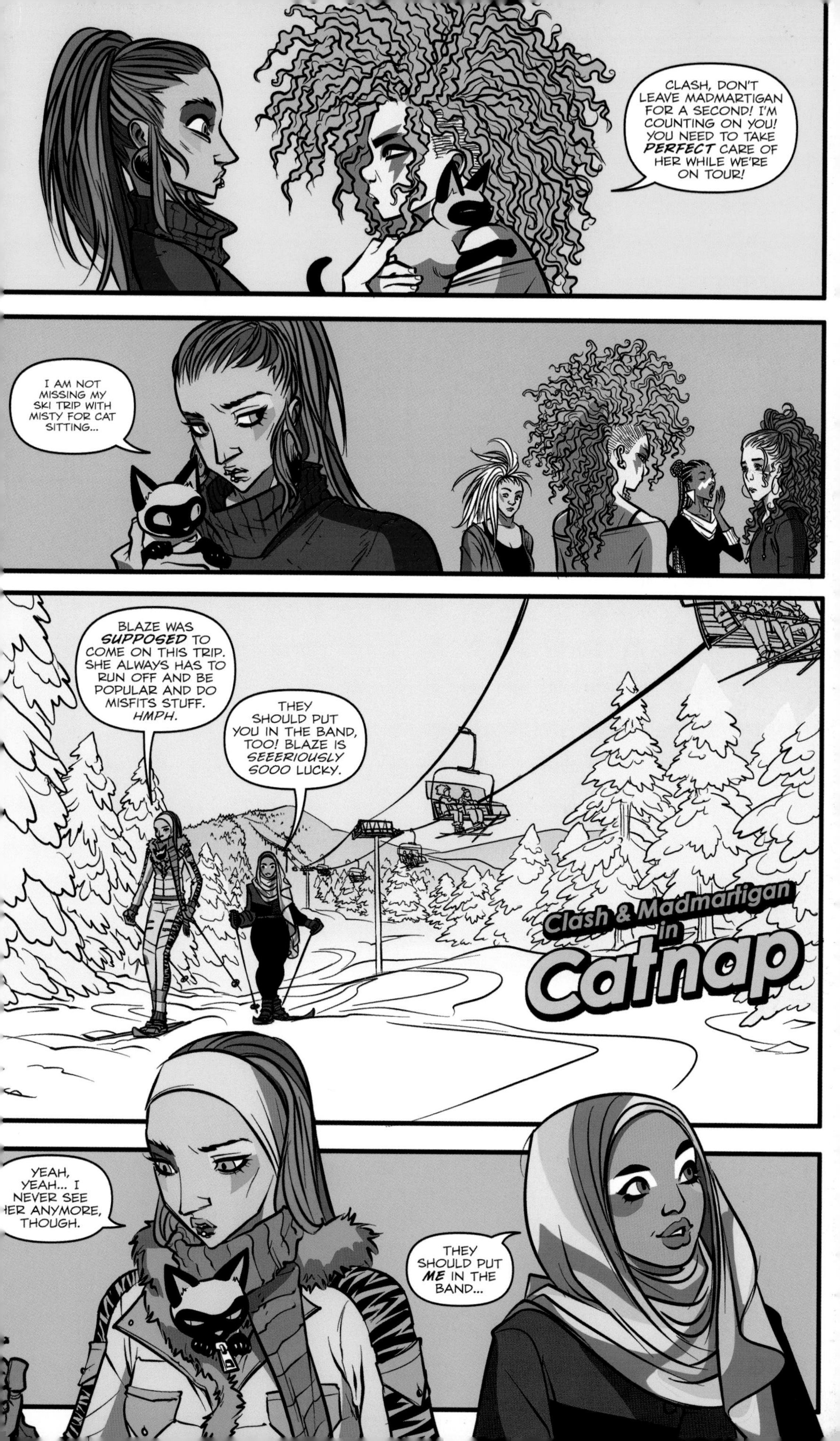
CLASH, DON'T LEAVE MADMARTIGAN FOR A SECOND! I'M COUNTING ON YOU! YOU NEED TO TAKE PERFECT CARE OF HER WHILE WE'RE ON TOUR!
I AM NOT MISSING MY SKI TRIP WITH MISTY FOR CAT SITTING...
BLAZE WAS SUPPOSED TO COME ON THIS TRIP. SHE ALWAYS HAS TO RUN OFF AND BE POPULAR AND DO MISFITS STUFF. HMPH.
THEY SHOULD PUT YOU IN THE BAND, TOO! BLAZE IS SEEERIOUSLY SOOO LUCKY.
Clash & Madmartigan in Catnap
YEAH, YEAH... I NEVER SEE HER ANYMORE, THOUGH.
THEY SHOULD PUT ME IN THE BAND...

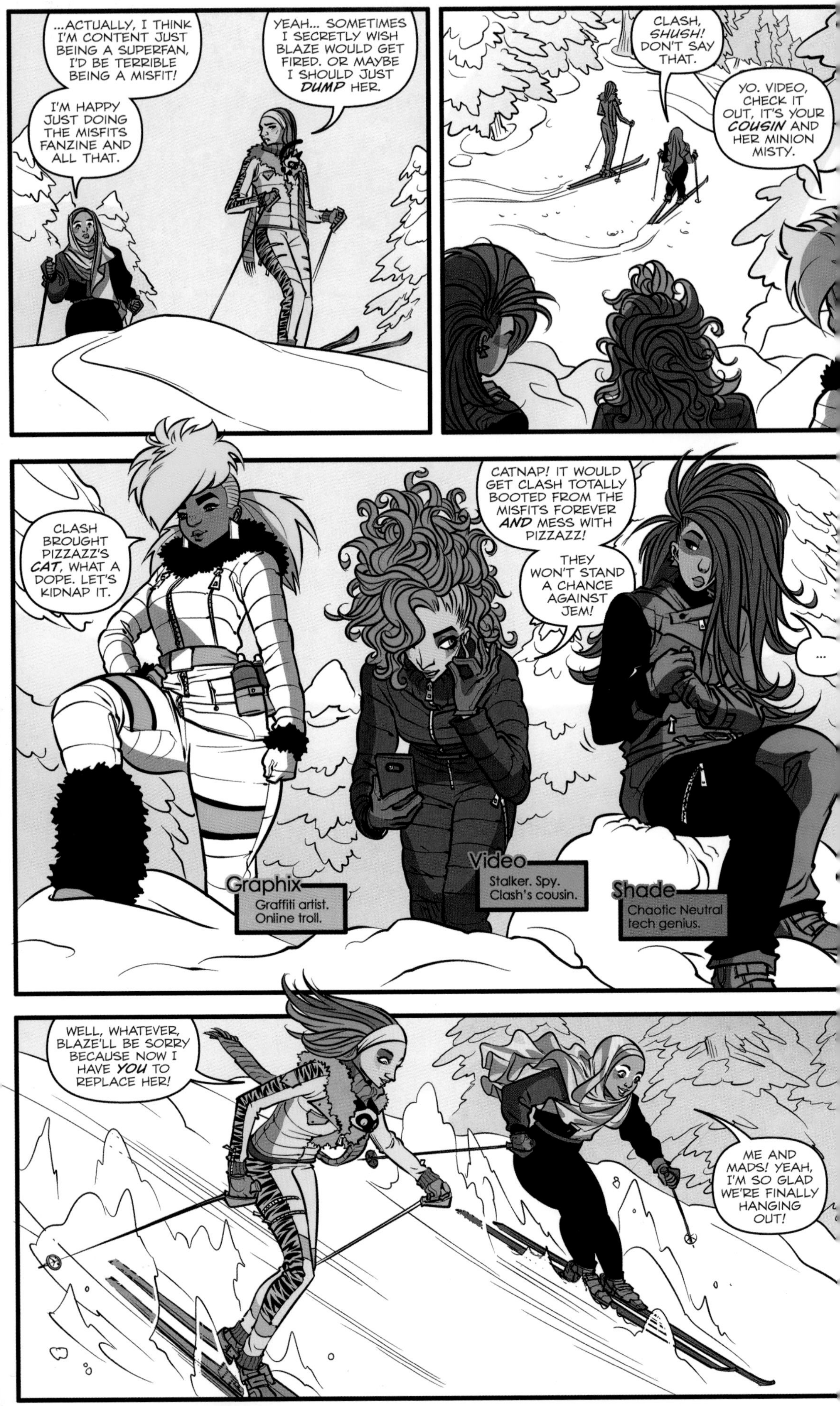
...ACTUALLY, I THINK I'M CONTENT JUST BEING A SUPERFAN, I'D BE TERRIBLE BEING A MISFIT!
I'M HAPPY JUST DOING THE MISFITS FANZINE AND ALL THAT.
YEAH... SOMETIMES I SECRETLY WISH BLAZE WOULD GET FIRED. OR MAYBE I SHOULD JUST DUMP HER.
CLASH, SHUSH! DON'T SAY THAT.
YO. VIDEO, CHECK IT OUT, IT'S YOUR COUSIN AND HER MINION MISTY.
CLASH BROUGHT PIZZAZZ'S CAT, WHAT A DOPE. LET'S KIDNAP IT.
CATNAP! IT WOULD GET CLASH TOTALLY BOOTED FROM THE MISFITS FOREVER AND MESS WITH PIZZAZZ!
THEY WON'T STAND A CHANCE AGAINST JEM!
...
Graphix
Graffiti artist. Online troll.
Video
Stalker. Spy. Clash's cousin.
Shade
Chaotic Neutral tech genius.
WELL, WHATEVER, BLAZE'LL BE SORRY BECAUSE NOW I HAVE YOU TO REPLACE HER!
ME AND MADS! YEAH, I'M SO GLAD WE'RE FINALLY HANGING OUT!

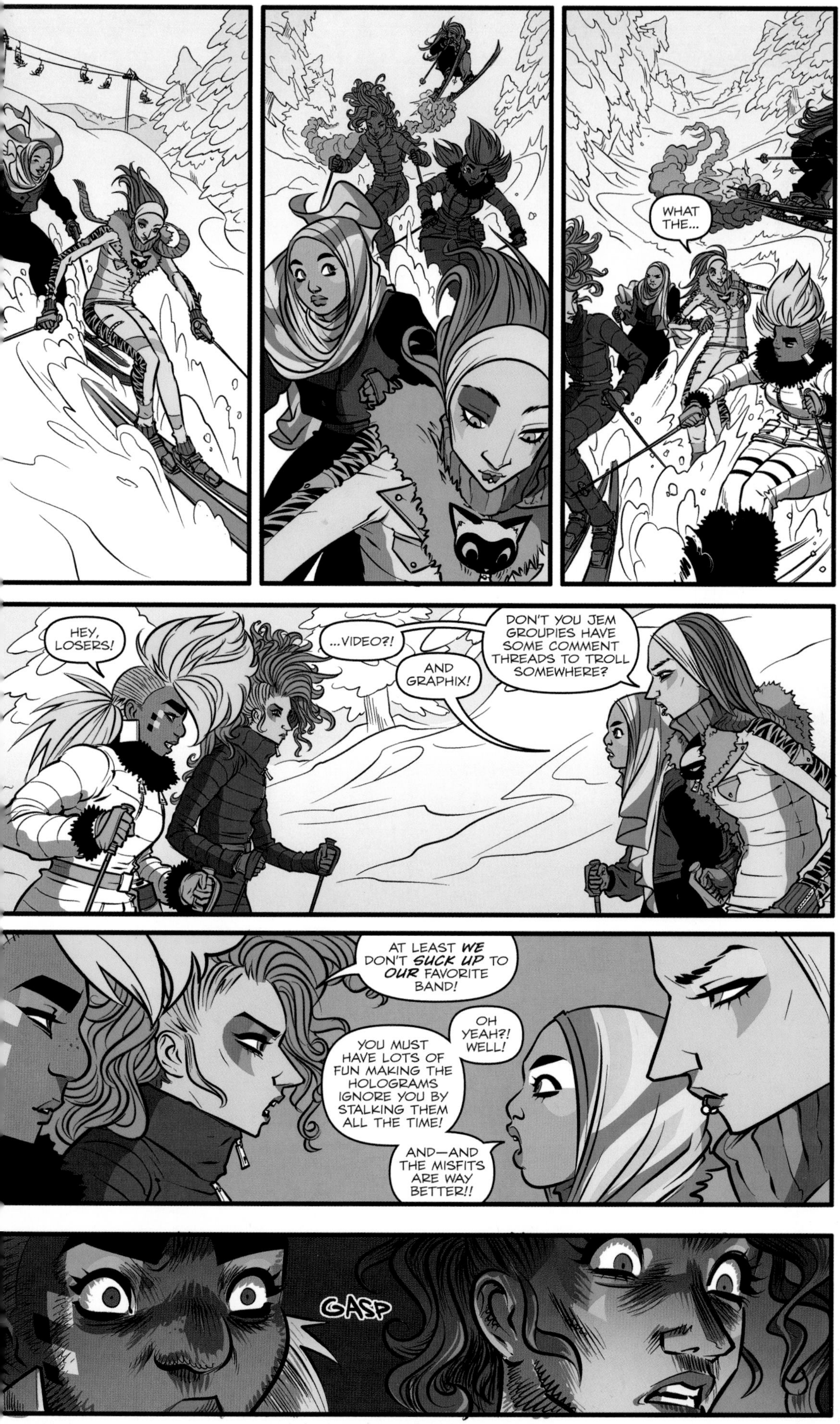
WHAT THE...
HEY, LOSERS!
...VIDEO?!
AND GRAPHIX!
DON'T YOU JEM GROUPIES HAVE SOME COMMENT THREADS TO TROLL SOMEWHERE?
AT LEAST WE DON'T SUCK UP TO OUR FAVORITE BAND!
OH YEAH?! WELL!
YOU MUST HAVE LOTS OF FUN MAKING THE HOLOGRAMS IGNORE YOU BY STALKING THEM ALL THE TIME!
AND—AND THE MISFITS ARE WAY BETTER!!
GASP

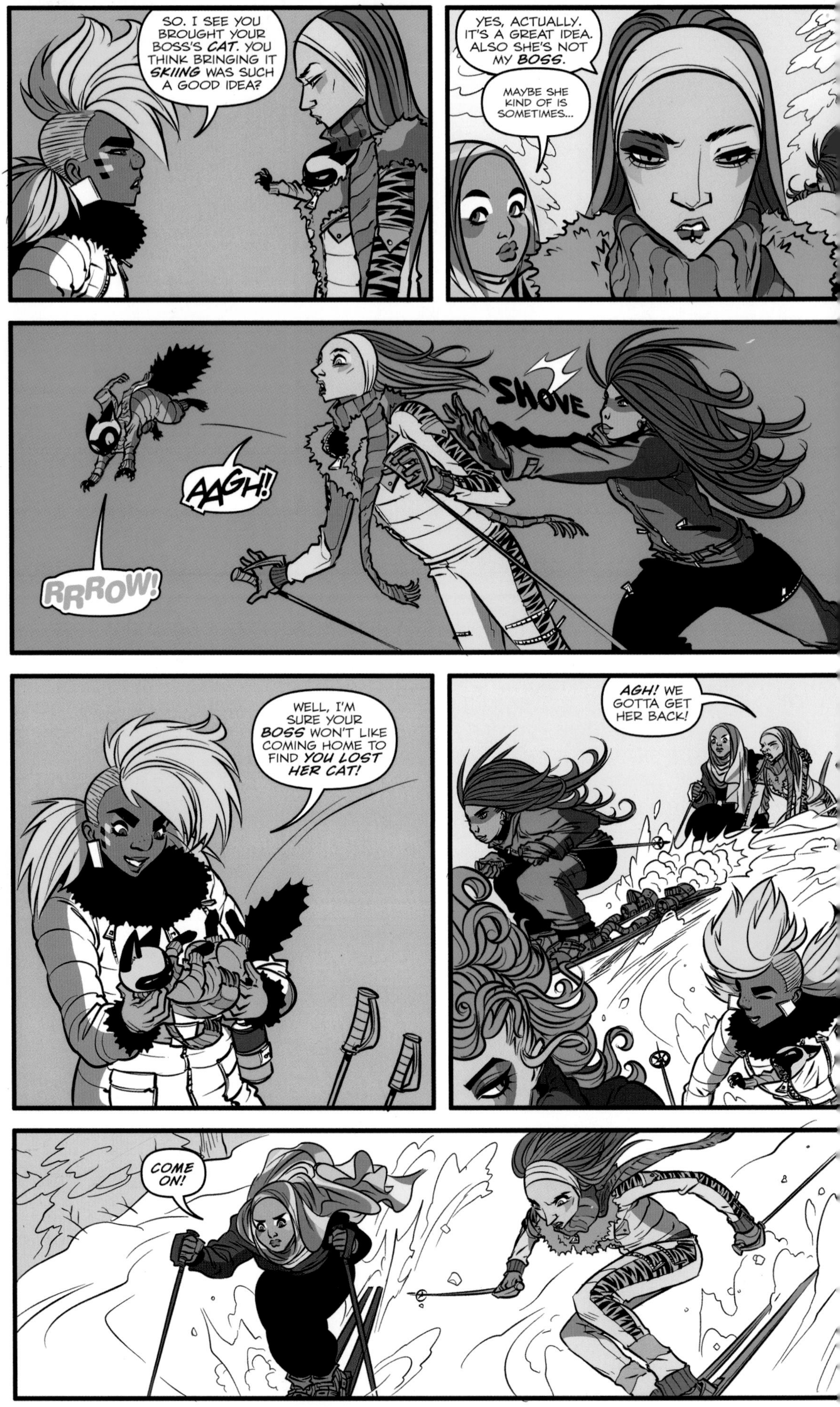
SO. I SEE YOU BROUGHT YOUR BOSS'S CAT. YOU THINK BRINGING IT SKIING WAS SUCH A GOOD IDEA?
YES, ACTUALLY. IT'S A GREAT IDEA. ALSO SHE'S NOT MY BOSS.
MAYBE SHE KIND OF IS SOMETIMES...
SHOVE
AAGH!
RRROW!
WELL, I'M SURE YOUR BOSS WON'T LIKE COMING HOME TO FIND YOU LOST HER CAT!
AGH! WE GOTTA GET HER BACK!
COME ON!

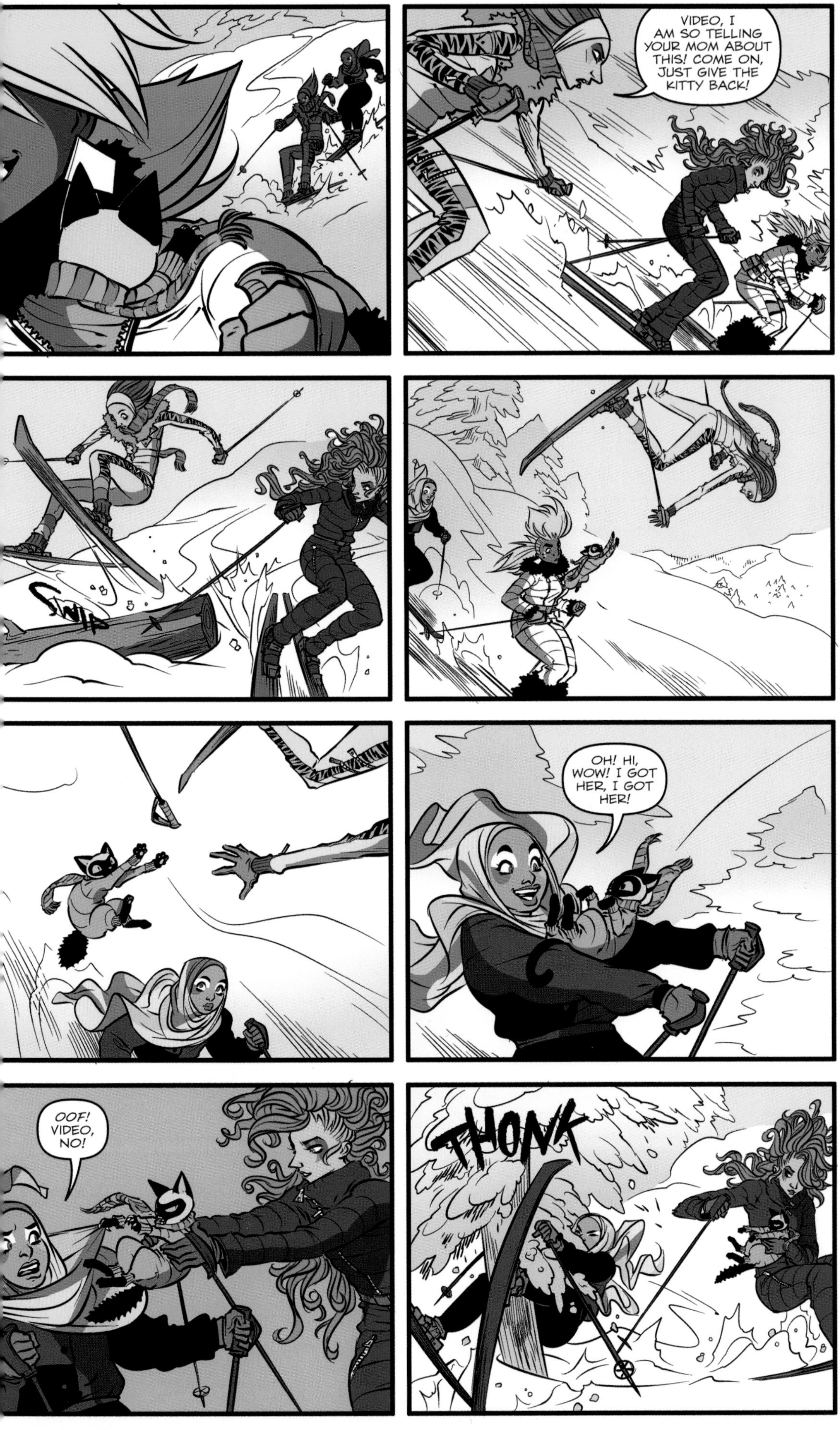
VIDEO, I AM SO TELLING YOUR MOM ABOUT THIS! COME ON, JUST GIVE THE KITTY BACK!
SNIP
OH! HI, WOW! I GOT HER, I GOT HER!
OOF! VIDEO, NO!
THONK

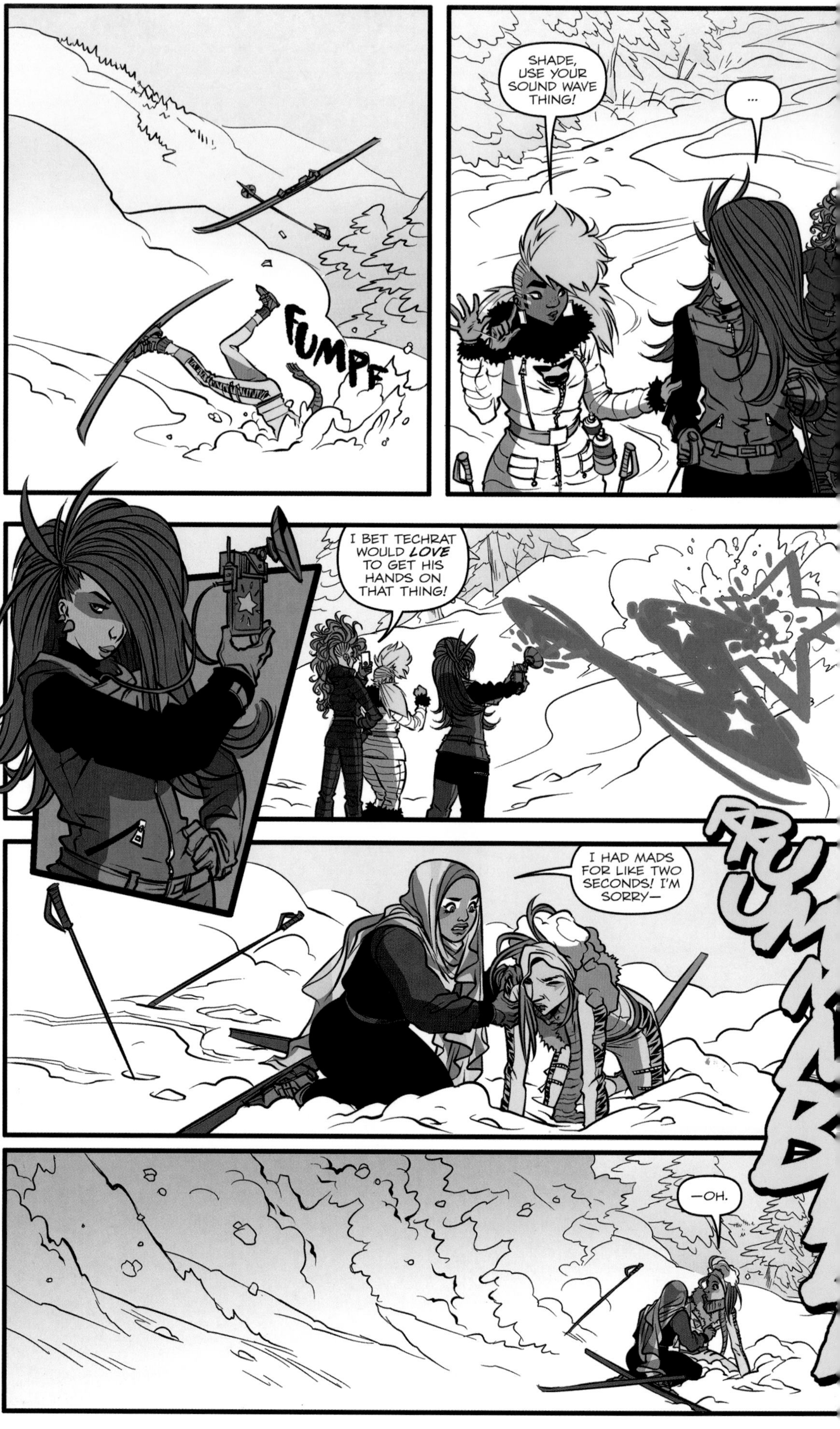
FUMPF
SHADE, USE YOUR SOUND WAVE THING!
...
I BET TECHRAT WOULD LOVE TO GET HIS HANDS ON THAT THING!
RRUMMBBB
I HAD MADS FOR LIKE TWO SECONDS! I'M SORRY—
—OH.

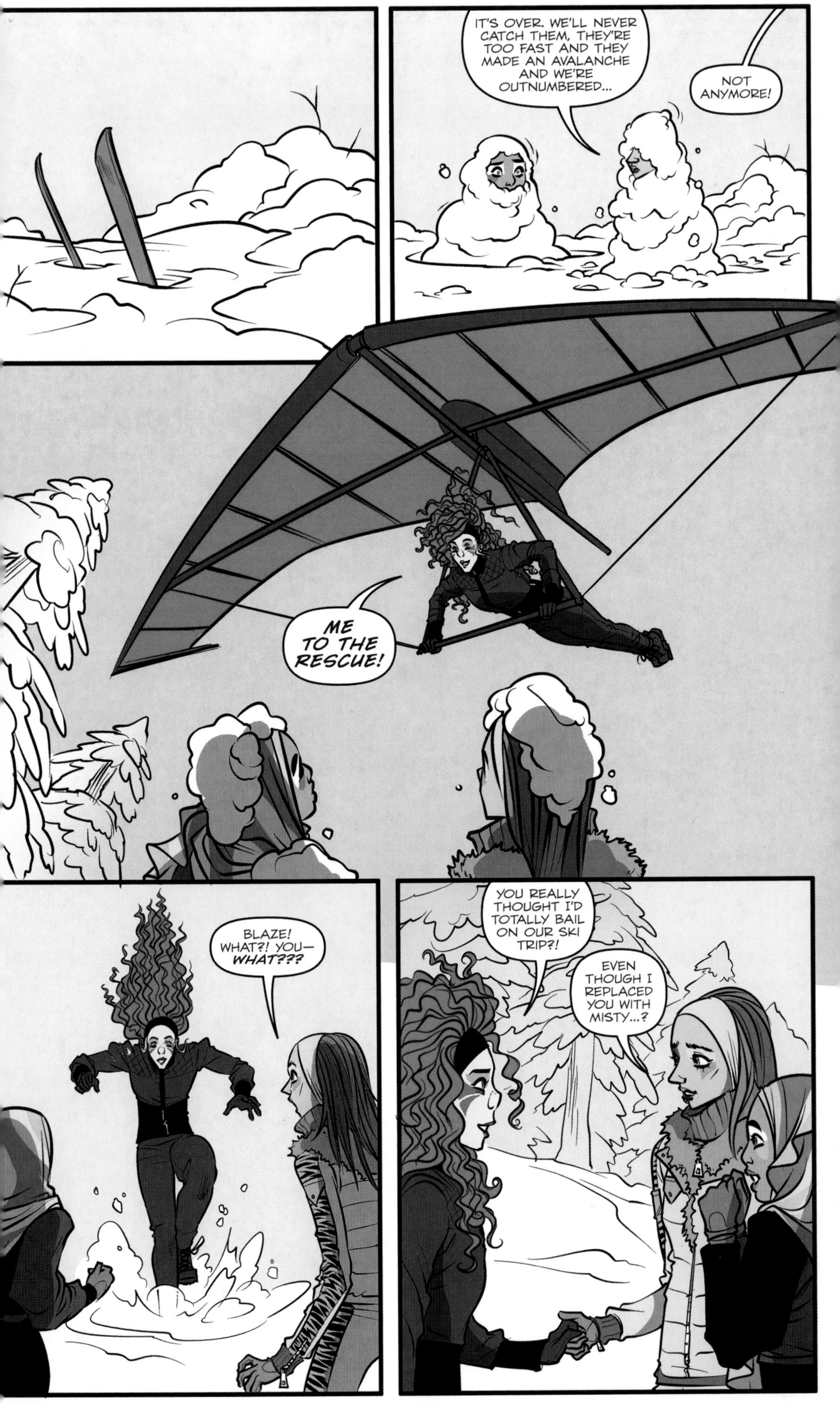
IT'S OVER. WE'LL NEVER CATCH THEM, THEY'RE TOO FAST AND THEY MADE AN AVALANCHE AND WE'RE OUTNUMBERED...
NOT ANYMORE!
ME TO THE RESCUE!
BLAZE! WHAT?! YOU— WHAT???
YOU REALLY THOUGHT I'D TOTALLY BAIL ON OUR SKI TRIP?!
EVEN THOUGH I REPLACED YOU WITH MISTY...?

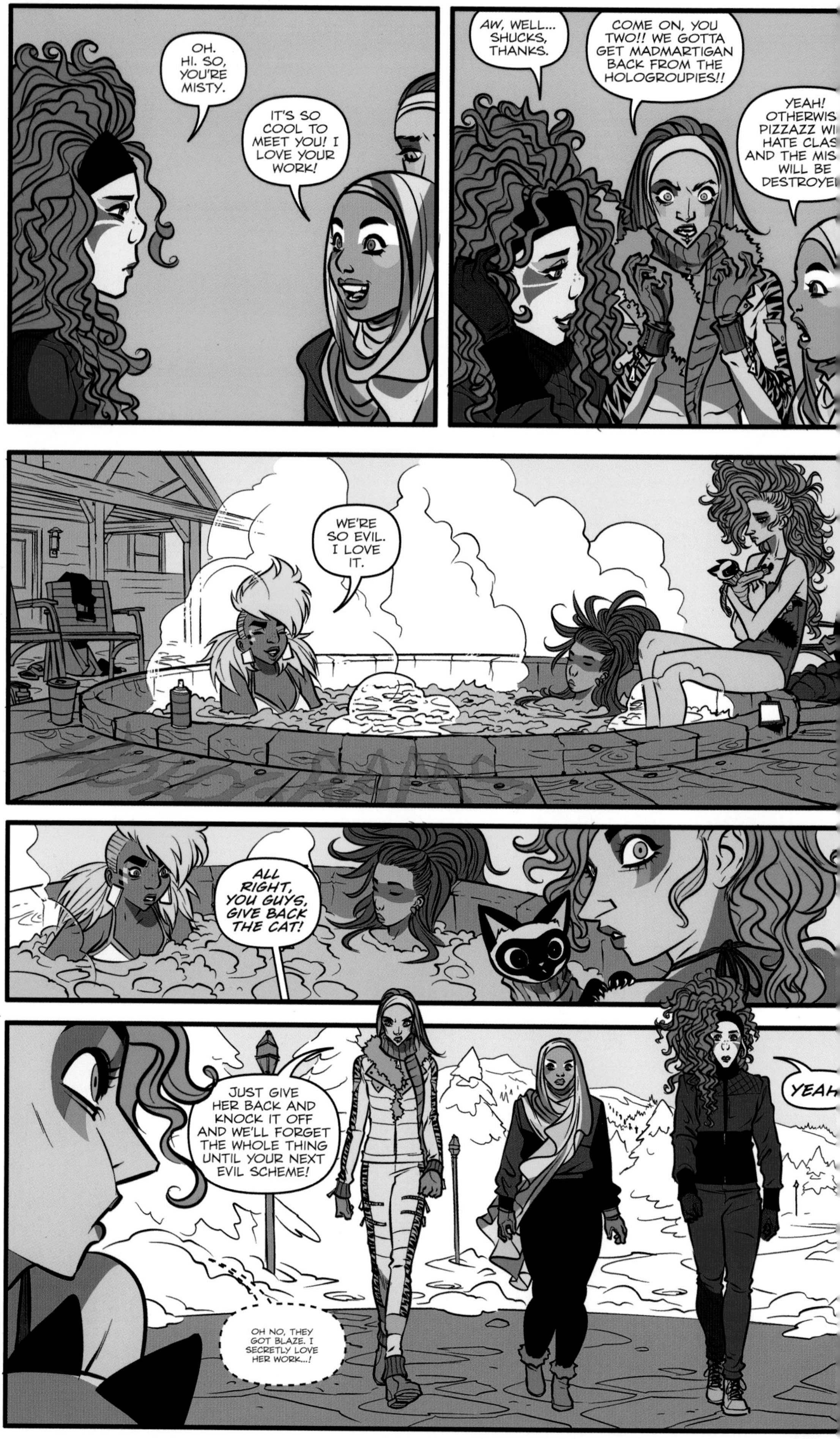
OH. HI. SO, YOU'RE MISTY.
IT'S SO COOL TO MEET YOU! I LOVE YOUR WORK!
AW, WELL... SHUCKS, THANKS.
COME ON, YOU TWO!! WE GOTTA GET MADMARTIGAN BACK FROM THE HOLOGROUPIES!!
WE'RE SO EVIL. I LOVE IT.
ALL RIGHT, YOU GUYS, GIVE BACK THE CAT!
JUST GIVE HER BACK AND KNOCK IT OFF AND WE'LL FORGET THE WHOLE THING UNTIL YOUR NEXT EVIL SCHEME!
OH NO, THEY GOT BLAZE. I SECRETLY LOVE HER WORK...!

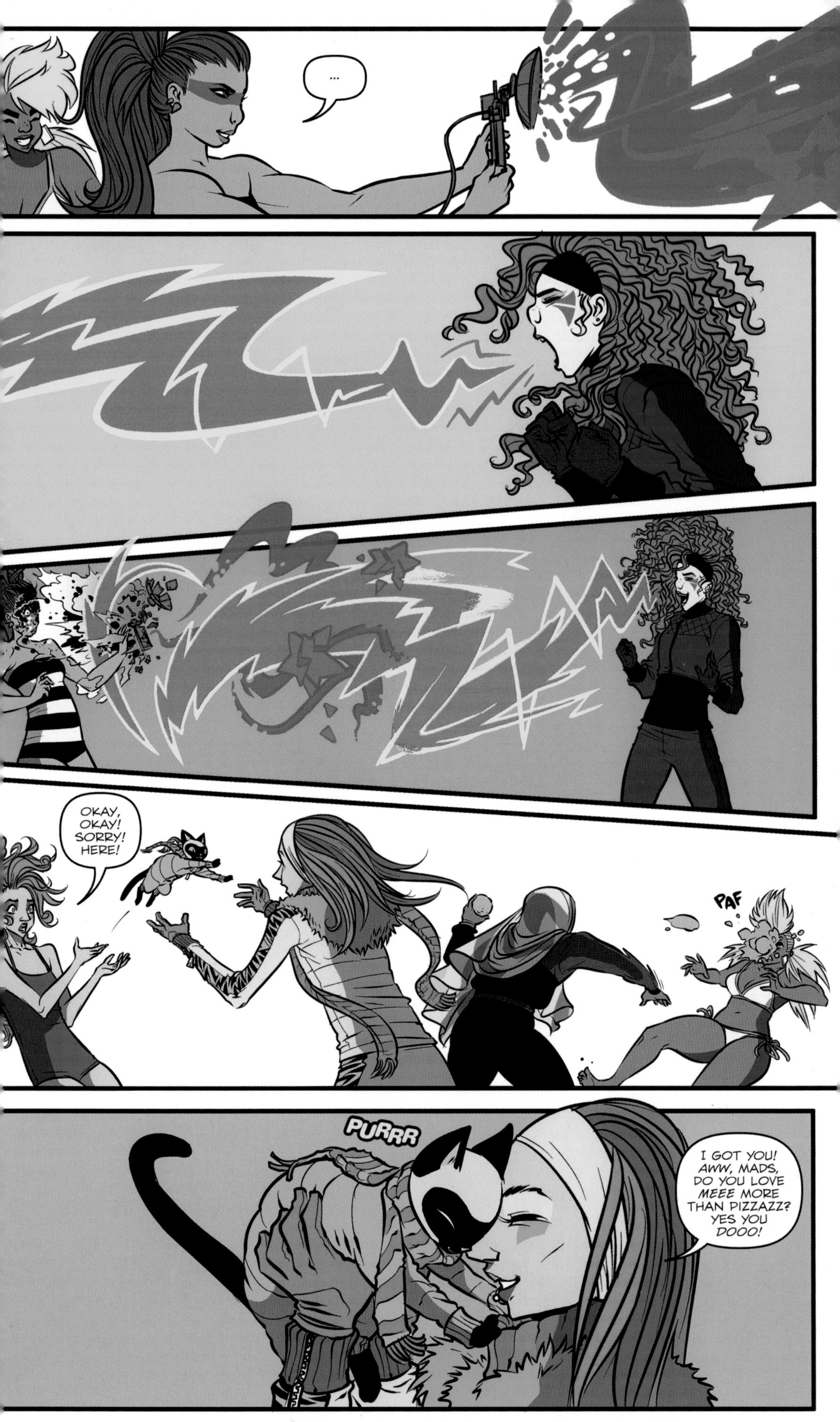
...
OKAY, OKAY! SORRY! HERE!
PAF
PURRR
I GOT YOU! AWW, MADS, DO YOU LOVE MEEE MORE THAN PIZZAZZ? YES YOU DOOO!

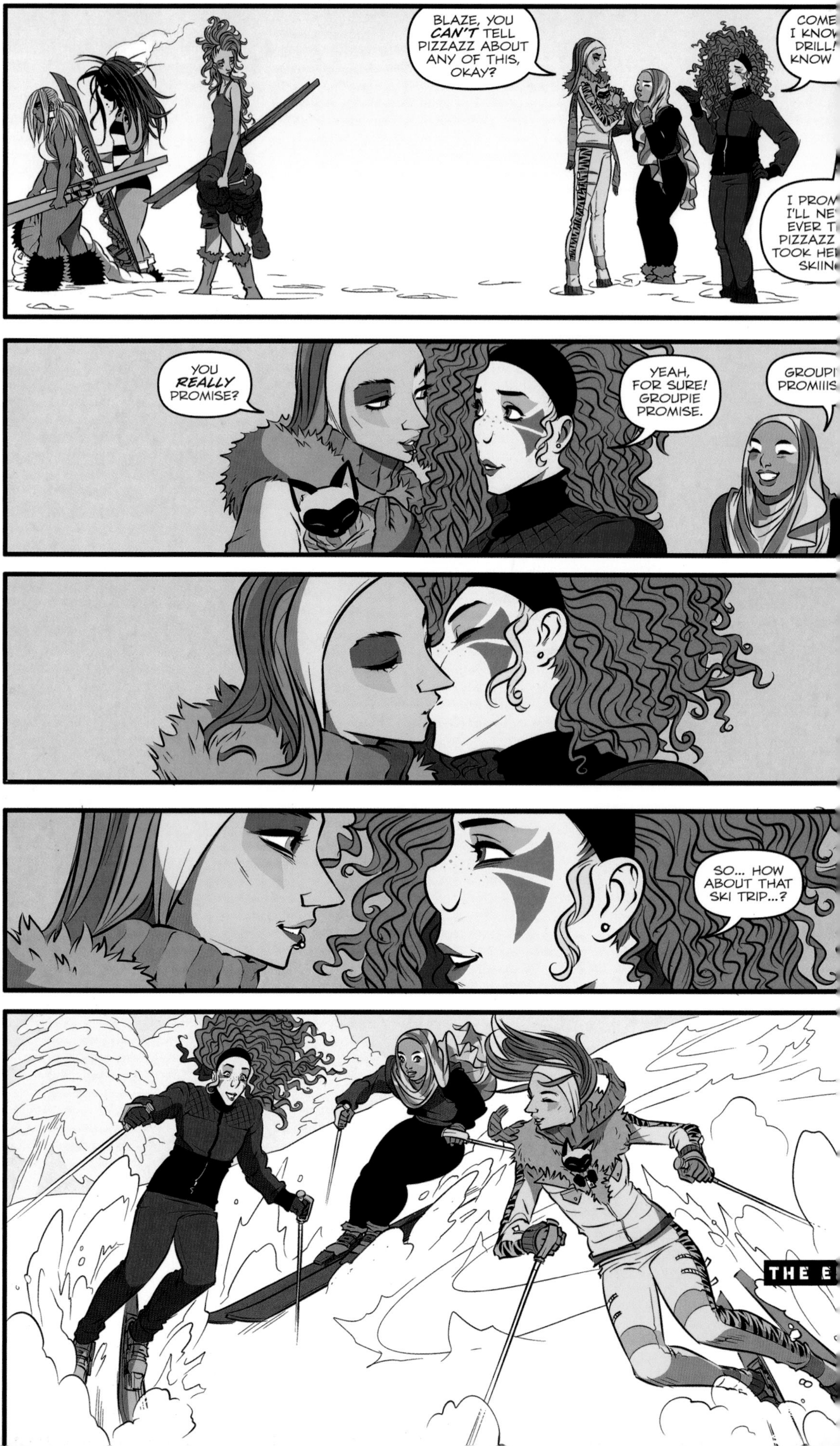
BLAZE, YOU *CAN'T* TELL PIZZAZZ ABOUT ANY OF THIS, OKAY?
COME I KNO DRILL! KNOW
I PROM I'LL NE EVER T PIZZAZZ TOOK HE SKIIN
YOU *REALLY* PROMISE?
YEAH, FOR SURE! GROUPIE PROMISE.
GROUPI PROMIIIS
SO... HOW ABOUT THAT SKI TRIP...?

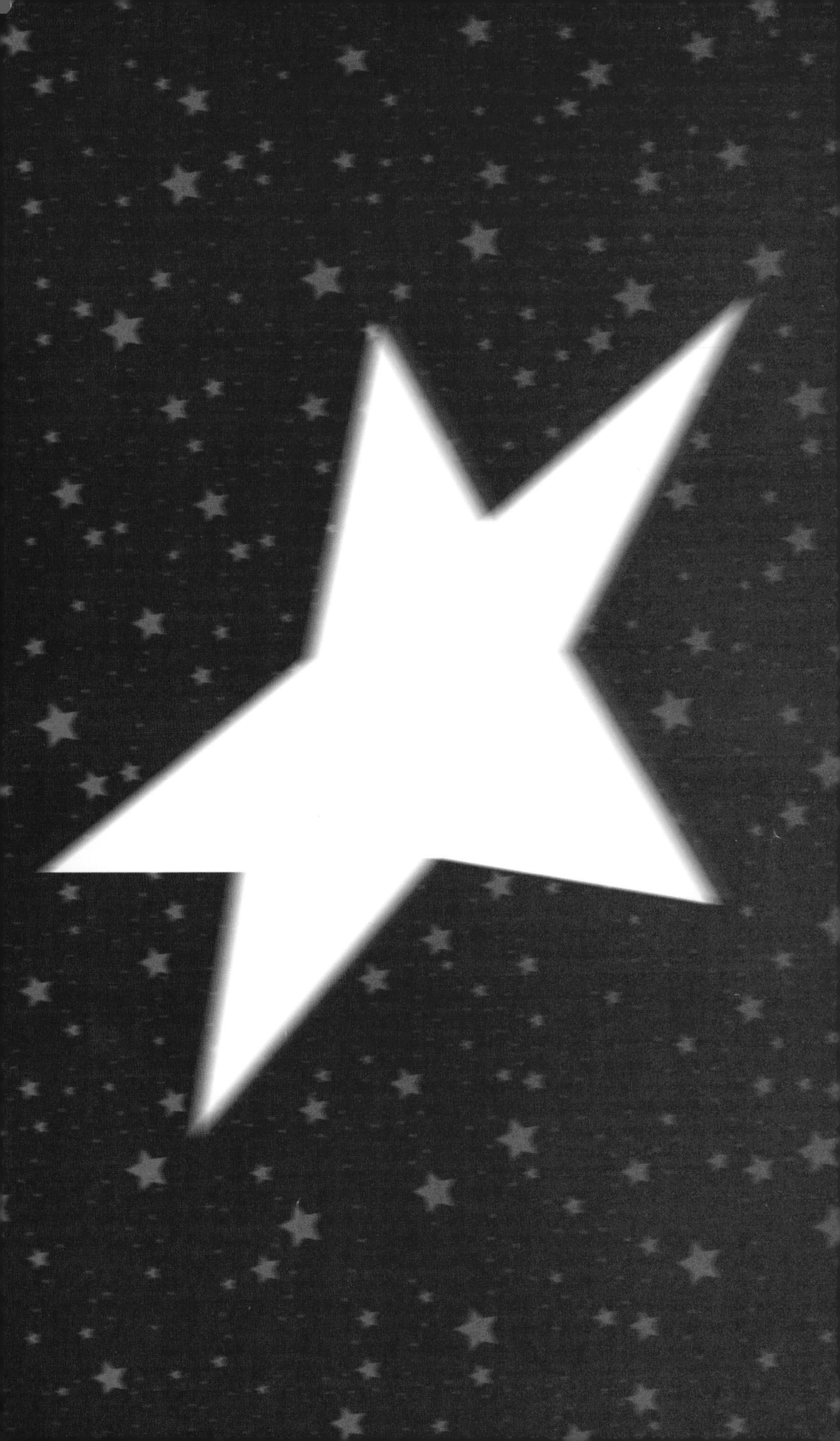

ART BY **TANA FORD**

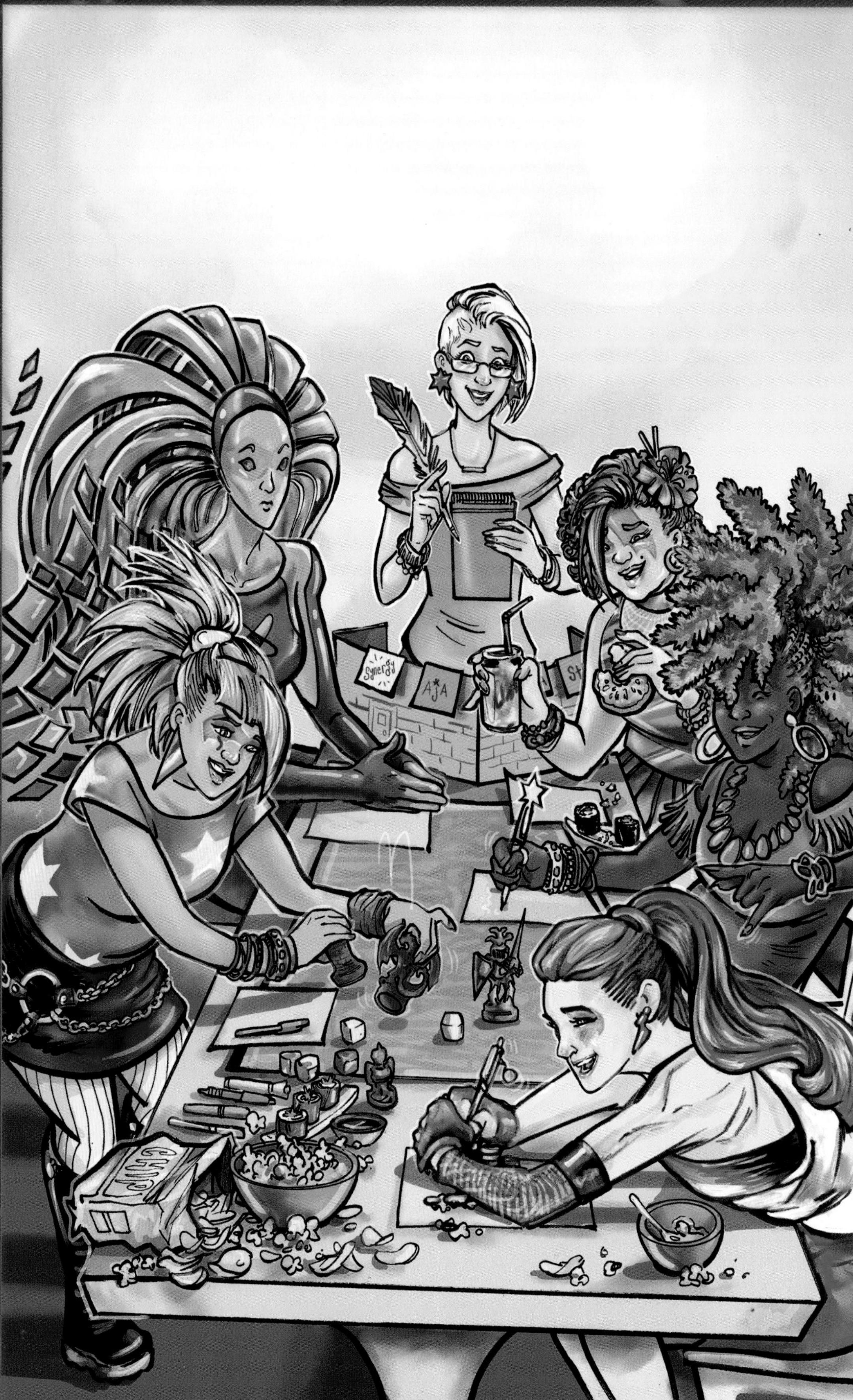
Synergy

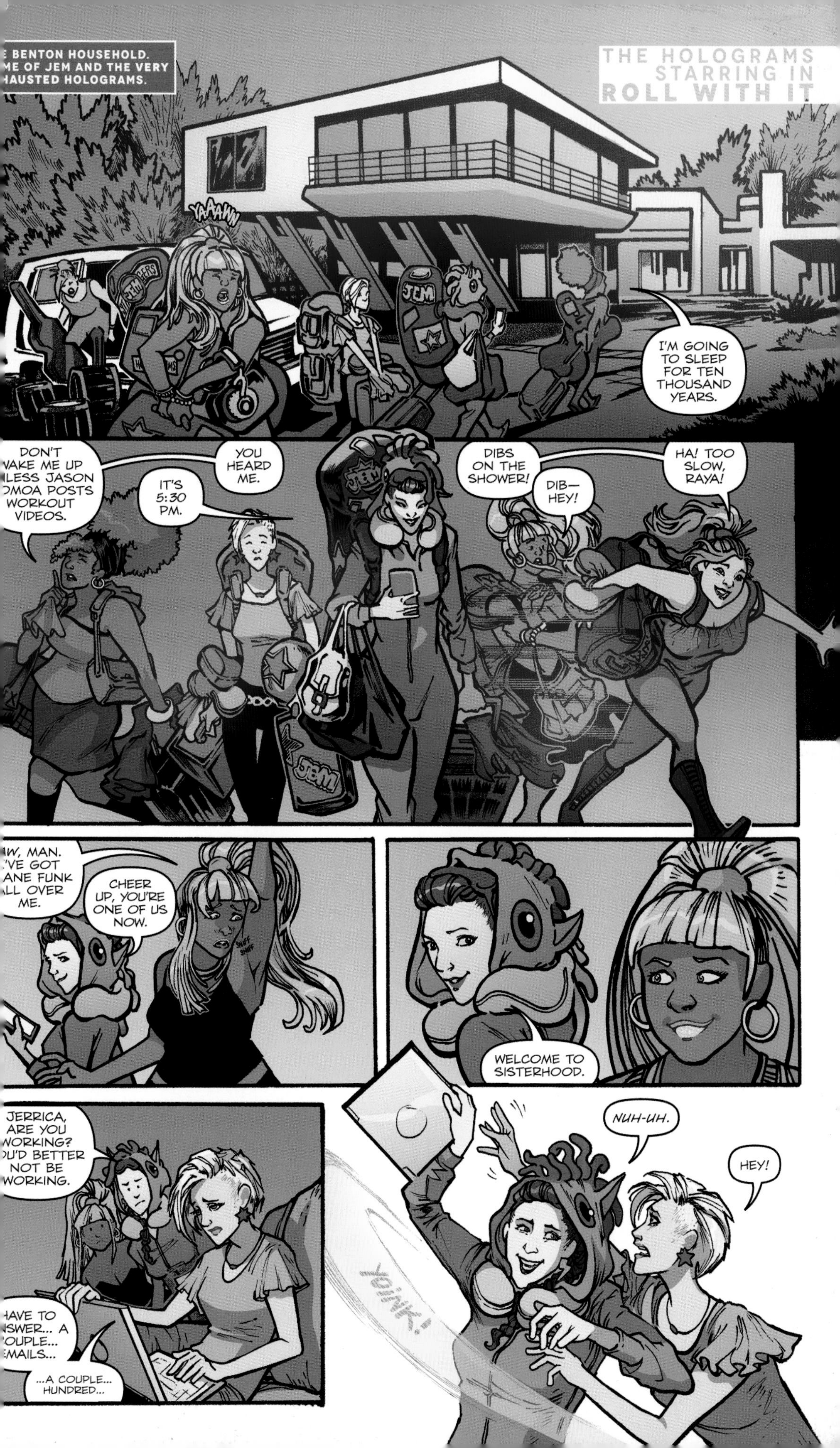
E BENTON HOUSEHOLD.
ME OF JEM AND THE VERY
HAUSTED HOLOGRAMS.
THE HOLOGRAMS
STARRING IN
ROLL WITH IT
YAAAWN
I'M GOING TO SLEEP FOR TEN THOUSAND YEARS.
DON'T WAKE ME UP LESS JASON OMOA POSTS WORKOUT VIDEOS.
IT'S 5:30 PM.
YOU HEARD ME.
DIBS ON THE SHOWER!
DIB— HEY!
HA! TOO SLOW, RAYA!
W, MAN. 'VE GOT ANE FUNK LL OVER ME.
CHEER UP, YOU'RE ONE OF US NOW.
SNIFF SNIFF
WELCOME TO SISTERHOOD.
JERRICA, ARE YOU WORKING? U'D BETTER NOT BE WORKING.
HAVE TO NSWER... A OUPLE... EMAILS...
...A COUPLE... HUNDRED...
NUH-UH.
HEY!
YOINK!

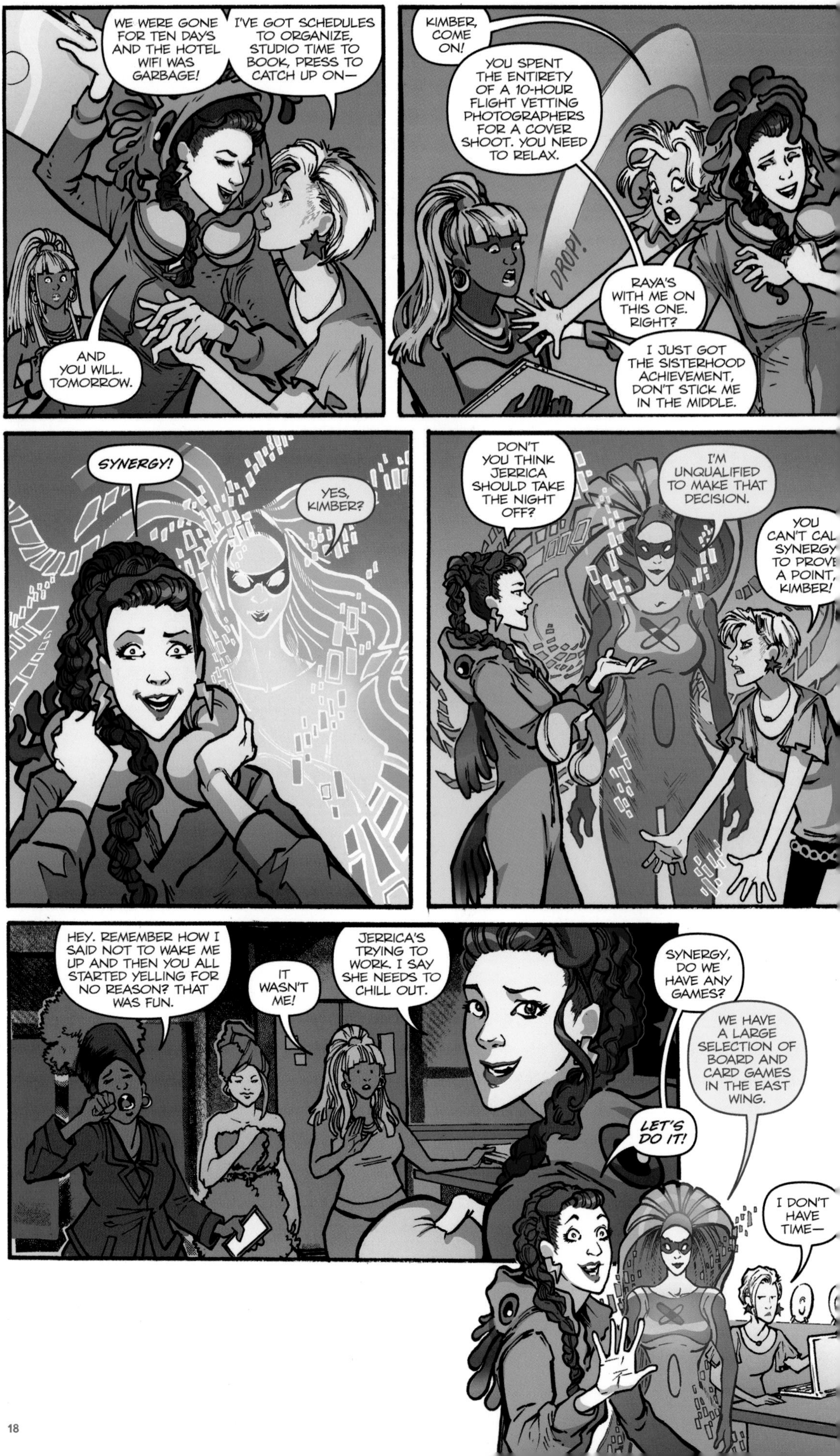
WE WERE GONE FOR TEN DAYS AND THE HOTEL WIFI WAS GARBAGE!
I'VE GOT SCHEDULES TO ORGANIZE, STUDIO TIME TO BOOK, PRESS TO CATCH UP ON—
AND YOU WILL. TOMORROW.
KIMBER, COME ON!
YOU SPENT THE ENTIRETY OF A 10-HOUR FLIGHT VETTING PHOTOGRAPHERS FOR A COVER SHOOT. YOU NEED TO RELAX.
DROP!
RAYA'S WITH ME ON THIS ONE. RIGHT?
I JUST GOT THE SISTERHOOD ACHIEVEMENT, DON'T STICK ME IN THE MIDDLE.
SYNERGY!
YES, KIMBER?
DON'T YOU THINK JERRICA SHOULD TAKE THE NIGHT OFF?
I'M UNQUALIFIED TO MAKE THAT DECISION.
YOU CAN'T CAL SYNERGY TO PROVE A POINT, KIMBER!
HEY. REMEMBER HOW I SAID NOT TO WAKE ME UP AND THEN YOU ALL STARTED YELLING FOR NO REASON? THAT WAS FUN.
IT WASN'T ME!
JERRICA'S TRYING TO WORK. I SAY SHE NEEDS TO CHILL OUT.
SYNERGY, DO WE HAVE ANY GAMES?
WE HAVE A LARGE SELECTION OF BOARD AND CARD GAMES IN THE EAST WING.
LET'S DO IT!
I DON'T HAVE TIME—

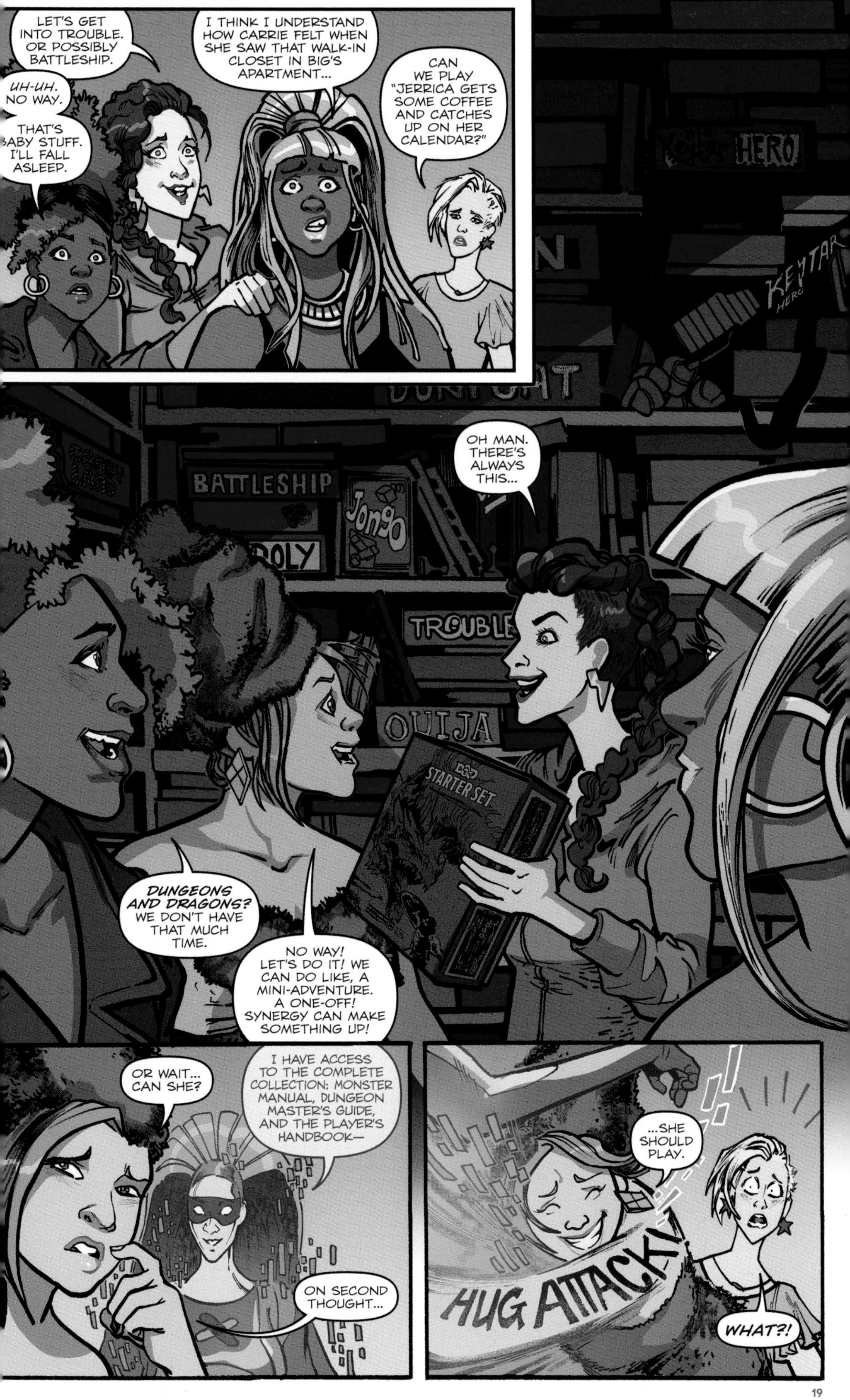

LET'S GET INTO TROUBLE. OR POSSIBLY BATTLESHIP.
UH-UH. NO WAY.
THAT'S BABY STUFF. I'LL FALL ASLEEP.
I THINK I UNDERSTAND HOW CARRIE FELT WHEN SHE SAW THAT WALK-IN CLOSET IN BIG'S APARTMENT...
CAN WE PLAY "JERRICA GETS SOME COFFEE AND CATCHES UP ON HER CALENDAR?"
HERO
KEYTAR HERO
BATTLESHIP
Jongo
TROUBLE
OUIJA
STARTER SET
OH MAN. THERE'S ALWAYS THIS...
DUNGEONS AND DRAGONS? WE DON'T HAVE THAT MUCH TIME.
NO WAY! LET'S DO IT! WE CAN DO LIKE, A MINI-ADVENTURE. A ONE-OFF! SYNERGY CAN MAKE SOMETHING UP!
OR WAIT... CAN SHE?
I HAVE ACCESS TO THE COMPLETE COLLECTION: MONSTER MANUAL, DUNGEON MASTER'S GUIDE, AND THE PLAYER'S HANDBOOK—
ON SECOND THOUGHT...
...SHE SHOULD PLAY.
HUG ATTACK!
WHAT?!

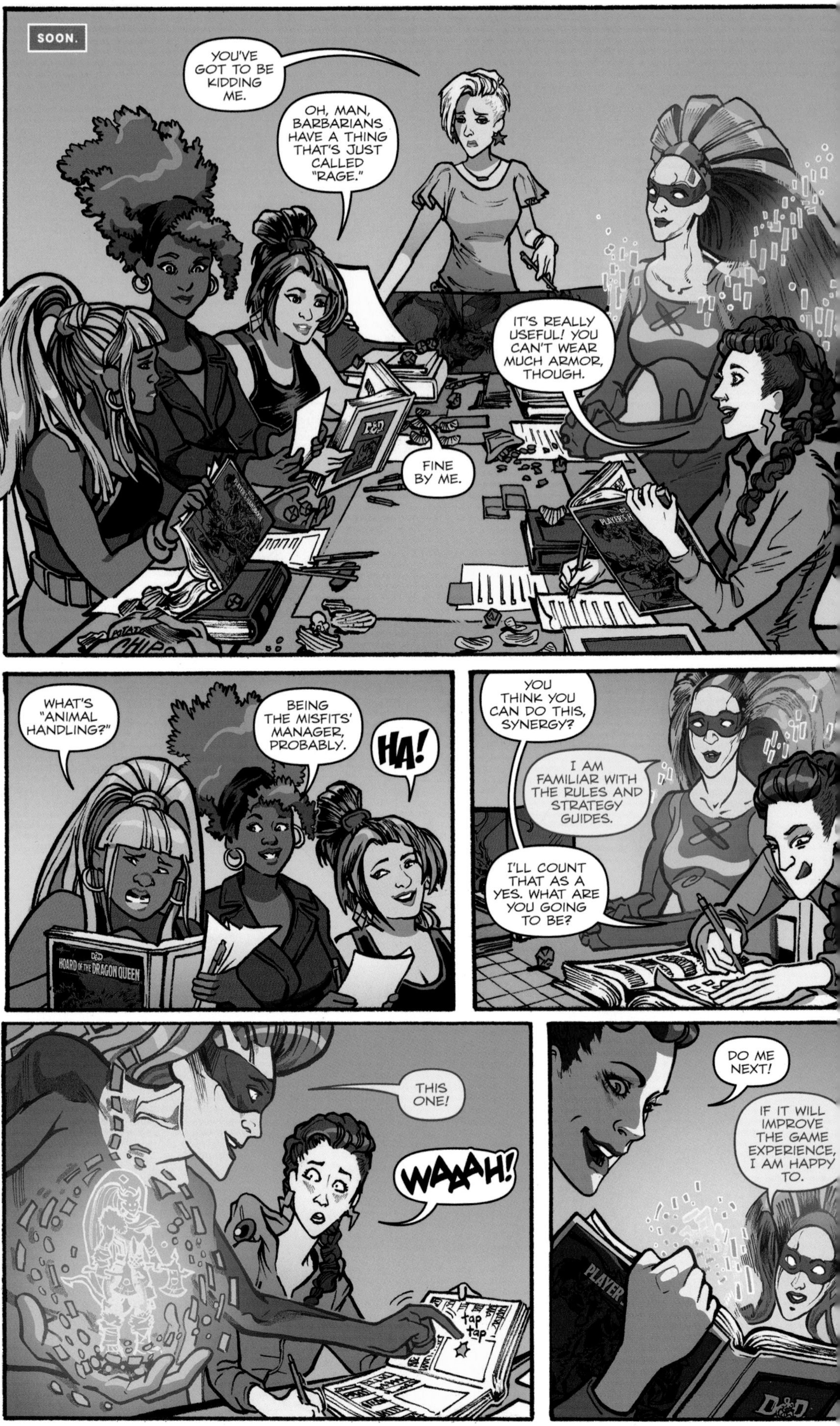
SOON.
YOU'VE GOT TO BE KIDDING ME.
OH, MAN, BARBARIANS HAVE A THING THAT'S JUST CALLED "RAGE."
IT'S REALLY USEFUL! YOU CAN'T WEAR MUCH ARMOR, THOUGH.
FINE BY ME.
WHAT'S "ANIMAL HANDLING?"
BEING THE MISFITS' MANAGER, PROBABLY.
HA!
HOARD OF THE DRAGON QUEEN
YOU THINK YOU CAN DO THIS, SYNERGY?
I AM FAMILIAR WITH THE RULES AND STRATEGY GUIDES.
I'LL COUNT THAT AS A YES. WHAT ARE YOU GOING TO BE?
THIS ONE!
WAAAH!
tap tap
DO ME NEXT!
IF IT WILL IMPROVE THE GAME EXPERIENCE, I AM HAPPY TO.

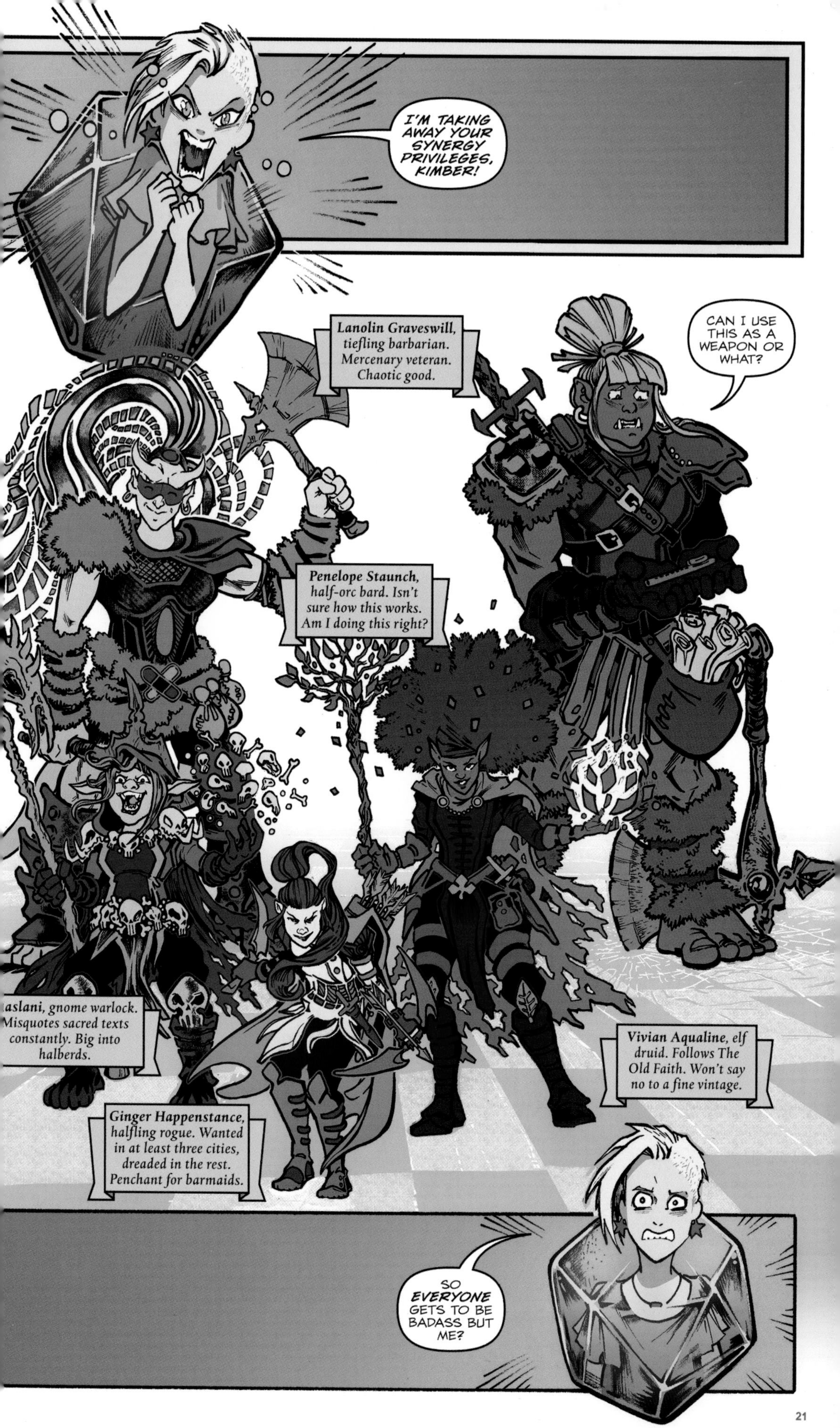
I'M TAKING AWAY YOUR SYNERGY PRIVILEGES, KIMBER!
Lanolin Graveswill, tiefling barbarian. Mercenary veteran. Chaotic good.
CAN I USE THIS AS A WEAPON OR WHAT?
Penelope Staunch, half-orc bard. Isn't sure how this works. Am I doing this right?
aslani, gnome warlock. Misquotes sacred texts constantly. Big into halberds.
Vivian Aqualine, elf druid. Follows The Old Faith. Won't say no to a fine vintage.
Ginger Happenstance, halfling rogue. Wanted in at least three cities, dreaded in the rest. Penchant for barmaids.
SO EVERYONE GETS TO BE BADASS BUT ME?

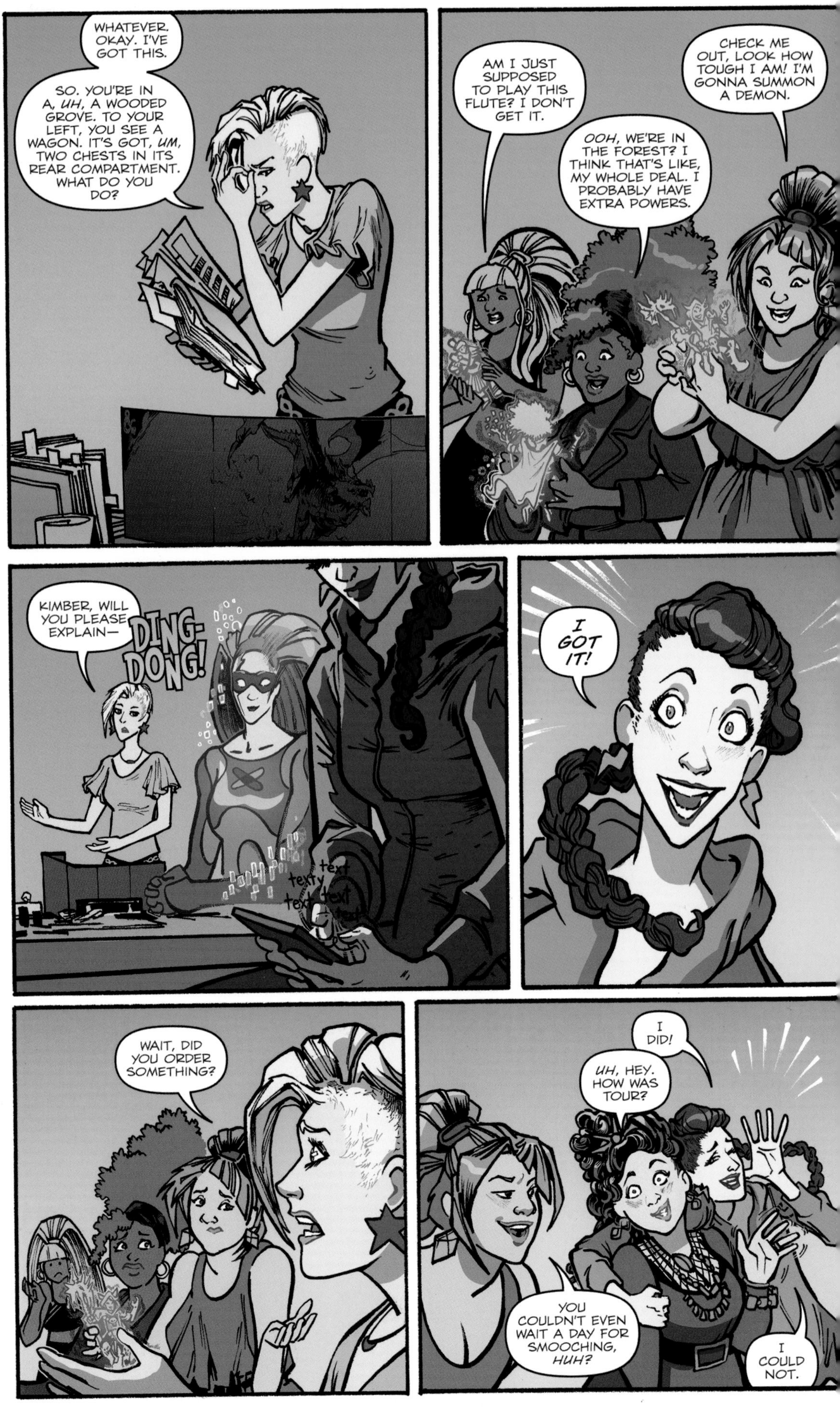

WHATEVER. OKAY. I'VE GOT THIS.
SO. YOU'RE IN A, *UH*, A WOODED GROVE. TO YOUR LEFT, YOU SEE A WAGON. IT'S GOT, *UM*, TWO CHESTS IN ITS REAR COMPARTMENT. WHAT DO YOU DO?
AM I JUST SUPPOSED TO PLAY THIS FLUTE? I DON'T GET IT.
OOH, WE'RE IN THE FOREST? I THINK THAT'S LIKE, MY WHOLE DEAL. I PROBABLY HAVE EXTRA POWERS.
CHECK ME OUT, LOOK HOW TOUGH I AM! I'M GONNA SUMMON A DEMON.
KIMBER, WILL YOU PLEASE EXPLAIN—
DING-DONG!
text
text
text
text
I GOT IT!
WAIT, DID YOU ORDER SOMETHING?
I DID!
UH, HEY. HOW WAS TOUR?
YOU COULDN'T EVEN WAIT A DAY FOR SMOOCHING, *HUH*?
I COULD NOT.

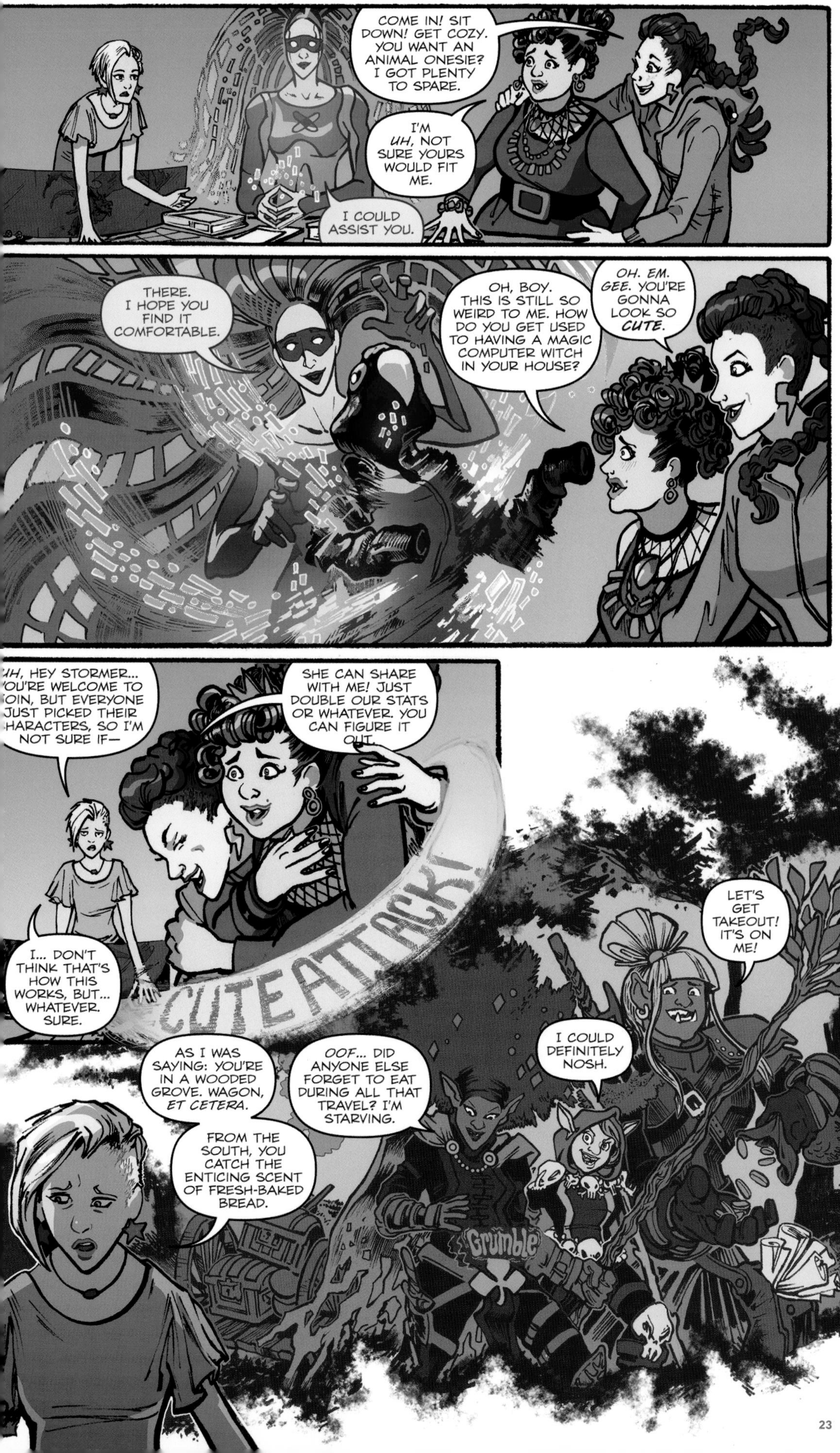

COME IN! SIT DOWN! GET COZY. YOU WANT AN ANIMAL ONESIE? I GOT PLENTY TO SPARE.
I'M *UH*, NOT SURE YOURS WOULD FIT ME.
I COULD ASSIST YOU.
THERE. I HOPE YOU FIND IT COMFORTABLE.
OH, BOY. THIS IS STILL SO WEIRD TO ME. HOW DO YOU GET USED TO HAVING A MAGIC COMPUTER WITCH IN YOUR HOUSE?
OH. EM. GEE. YOU'RE GONNA LOOK SO *CUTE*.
UH, HEY STORMER... YOU'RE WELCOME TO JOIN, BUT EVERYONE JUST PICKED THEIR CHARACTERS, SO I'M NOT SURE IF—
SHE CAN SHARE WITH ME! JUST DOUBLE OUR STATS OR WHATEVER. YOU CAN FIGURE IT OUT.
CUTE ATTACK!
I... DON'T THINK THAT'S HOW THIS WORKS, BUT... WHATEVER. SURE.
LET'S GET TAKEOUT! IT'S ON ME!
I COULD DEFINITELY NOSH.
AS I WAS SAYING: YOU'RE IN A WOODED GROVE. WAGON, *ET CETERA*.
FROM THE SOUTH, YOU CATCH THE ENTICING SCENT OF FRESH-BAKED BREAD.
OOF... DID ANYONE ELSE FORGET TO EAT DURING ALL THAT TRAVEL? I'M STARVING.
Grumble

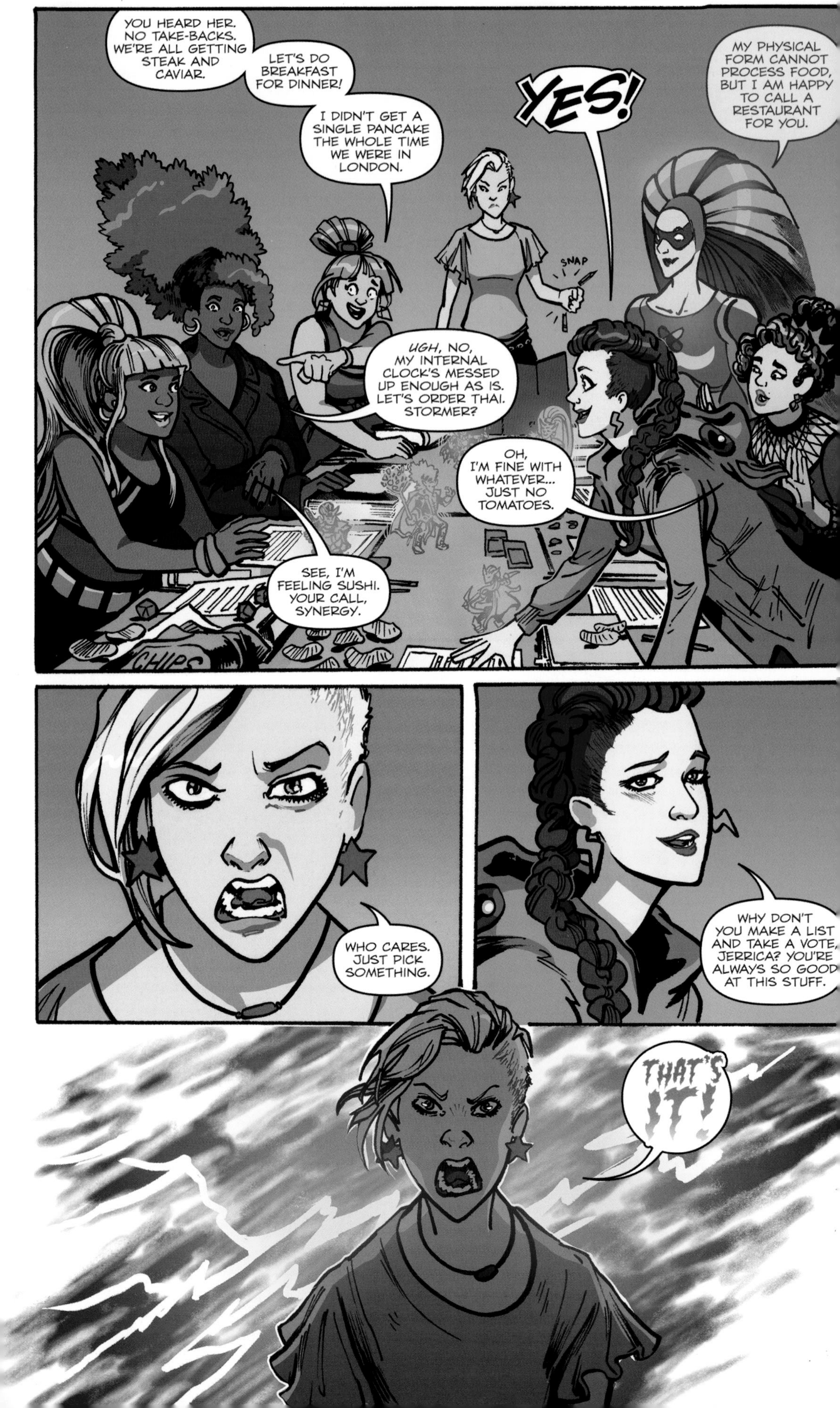
YOU HEARD HER. NO TAKE-BACKS. WE'RE ALL GETTING STEAK AND CAVIAR.
LET'S DO BREAKFAST FOR DINNER!
I DIDN'T GET A SINGLE PANCAKE THE WHOLE TIME WE WERE IN LONDON.
YES!
MY PHYSICAL FORM CANNOT PROCESS FOOD, BUT I AM HAPPY TO CALL A RESTAURANT FOR YOU.
SNAP
UGH, NO, MY INTERNAL CLOCK'S MESSED UP ENOUGH AS IS. LET'S ORDER THAI. STORMER?
OH, I'M FINE WITH WHATEVER... JUST NO TOMATOES.
SEE, I'M FEELING SUSHI. YOUR CALL, SYNERGY.
CHIPS
WHO CARES. JUST PICK SOMETHING.
WHY DON'T YOU MAKE A LIST AND TAKE A VOTE, JERRICA? YOU'RE ALWAYS SO GOOD AT THIS STUFF.
THAT'S IT!

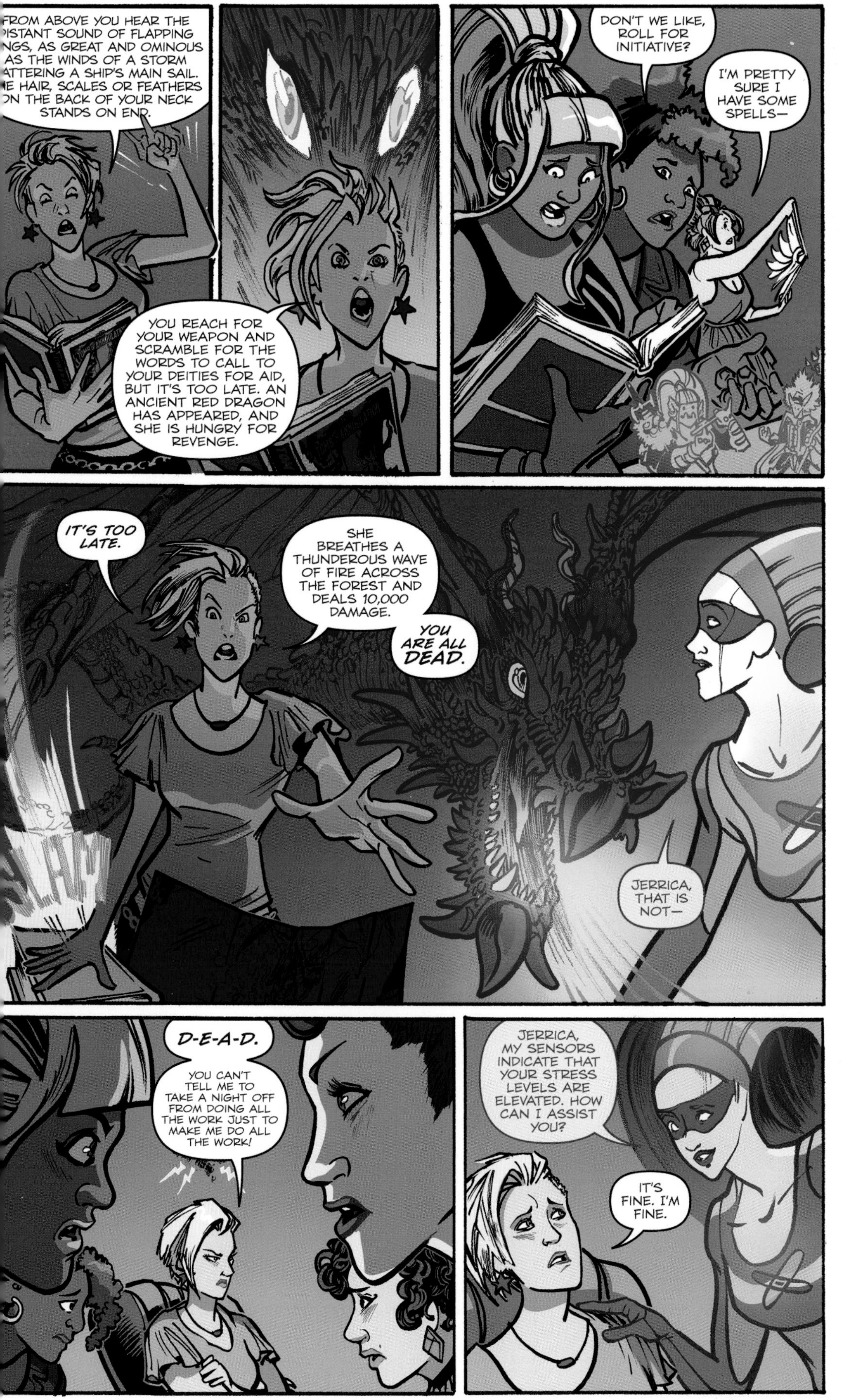
FROM ABOVE YOU HEAR THE ISTANT SOUND OF FLAPPING NGS, AS GREAT AND OMINOUS AS THE WINDS OF A STORM ATTERING A SHIP'S MAIN SAIL. E HAIR, SCALES OR FEATHERS ON THE BACK OF YOUR NECK STANDS ON END.
YOU REACH FOR YOUR WEAPON AND SCRAMBLE FOR THE WORDS TO CALL TO YOUR DEITIES FOR AID, BUT IT'S TOO LATE. AN ANCIENT RED DRAGON HAS APPEARED, AND SHE IS HUNGRY FOR REVENGE.
DON'T WE LIKE, ROLL FOR INITIATIVE?
I'M PRETTY SURE I HAVE SOME SPELLS—
IT'S TOO LATE.
SHE BREATHES A THUNDEROUS WAVE OF FIRE ACROSS THE FOREST AND DEALS 10,000 DAMAGE.
YOU ARE ALL DEAD.
JERRICA, THAT IS NOT—
D-E-A-D.
YOU CAN'T TELL ME TO TAKE A NIGHT OFF FROM DOING ALL THE WORK JUST TO MAKE ME DO ALL THE WORK!
JERRICA, MY SENSORS INDICATE THAT YOUR STRESS LEVELS ARE ELEVATED. HOW CAN I ASSIST YOU?
IT'S FINE. I'M FINE.

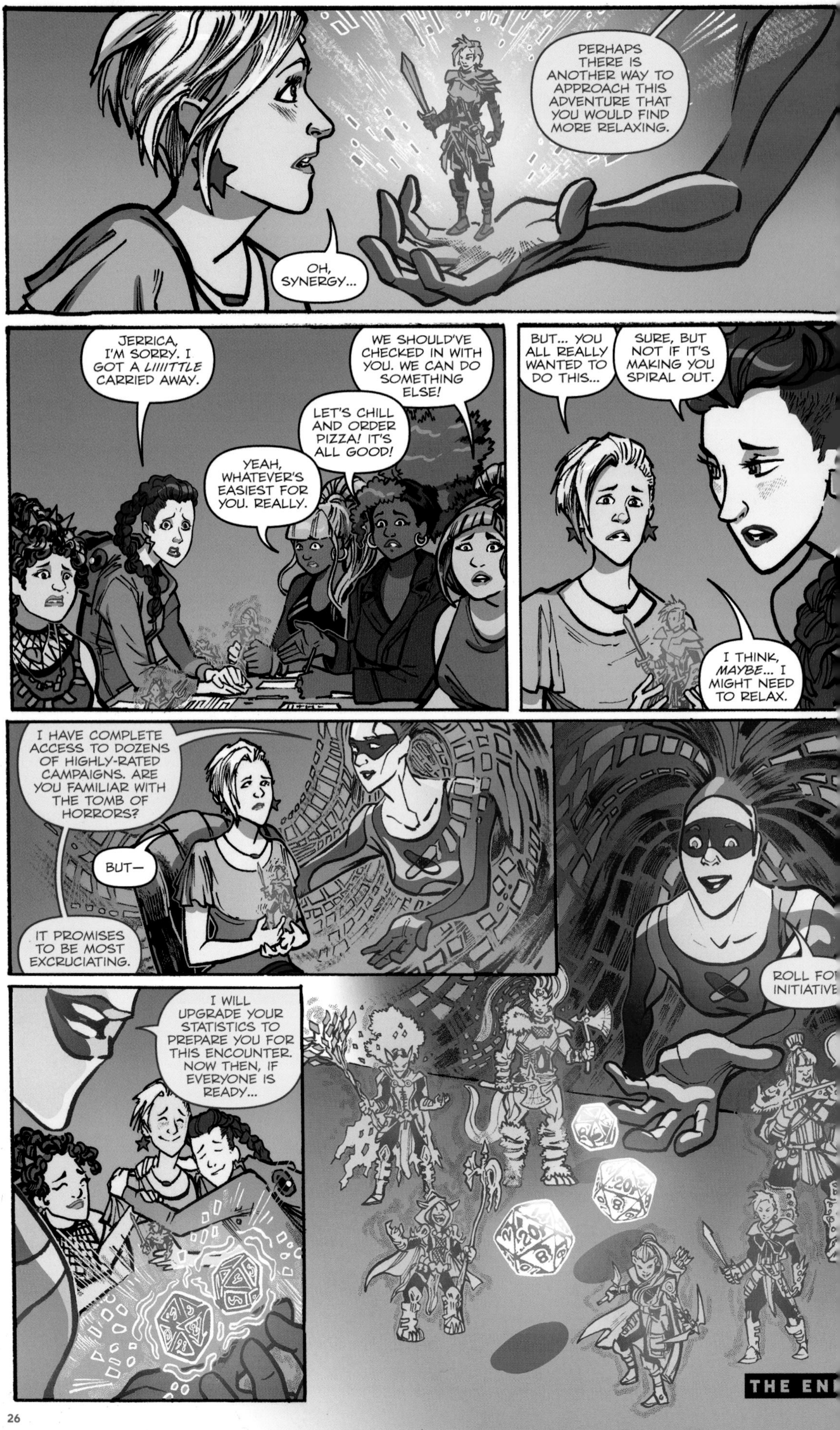
PERHAPS THERE IS ANOTHER WAY TO APPROACH THIS ADVENTURE THAT YOU WOULD FIND MORE RELAXING.
OH, SYNERGY...
JERRICA, I'M SORRY. I GOT A *LIIIITTLE* CARRIED AWAY.
WE SHOULD'VE CHECKED IN WITH YOU. WE CAN DO SOMETHING ELSE!
LET'S CHILL AND ORDER PIZZA! IT'S ALL GOOD!
YEAH, WHATEVER'S EASIEST FOR YOU. REALLY.
BUT... YOU ALL REALLY WANTED TO DO THIS...
SURE, BUT NOT IF IT'S MAKING YOU SPIRAL OUT.
I THINK, *MAYBE*... I MIGHT NEED TO RELAX.
I HAVE COMPLETE ACCESS TO DOZENS OF HIGHLY-RATED CAMPAIGNS. ARE YOU FAMILIAR WITH THE TOMB OF HORRORS?
BUT—
IT PROMISES TO BE MOST EXCRUCIATING.
I WILL UPGRADE YOUR STATISTICS TO PREPARE YOU FOR THIS ENCOUNTER. NOW THEN, IF EVERYONE IS READY...
ROLL FO
INITIATIVE
THE EN

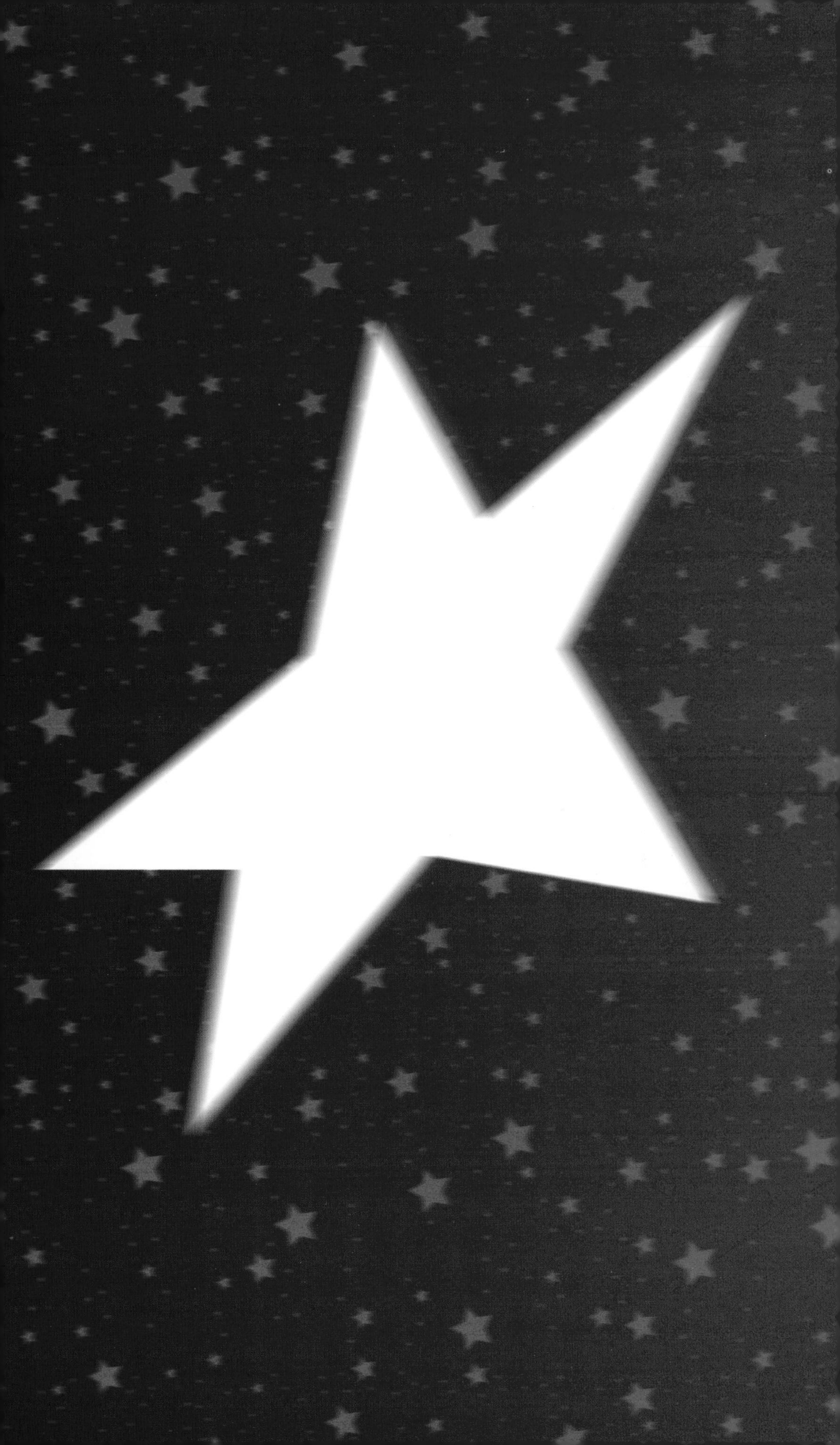

ART BY **SIOBHAN KEENAN**

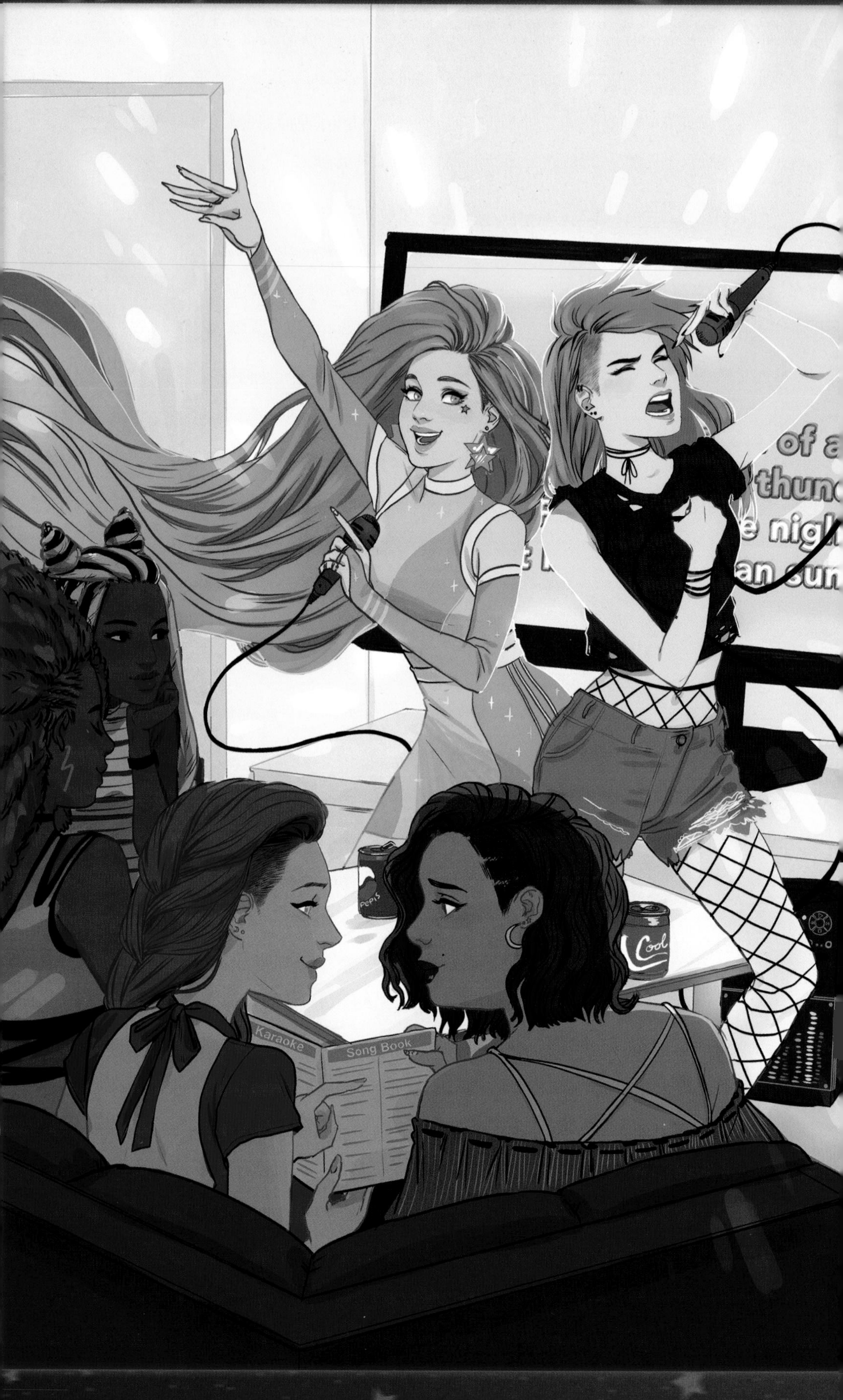
Karaoke
Song Book
PEPIS
Cool

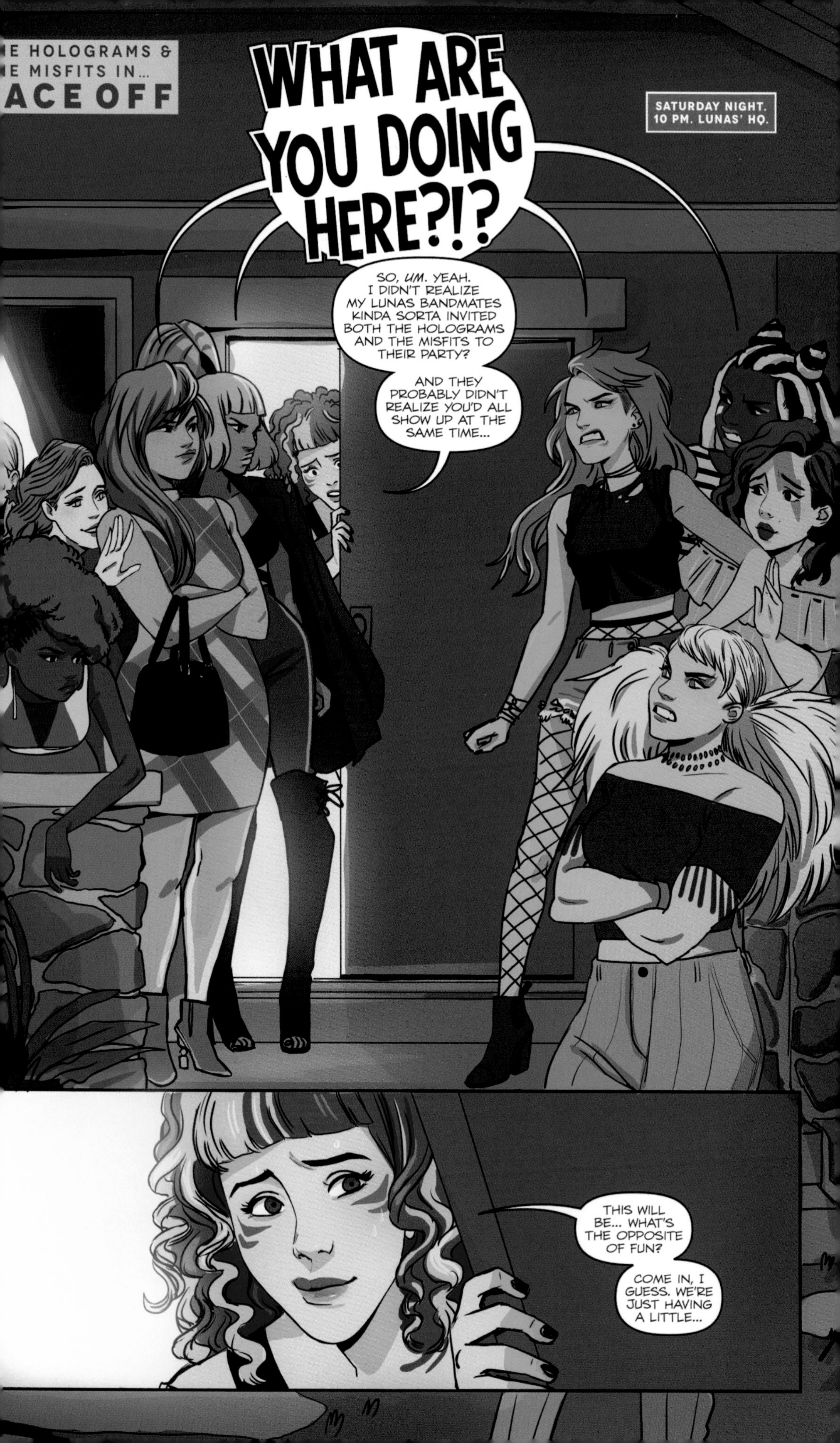
E HOLOGRAMS &
E MISFITS IN...
ACE OFF
WHAT ARE YOU DOING HERE?!?
SATURDAY NIGHT. 10 PM. LUNAS' HQ.
SO, UM. YEAH. I DIDN'T REALIZE MY LUNAS BANDMATES KINDA SORTA INVITED BOTH THE HOLOGRAMS AND THE MISFITS TO THEIR PARTY?
AND THEY PROBABLY DIDN'T REALIZE YOU'D ALL SHOW UP AT THE SAME TIME...
THIS WILL BE... WHAT'S THE OPPOSITE OF FUN?
COME IN, I GUESS. WE'RE JUST HAVING A LITTLE...

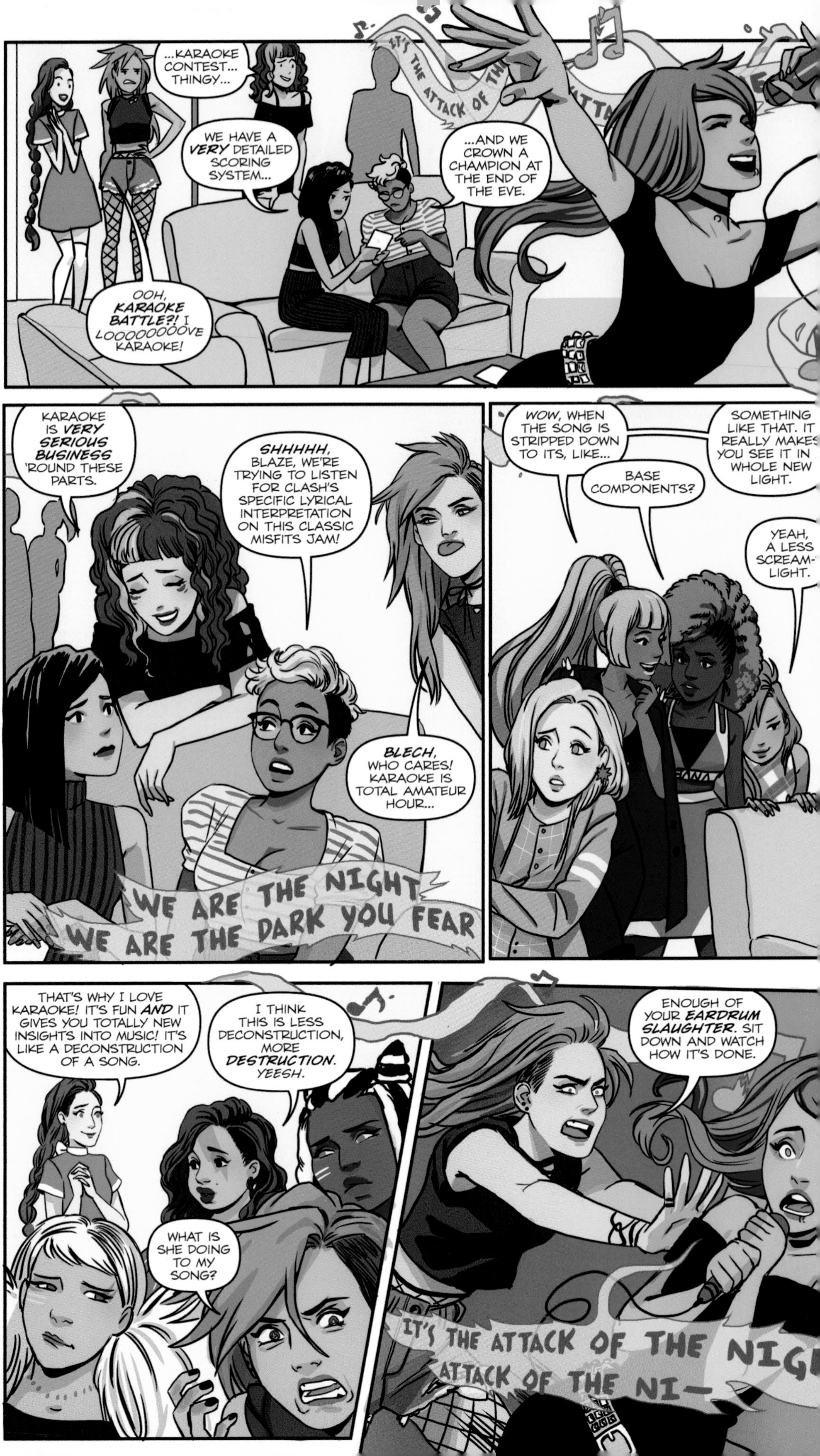
...KARAOKE CONTEST... THINGY...
WE HAVE A VERY DETAILED SCORING SYSTEM...
...AND WE CROWN A CHAMPION AT THE END OF THE EVE.
IT'S THE ATTACK OF THE
OOH, KARAOKE BATTLE?! I LOOOOOOOOVE KARAOKE!
KARAOKE IS VERY SERIOUS BUSINESS 'ROUND THESE PARTS.
SHHHHH, BLAZE, WE'RE TRYING TO LISTEN FOR CLASH'S SPECIFIC LYRICAL INTERPRETATION ON THIS CLASSIC MISFITS JAM!
BLECH, WHO CARES! KARAOKE IS TOTAL AMATEUR HOUR...
WE ARE THE NIGHT
WE ARE THE DARK YOU FEAR
WOW, WHEN THE SONG IS STRIPPED DOWN TO ITS, LIKE...
BASE COMPONENTS?
SOMETHING LIKE THAT. IT REALLY MAKES YOU SEE IT IN WHOLE NEW LIGHT.
YEAH, A LESS SCREAM-LIGHT.
THAT'S WHY I LOVE KARAOKE! IT'S FUN AND IT GIVES YOU TOTALLY NEW INSIGHTS INTO MUSIC! IT'S LIKE A DECONSTRUCTION OF A SONG.
I THINK THIS IS LESS DECONSTRUCTION, MORE DESTRUCTION. YEESH.
WHAT IS SHE DOING TO MY SONG?
ENOUGH OF YOUR EARDRUM SLAUGHTER. SIT DOWN AND WATCH HOW IT'S DONE.
IT'S THE ATTACK OF THE NIGH
ATTACK OF THE NI—

SEEPING IN YOUR HEAD
CRAWLING IN YOUR BED

ARE WE FOR REAL WATCHING PIZZAZZ *KARAOKE HER OWN SONG?*

LET'S GO HOME. ANYTHING IS BETTER THAN THIS. NETFLIX AND NACHOS.

AND WHEN YOU SAY "NETFLIX," YOU OF COURSE MEAN "ARGUING FOR THREE HOURS ABOUT WHAT TO WATCH ON NETFLIX, THEN PUTTING IT TO A VOTE THAT ENDS IN A FIVE-WAY TIE."

...AND NACHOS.

HOLOGRAMS!

THINK YOU CAN TOP THAT?

I ALREADY KNOW THE ANSWER.

THE ANSWER IS NO. *DUH.*

WE'LL SEE ABOUT THAT!

AJA! WHAT ARE YOU DOING...

I THOUGHT WE WERE GOING HOME!

SHE JUST TALKED SOME SMACK. SMACK TALK AT THIS SMACKDOWN WILL NOT GO *UNSMACKED!* ER, UNCHALLENGED.

DID YOU JUST WHIP OUT *YOUR OWN MICROPHONE?!*

JUST A LITTLE SOMETHING I'VE BEEN TINKERING WITH.

OF COURSE YOU LOT NEED HELP TO WIN!

NOT HELP.

INGENUITY.

I DOUBT YOU'LL FIND ANY HOLOGRAMS SONGS IN THERE, SINCE YOU GUYS HAVEN'T BEEN AROUND AS LONG OR MADE NEARLY THE IMPACT—

OH, I'M NOT SINGING MY OWN BAND'S SONGS. HOW HACKY WOULD THAT BE?

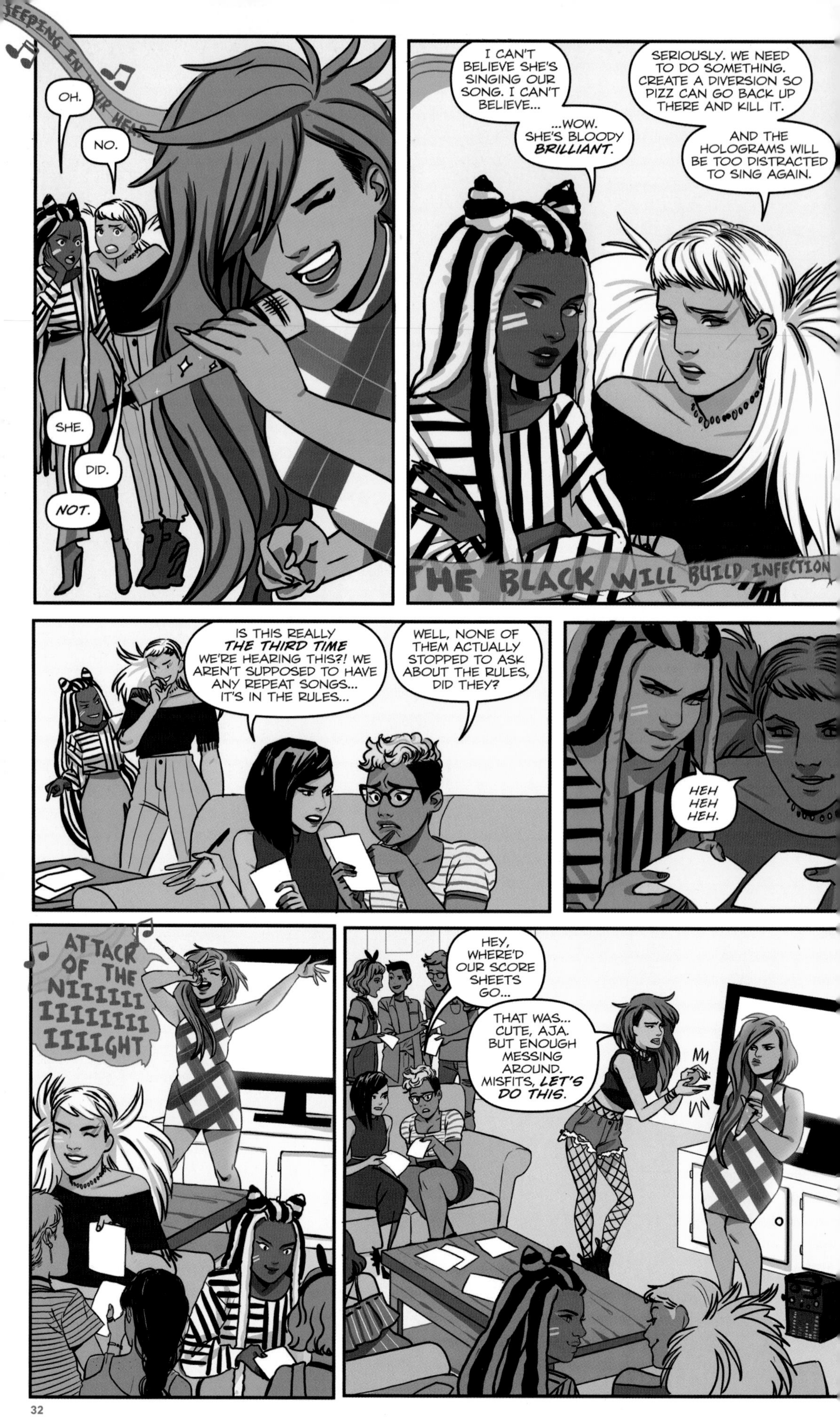
SEEPING IN YOUR HEAD
OH.
NO.
SHE.
DID.
NOT.
I CAN'T BELIEVE SHE'S SINGING OUR SONG. I CAN'T BELIEVE...
...WOW. SHE'S BLOODY BRILLIANT.
SERIOUSLY. WE NEED TO DO SOMETHING. CREATE A DIVERSION SO PIZZ CAN GO BACK UP THERE AND KILL IT.
AND THE HOLOGRAMS WILL BE TOO DISTRACTED TO SING AGAIN.
THE BLACK WILL BUILD INFECTION
IS THIS REALLY THE THIRD TIME WE'RE HEARING THIS?! WE AREN'T SUPPOSED TO HAVE ANY REPEAT SONGS... IT'S IN THE RULES...
WELL, NONE OF THEM ACTUALLY STOPPED TO ASK ABOUT THE RULES, DID THEY?
HEH HEH HEH.
ATTACK OF THE NIIIIIII IIIIIIII IIIIGHT
HEY, WHERE'D OUR SCORE SHEETS GO...
THAT WAS... CUTE, AJA. BUT ENOUGH MESSING AROUND. MISFITS, LET'S DO THIS.

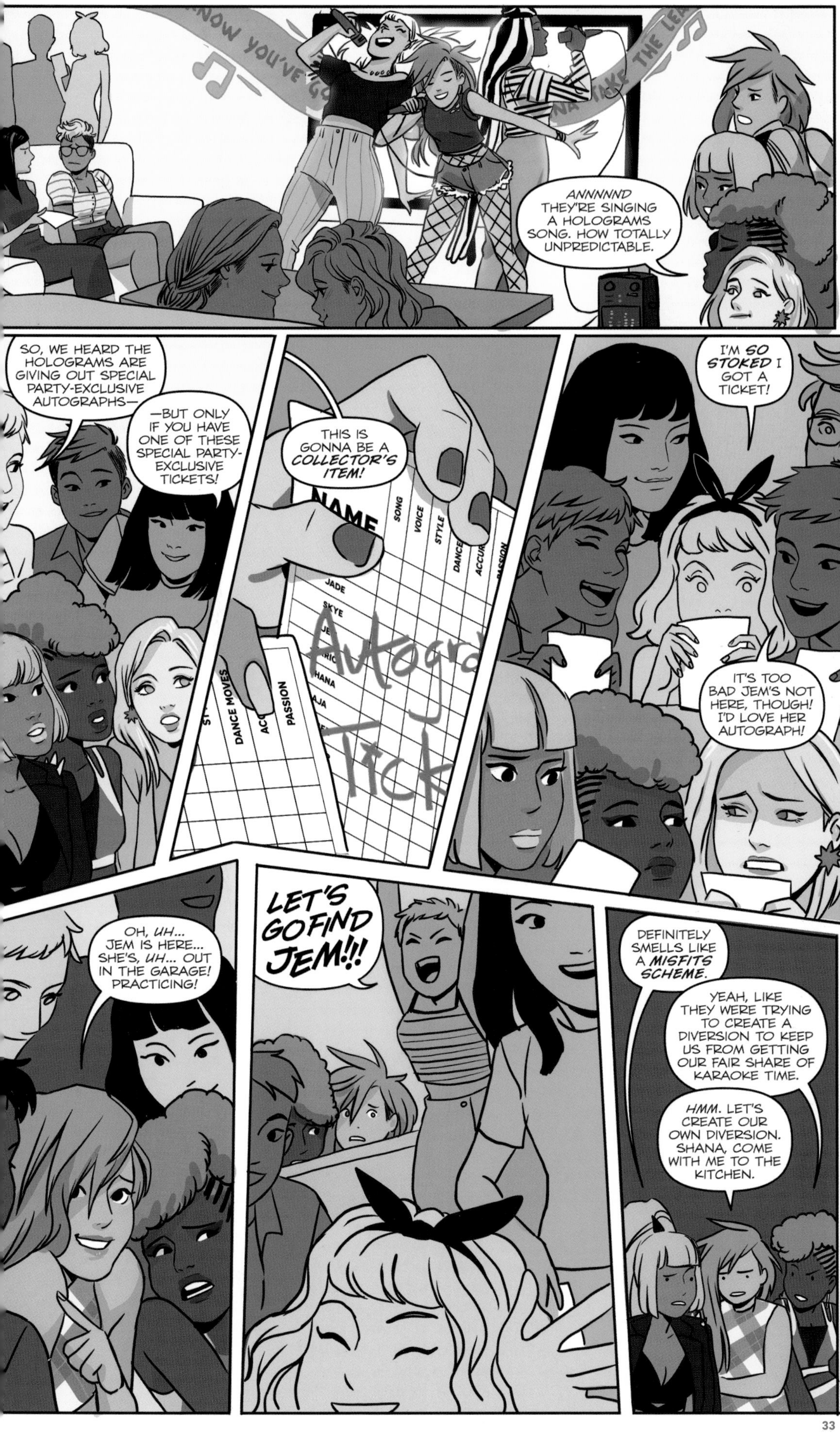
NOW YOU'VE GO
NA TAKE THE LEA
ANNNNND THEY'RE SINGING A HOLOGRAMS SONG. HOW TOTALLY UNPREDICTABLE.
SO, WE HEARD THE HOLOGRAMS ARE GIVING OUT SPECIAL PARTY-EXCLUSIVE AUTOGRAPHS—
—BUT ONLY IF YOU HAVE ONE OF THESE SPECIAL PARTY-EXCLUSIVE TICKETS!
THIS IS GONNA BE A COLLECTOR'S ITEM!
NAME
SONG
VOICE
STYLE
DANCE
ACCUR
PASSION
JADE
SKYE
HANA
AJA
DANCE MOVES
PASSION
I'M SO STOKED I GOT A TICKET!
IT'S TOO BAD JEM'S NOT HERE, THOUGH! I'D LOVE HER AUTOGRAPH!
OH, UH... JEM IS HERE... SHE'S, UH... OUT IN THE GARAGE! PRACTICING!
LET'S GO FIND JEM!!!
DEFINITELY SMELLS LIKE A MISFITS SCHEME.
YEAH, LIKE THEY WERE TRYING TO CREATE A DIVERSION TO KEEP US FROM GETTING OUR FAIR SHARE OF KARAOKE TIME.
HMM. LET'S CREATE OUR OWN DIVERSION. SHANA, COME WITH ME TO THE KITCHEN.

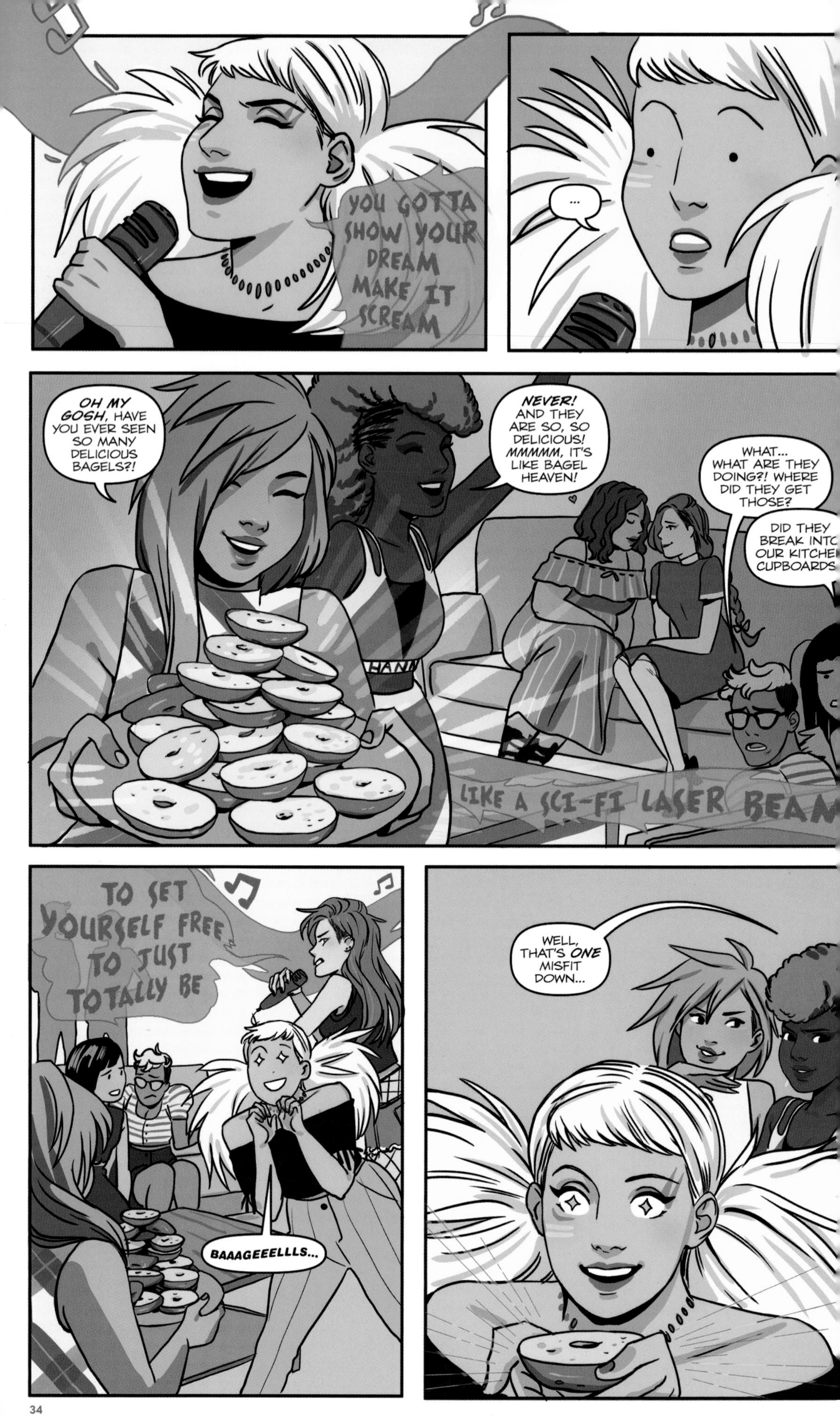
YOU GOTTA SHOW YOUR DREAM MAKE IT SCREAM
...
OH MY GOSH, HAVE YOU EVER SEEN SO MANY DELICIOUS BAGELS?!
NEVER! AND THEY ARE SO, SO DELICIOUS! MMMMM, IT'S LIKE BAGEL HEAVEN!
WHAT... WHAT ARE THEY DOING?! WHERE DID THEY GET THOSE?
DID THEY BREAK INTO OUR KITCHEN CUPBOARDS
LIKE A SCI-FI LASER BEAM
TO SET YOURSELF FREE TO JUST TOTALLY BE
BAAAGEEELLLS...
WELL, THAT'S ONE MISFIT DOWN...

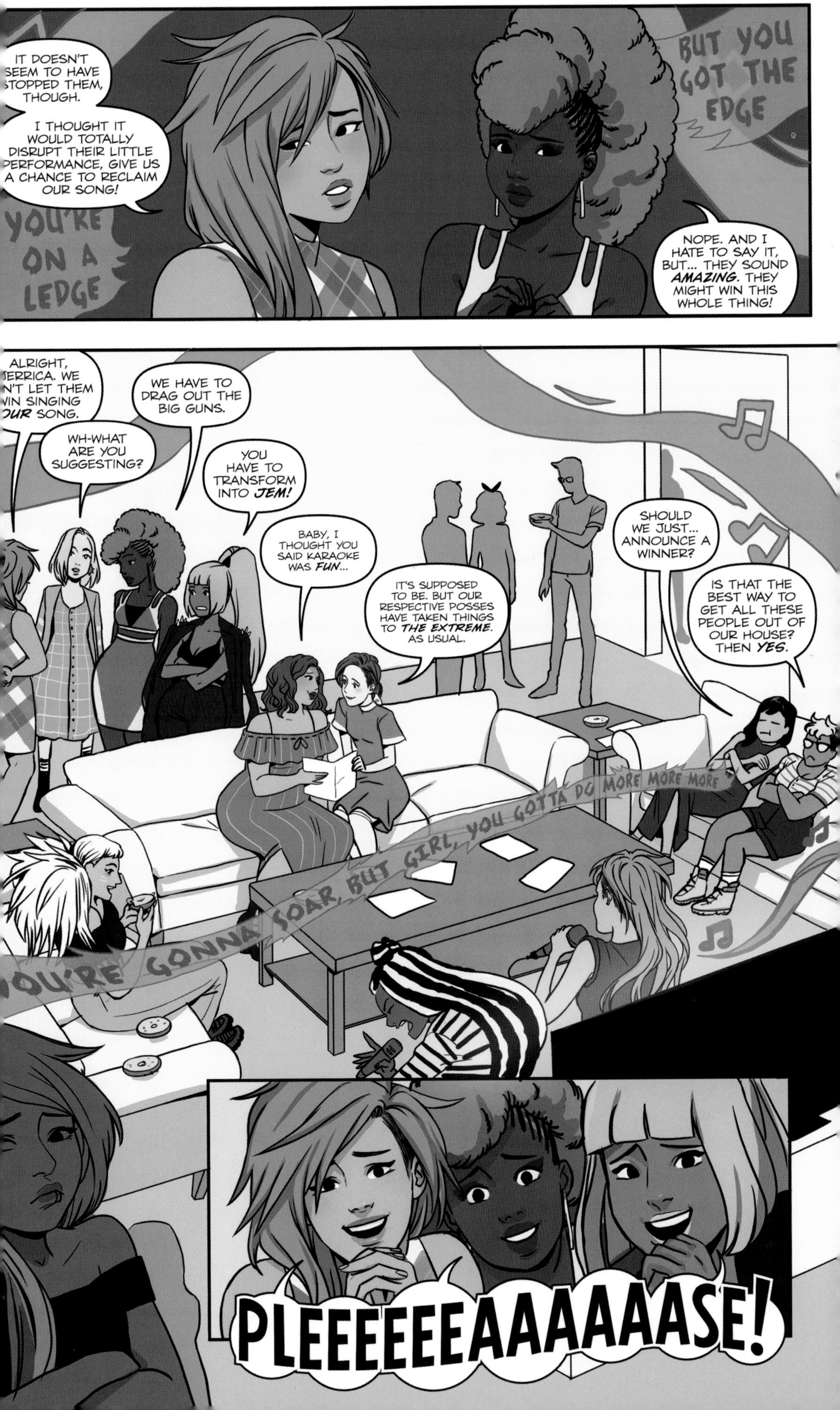

IT DOESN'T SEEM TO HAVE STOPPED THEM, THOUGH.
I THOUGHT IT WOULD TOTALLY DISRUPT THEIR LITTLE PERFORMANCE, GIVE US A CHANCE TO RECLAIM OUR SONG!
BUT YOU GOT THE EDGE
YOU'RE ON A LEDGE
NOPE. AND I HATE TO SAY IT, BUT... THEY SOUND AMAZING. THEY MIGHT WIN THIS WHOLE THING!
ALRIGHT, JERRICA. WE N'T LET THEM WIN SINGING OUR SONG.
WH-WHAT ARE YOU SUGGESTING?
WE HAVE TO DRAG OUT THE BIG GUNS.
YOU HAVE TO TRANSFORM INTO JEM!
BABY, I THOUGHT YOU SAID KARAOKE WAS FUN...
IT'S SUPPOSED TO BE. BUT OUR RESPECTIVE POSSES HAVE TAKEN THINGS TO THE EXTREME. AS USUAL.
SHOULD WE JUST... ANNOUNCE A WINNER?
IS THAT THE BEST WAY TO GET ALL THESE PEOPLE OUT OF OUR HOUSE? THEN YES.
YOU'RE GONNA SOAR, BUT GIRL, YOU GOTTA DO MORE MORE MORE
PLEEEEEEAAAAAASE!

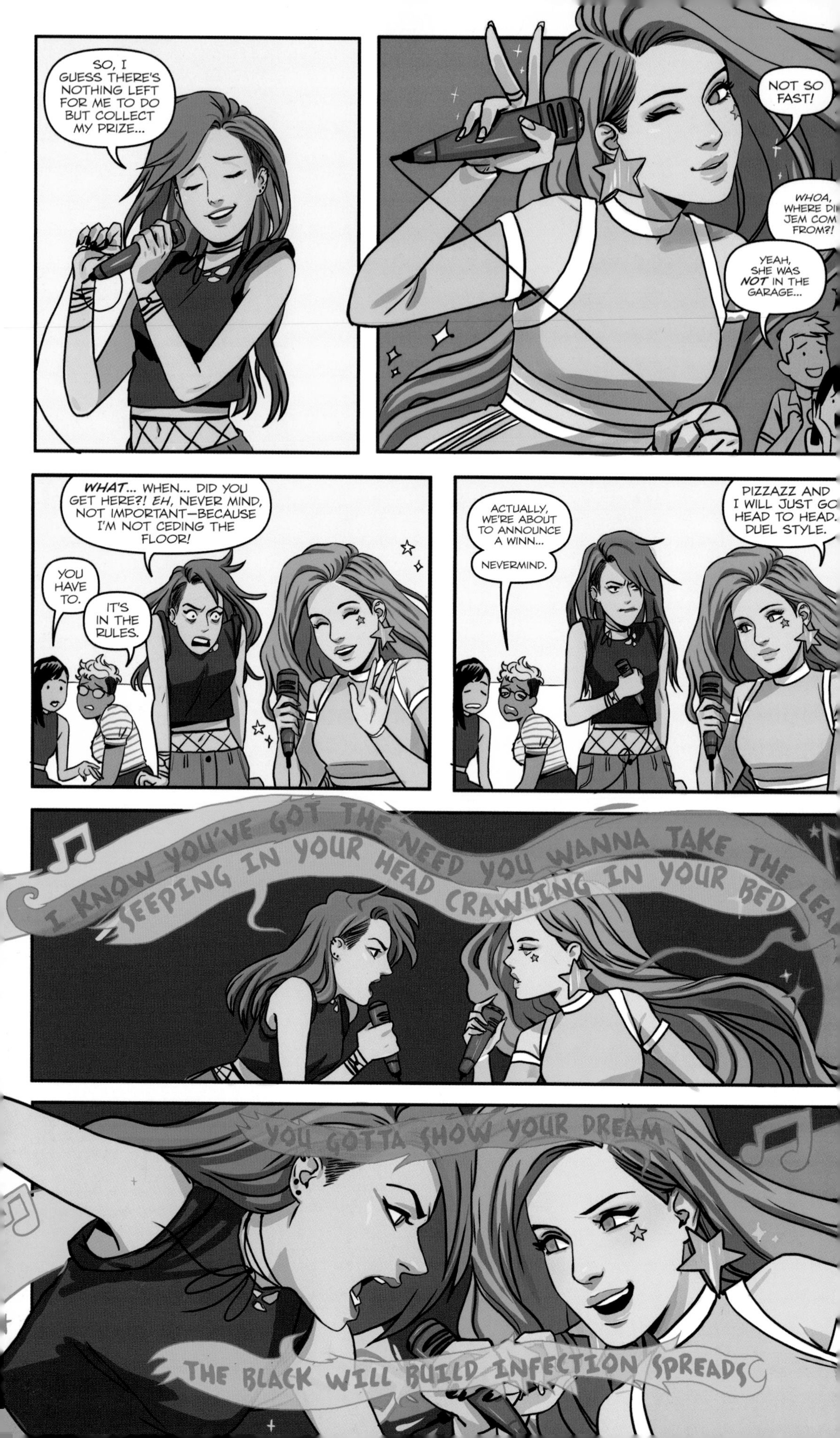

SO, I GUESS THERE'S NOTHING LEFT FOR ME TO DO BUT COLLECT MY PRIZE...
NOT SO FAST!
WHOA, WHERE DI JEM COM FROM?!
YEAH, SHE WAS NOT IN THE GARAGE...
WHAT... WHEN... DID YOU GET HERE?! EH, NEVER MIND, NOT IMPORTANT—BECAUSE I'M NOT CEDING THE FLOOR!
YOU HAVE TO.
IT'S IN THE RULES.
ACTUALLY, WE'RE ABOUT TO ANNOUNCE A WINN...
NEVERMIND.
PIZZAZZ AND I WILL JUST GO HEAD TO HEAD. DUEL STYLE.
I KNOW YOU'VE GOT THE NEED YOU WANNA TAKE THE LEA
SEEPING IN YOUR HEAD CRAWLING IN YOUR BED
YOU GOTTA SHOW YOUR DREAM
THE BLACK WILL BUILD INFECTION SPREADS

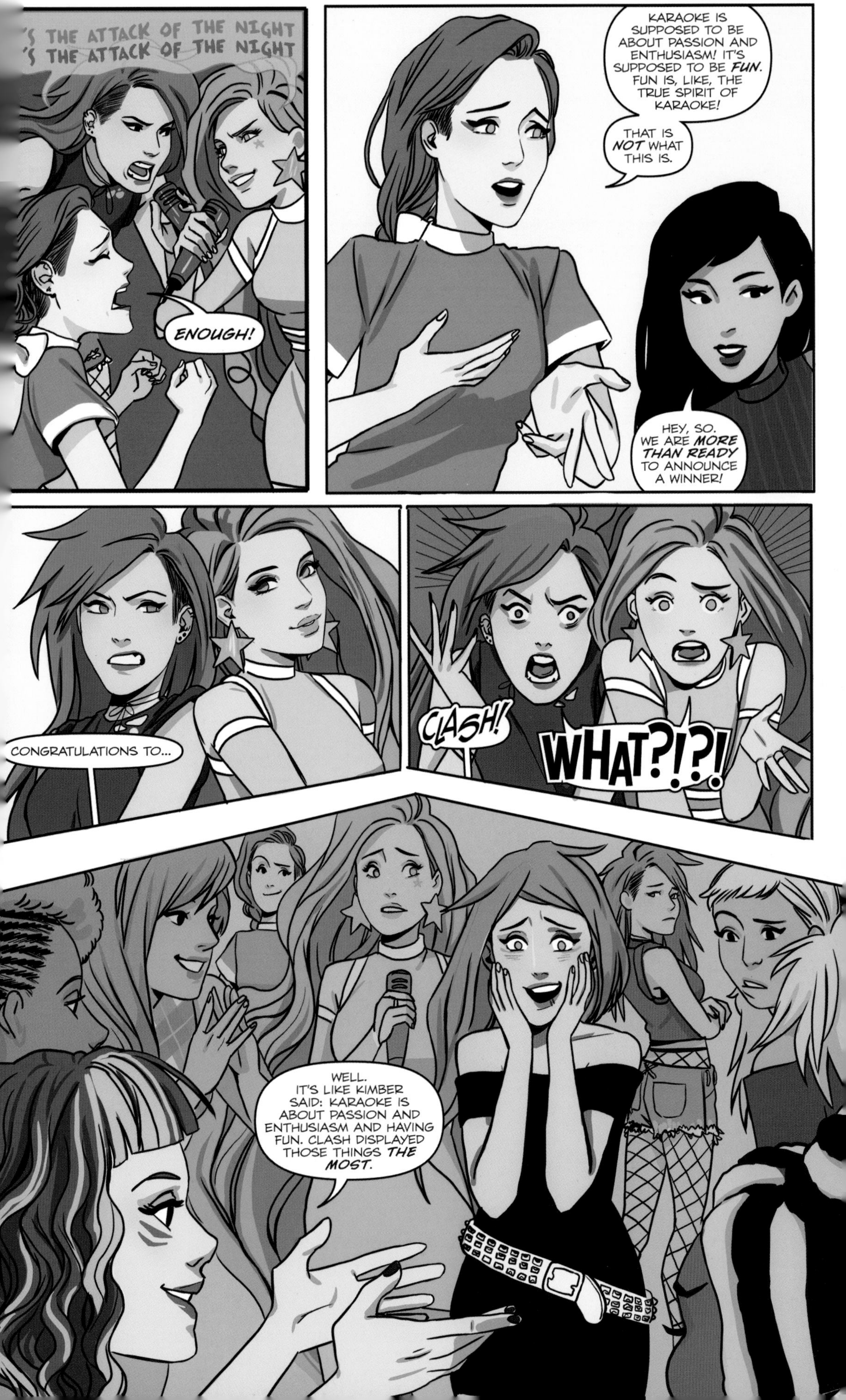

'S THE ATTACK OF THE NIGHT
'S THE ATTACK OF THE NIGHT
ENOUGH!
KARAOKE IS SUPPOSED TO BE ABOUT PASSION AND ENTHUSIASM! IT'S SUPPOSED TO BE FUN. FUN IS, LIKE, THE TRUE SPIRIT OF KARAOKE!
THAT IS NOT WHAT THIS IS.
HEY, SO. WE ARE MORE THAN READY TO ANNOUNCE A WINNER!
CONGRATULATIONS TO...
CLASH!
WHAT?!?!
WELL. IT'S LIKE KIMBER SAID: KARAOKE IS ABOUT PASSION AND ENTHUSIASM AND HAVING FUN. CLASH DISPLAYED THOSE THINGS THE MOST.

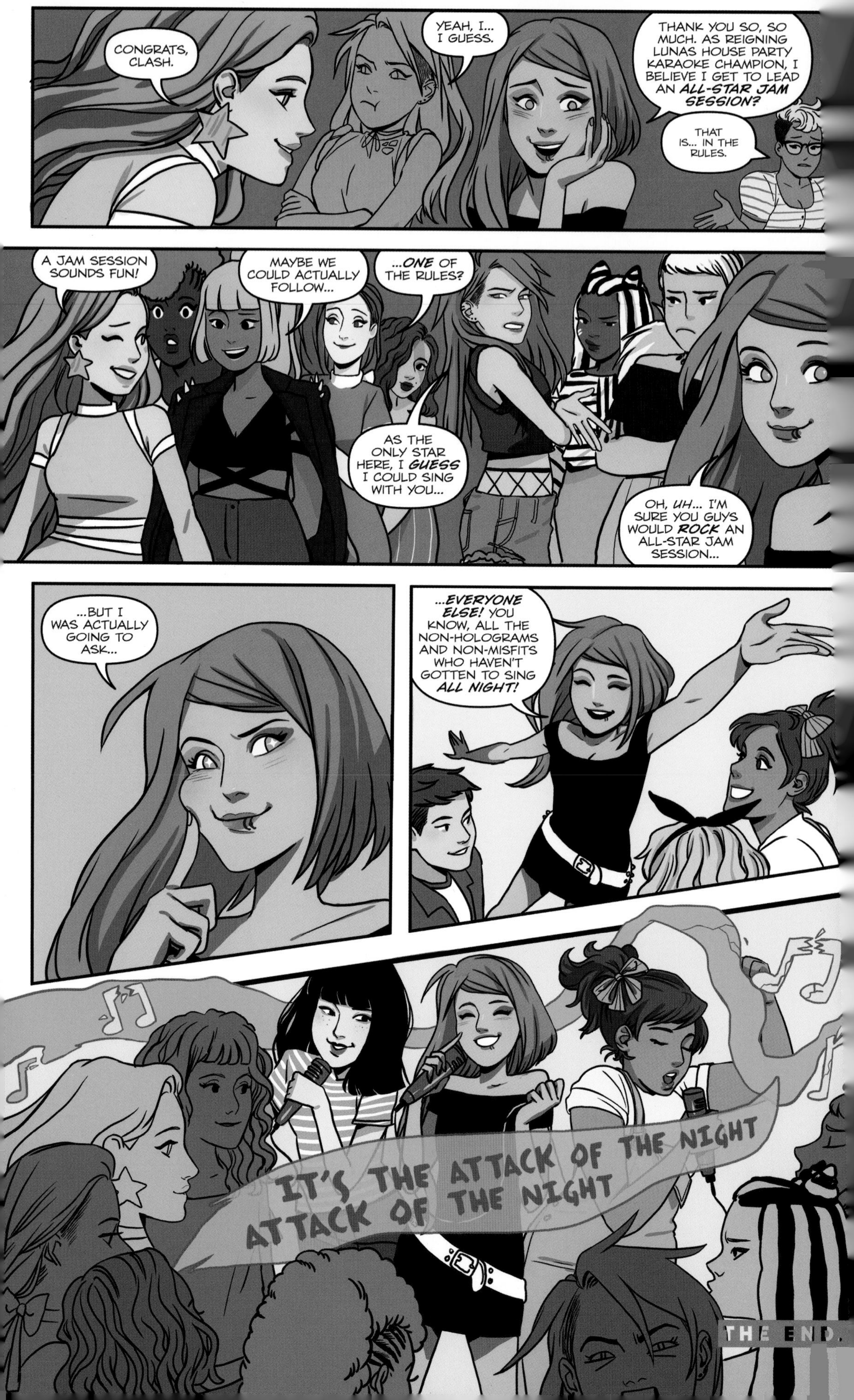
CONGRATS, CLASH.
YEAH, I... I GUESS.
THANK YOU SO, SO MUCH. AS REIGNING LUNAS HOUSE PARTY KARAOKE CHAMPION, I BELIEVE I GET TO LEAD AN ALL-STAR JAM SESSION?
THAT IS... IN THE RULES.
A JAM SESSION SOUNDS FUN!
MAYBE WE COULD ACTUALLY FOLLOW...
...ONE OF THE RULES?
AS THE ONLY STAR HERE, I GUESS I COULD SING WITH YOU...
OH, UH... I'M SURE YOU GUYS WOULD ROCK AN ALL-STAR JAM SESSION...
...BUT I WAS ACTUALLY GOING TO ASK...
...EVERYONE ELSE! YOU KNOW, ALL THE NON-HOLOGRAMS AND NON-MISFITS WHO HAVEN'T GOTTEN TO SING ALL NIGHT!
IT'S THE ATTACK OF THE NIGHT
ATTACK OF THE NIGHT
THE END.

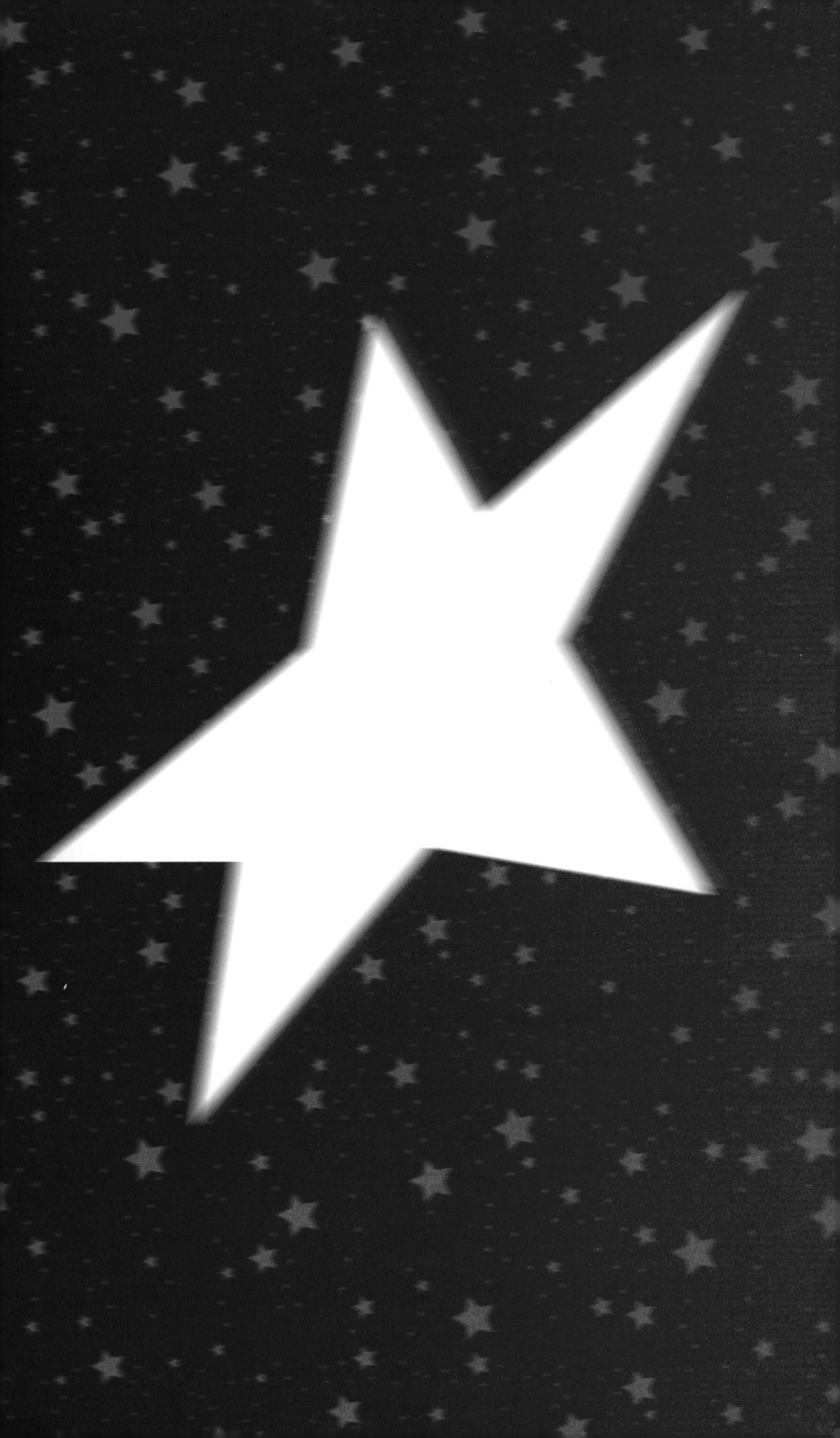

ART BY **SARAH WINIFRED SEARLE**

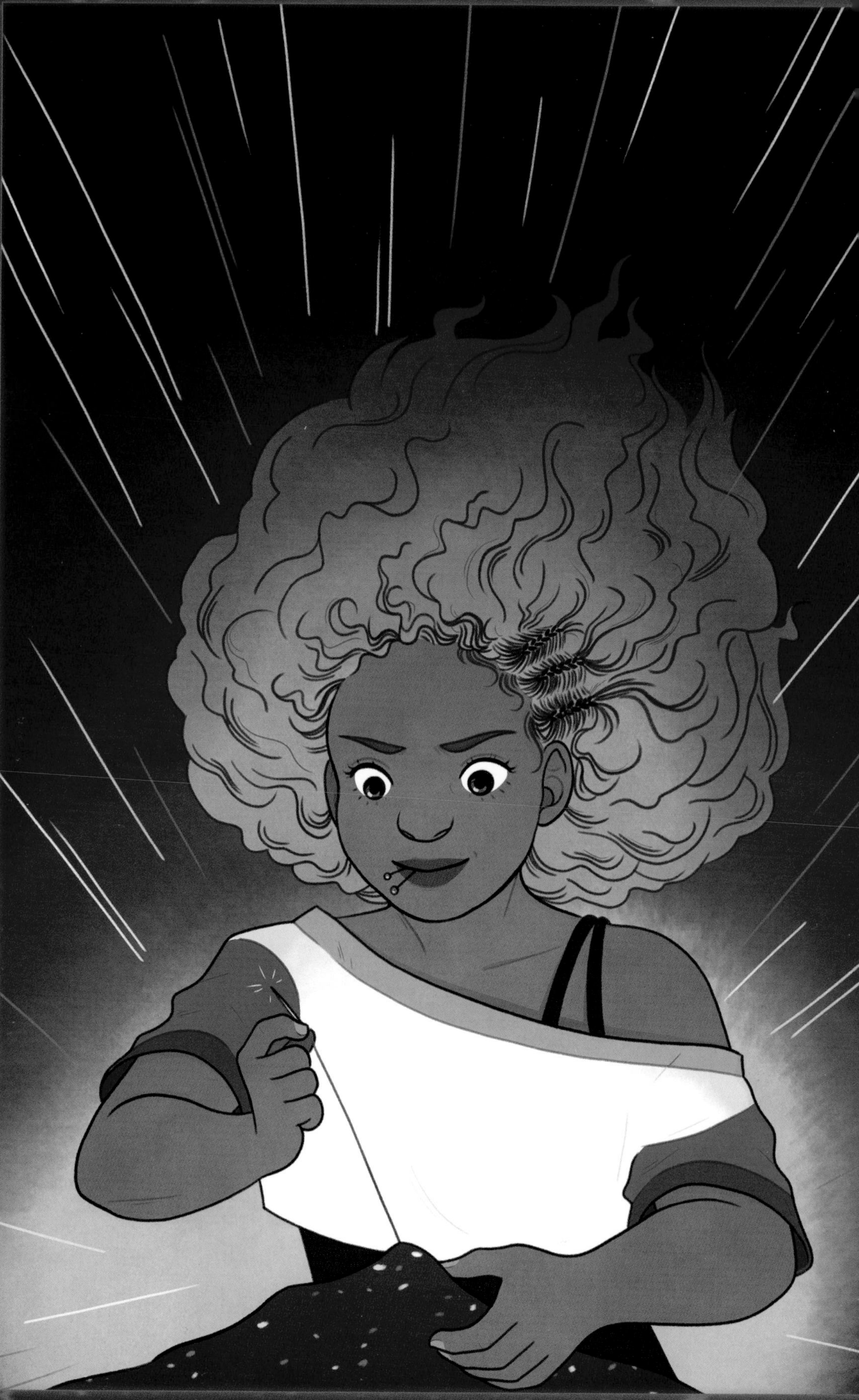

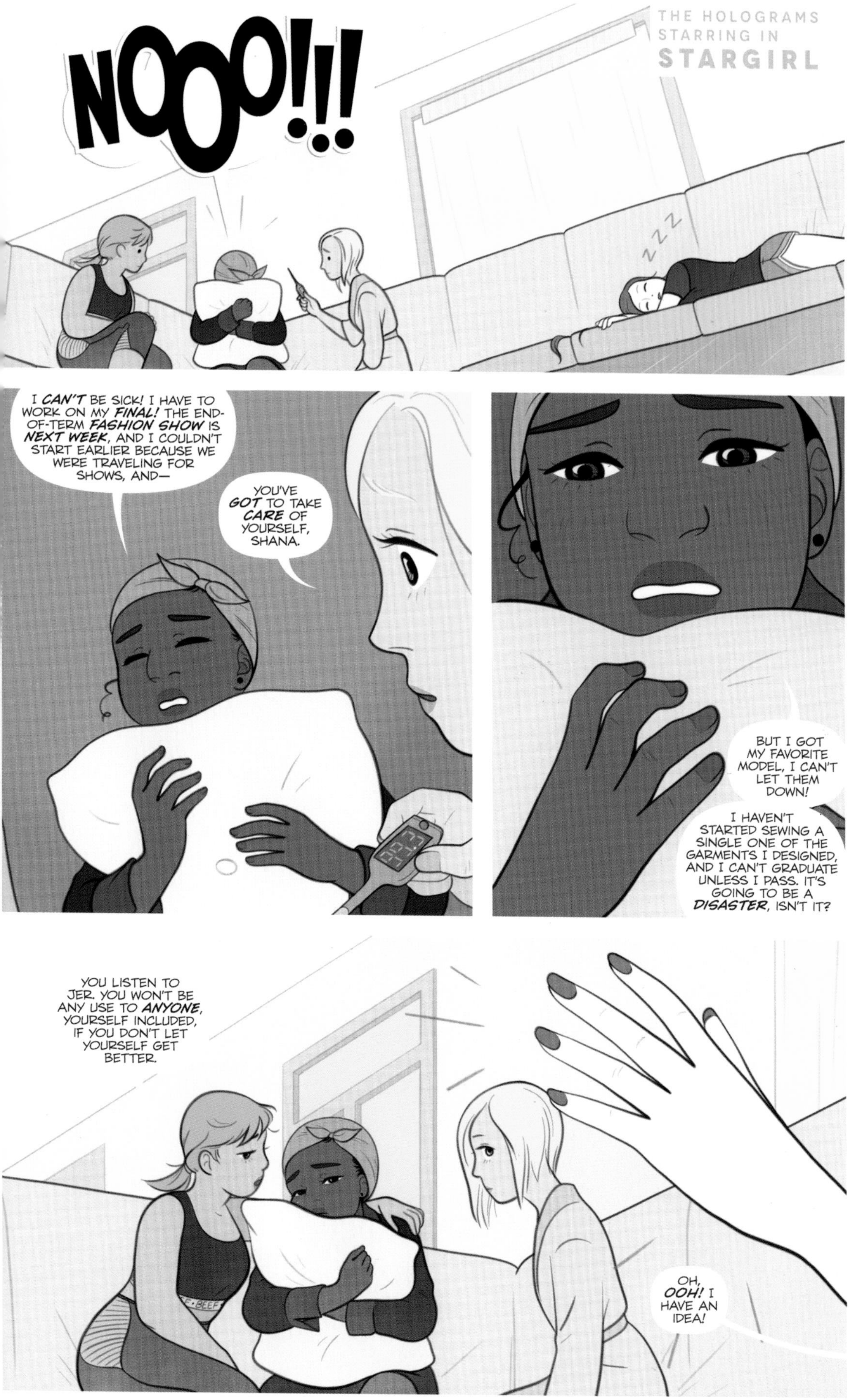
NOOO!!!
Z Z Z
I CAN'T BE SICK! I HAVE TO WORK ON MY FINAL! THE END-OF-TERM FASHION SHOW IS NEXT WEEK, AND I COULDN'T START EARLIER BECAUSE WE WERE TRAVELING FOR SHOWS, AND—
YOU'VE GOT TO TAKE CARE OF YOURSELF, SHANA.
BUT I GOT MY FAVORITE MODEL, I CAN'T LET THEM DOWN!
I HAVEN'T STARTED SEWING A SINGLE ONE OF THE GARMENTS I DESIGNED, AND I CAN'T GRADUATE UNLESS I PASS. IT'S GOING TO BE A DISASTER, ISN'T IT?
YOU LISTEN TO JER. YOU WON'T BE ANY USE TO ANYONE, YOURSELF INCLUDED, IF YOU DON'T LET YOURSELF GET BETTER.
OH, OOH! I HAVE AN IDEA!

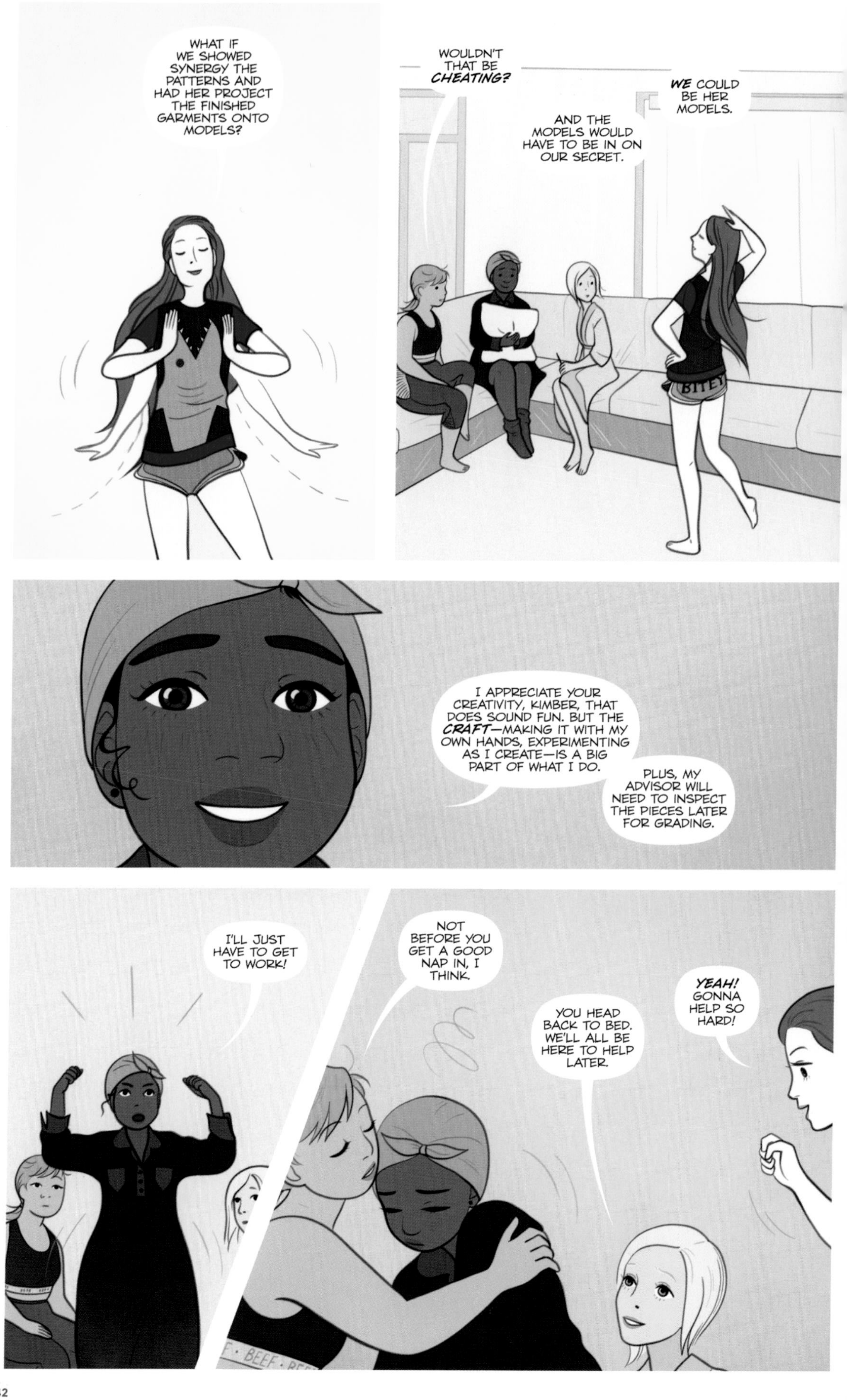
WHAT IF WE SHOWED SYNERGY THE PATTERNS AND HAD HER PROJECT THE FINISHED GARMENTS ONTO MODELS?
WOULDN'T THAT BE *CHEATING?*
AND THE MODELS WOULD HAVE TO BE IN ON OUR SECRET.
WE COULD BE HER MODELS.
BITEY
I APPRECIATE YOUR CREATIVITY, KIMBER, THAT DOES SOUND FUN. BUT THE *CRAFT*—MAKING IT WITH MY OWN HANDS, EXPERIMENTING AS I CREATE—IS A BIG PART OF WHAT I DO.
PLUS, MY ADVISOR WILL NEED TO INSPECT THE PIECES LATER FOR GRADING.
I'LL JUST HAVE TO GET TO WORK!
NOT BEFORE YOU GET A GOOD NAP IN, I THINK.
YOU HEAD BACK TO BED. WE'LL ALL BE HERE TO HELP LATER.
YEAH! GONNA HELP SO HARD!

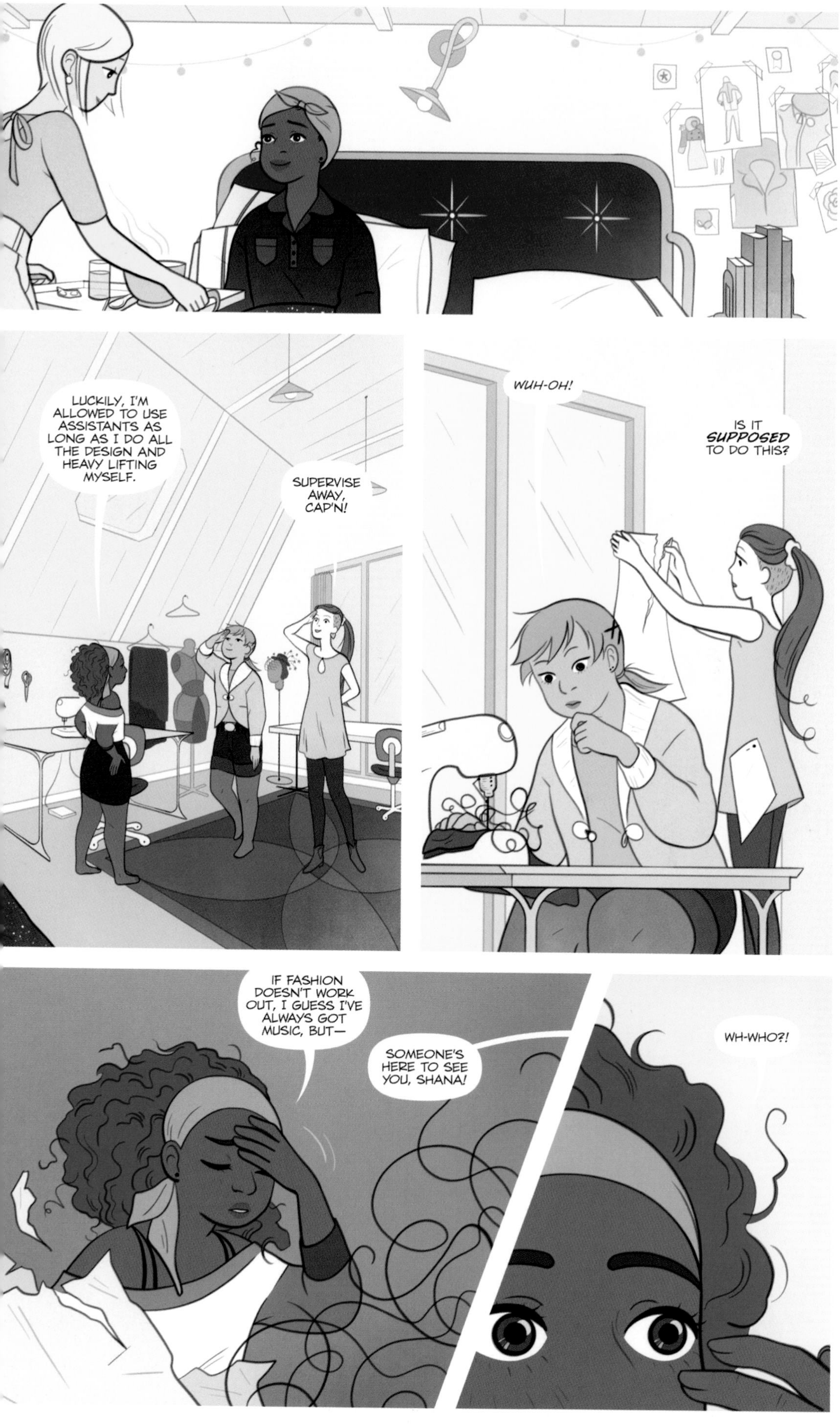

LUCKILY, I'M ALLOWED TO USE ASSISTANTS AS LONG AS I DO ALL THE DESIGN AND HEAVY LIFTING MYSELF.
SUPERVISE AWAY, CAP'N!
WUH-OH!
IS IT **SUPPOSED** TO DO THIS?
IF FASHION DOESN'T WORK OUT, I GUESS I'VE ALWAYS GOT MUSIC, BUT—
SOMEONE'S HERE TO SEE YOU, SHANA!
WH-WHO?!

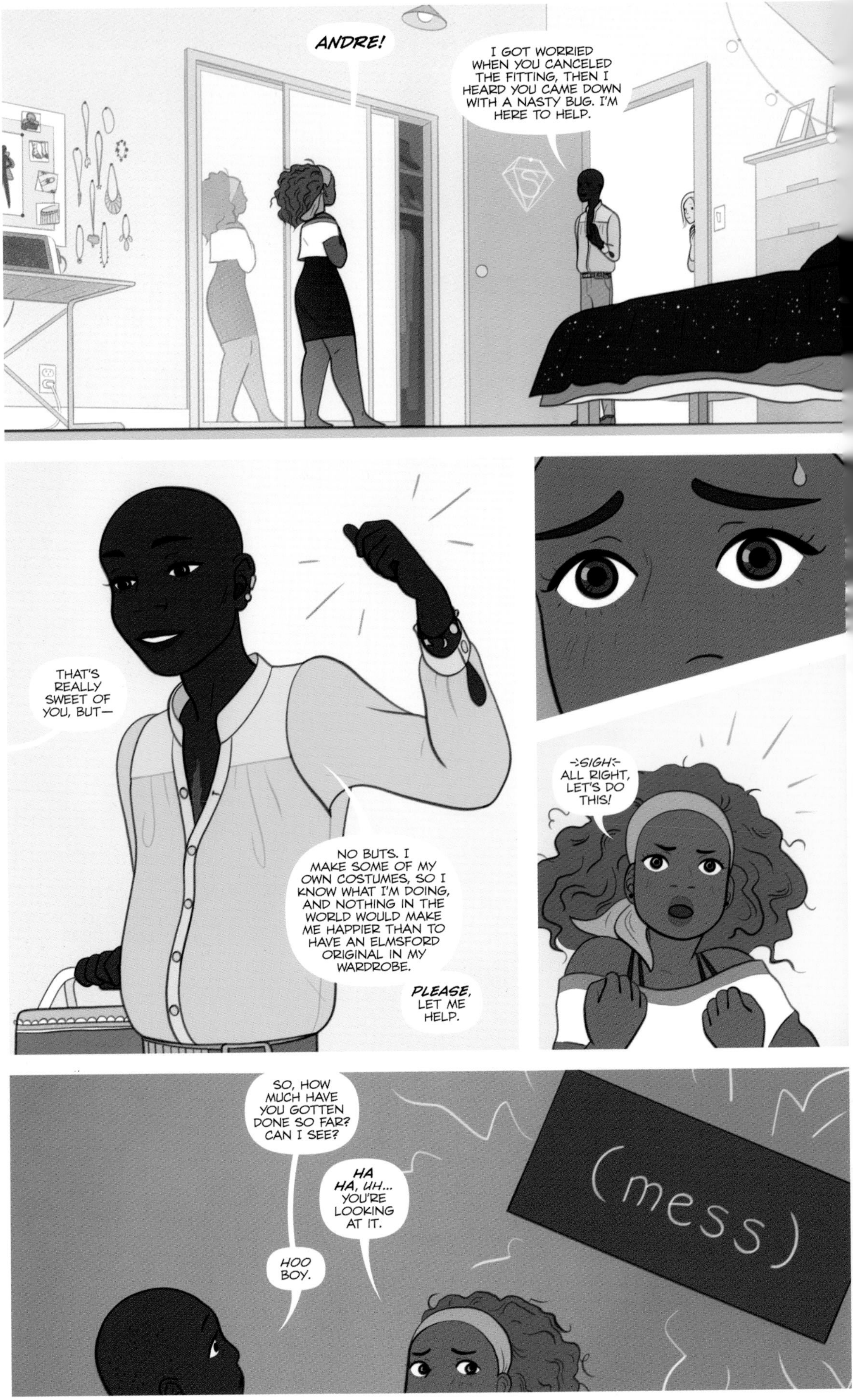
ANDRE!
I GOT WORRIED WHEN YOU CANCELED THE FITTING, THEN I HEARD YOU CAME DOWN WITH A NASTY BUG. I'M HERE TO HELP.
THAT'S REALLY SWEET OF YOU, BUT—
NO BUTS. I MAKE SOME OF MY OWN COSTUMES, SO I KNOW WHAT I'M DOING, AND NOTHING IN THE WORLD WOULD MAKE ME HAPPIER THAN TO HAVE AN ELMSFORD ORIGINAL IN MY WARDROBE.
PLEASE, LET ME HELP.
-SIGH- ALL RIGHT, LET'S DO THIS!
SO, HOW MUCH HAVE YOU GOTTEN DONE SO FAR? CAN I SEE?
HA HA, UH... YOU'RE LOOKING AT IT.
(mess)
HOO BOY.

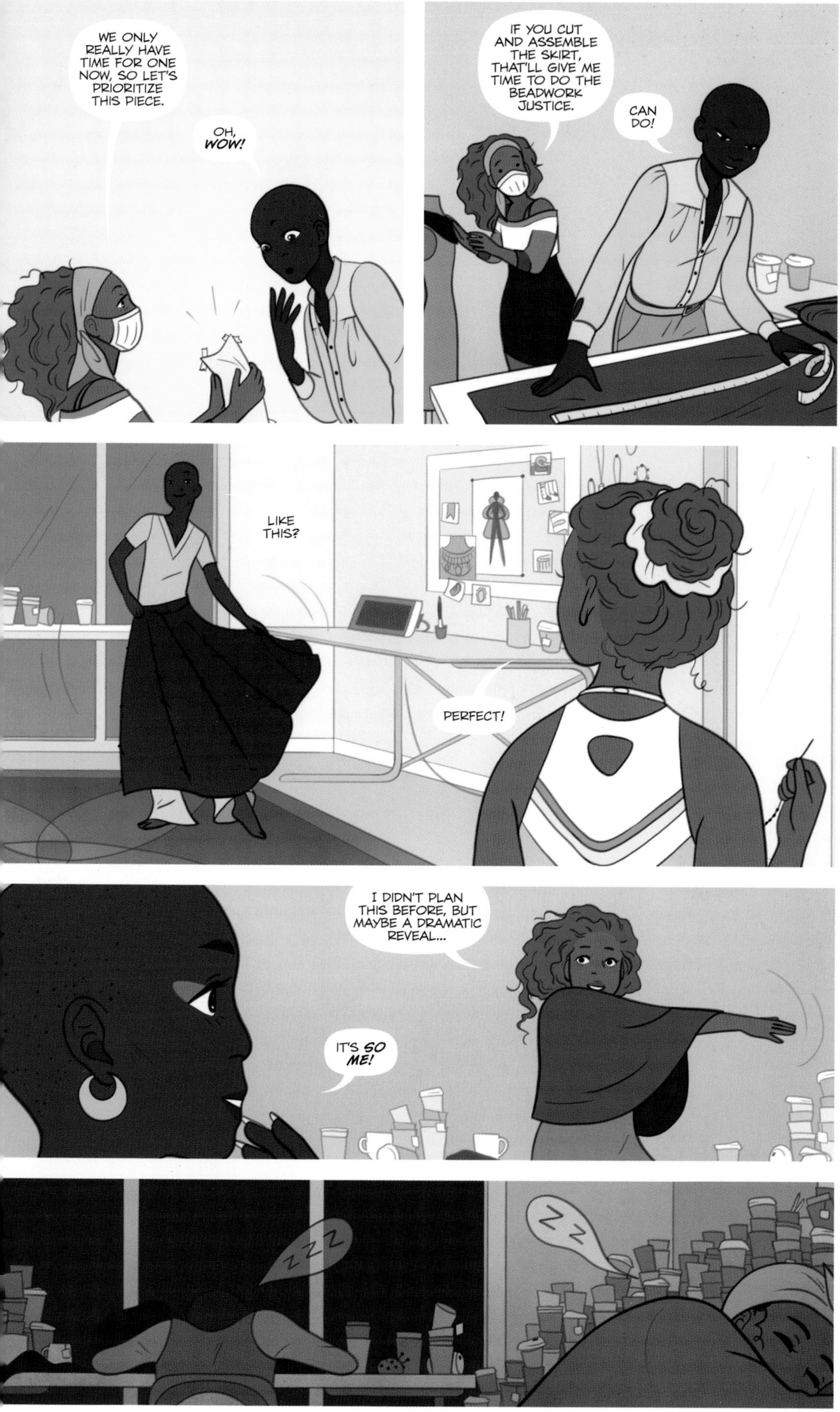
WE ONLY REALLY HAVE TIME FOR ONE NOW, SO LET'S PRIORITIZE THIS PIECE.
OH, *WOW!*
IF YOU CUT AND ASSEMBLE THE SKIRT, THAT'LL GIVE ME TIME TO DO THE BEADWORK JUSTICE.
CAN DO!
LIKE THIS?
PERFECT!
I DIDN'T PLAN THIS BEFORE, BUT MAYBE A DRAMATIC REVEAL...
IT'S *SO ME!*
ZZZ
ZZ

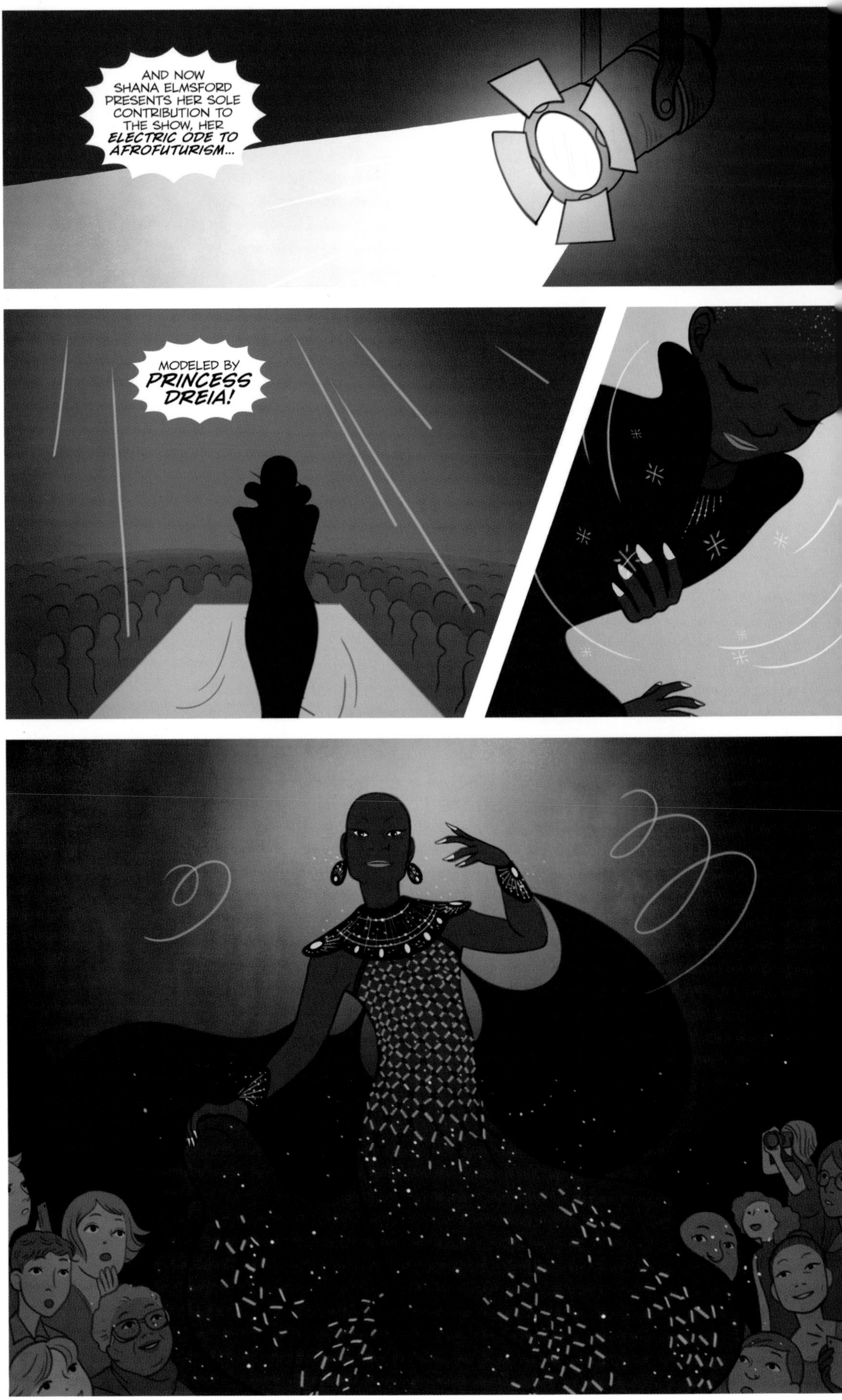
AND NOW SHANA ELMSFORD PRESENTS HER SOLE CONTRIBUTION TO THE SHOW, HER *ELECTRIC ODE TO AFROFUTURISM...*
MODELED BY *PRINCESS DREIA!*

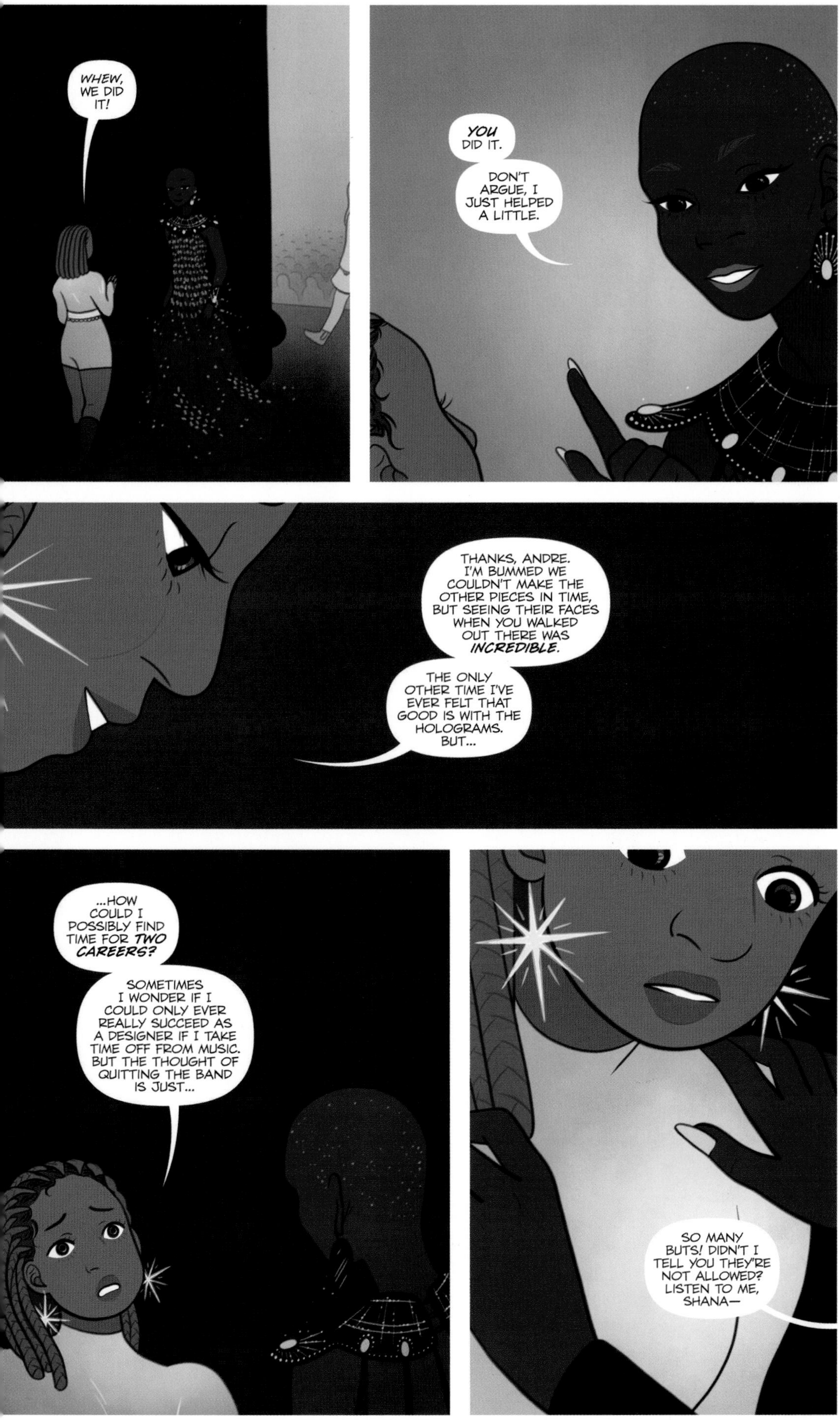
WHEW, WE DID IT!
YOU DID IT.
DON'T ARGUE, I JUST HELPED A LITTLE.
THANKS, ANDRE. I'M BUMMED WE COULDN'T MAKE THE OTHER PIECES IN TIME, BUT SEEING THEIR FACES WHEN YOU WALKED OUT THERE WAS INCREDIBLE.
THE ONLY OTHER TIME I'VE EVER FELT THAT GOOD IS WITH THE HOLOGRAMS. BUT...
...HOW COULD I POSSIBLY FIND TIME FOR TWO CAREERS?
SOMETIMES I WONDER IF I COULD ONLY EVER REALLY SUCCEED AS A DESIGNER IF I TAKE TIME OFF FROM MUSIC. BUT THE THOUGHT OF QUITTING THE BAND IS JUST...
SO MANY BUTS! DIDN'T I TELL YOU THEY'RE NOT ALLOWED? LISTEN TO ME, SHANA—

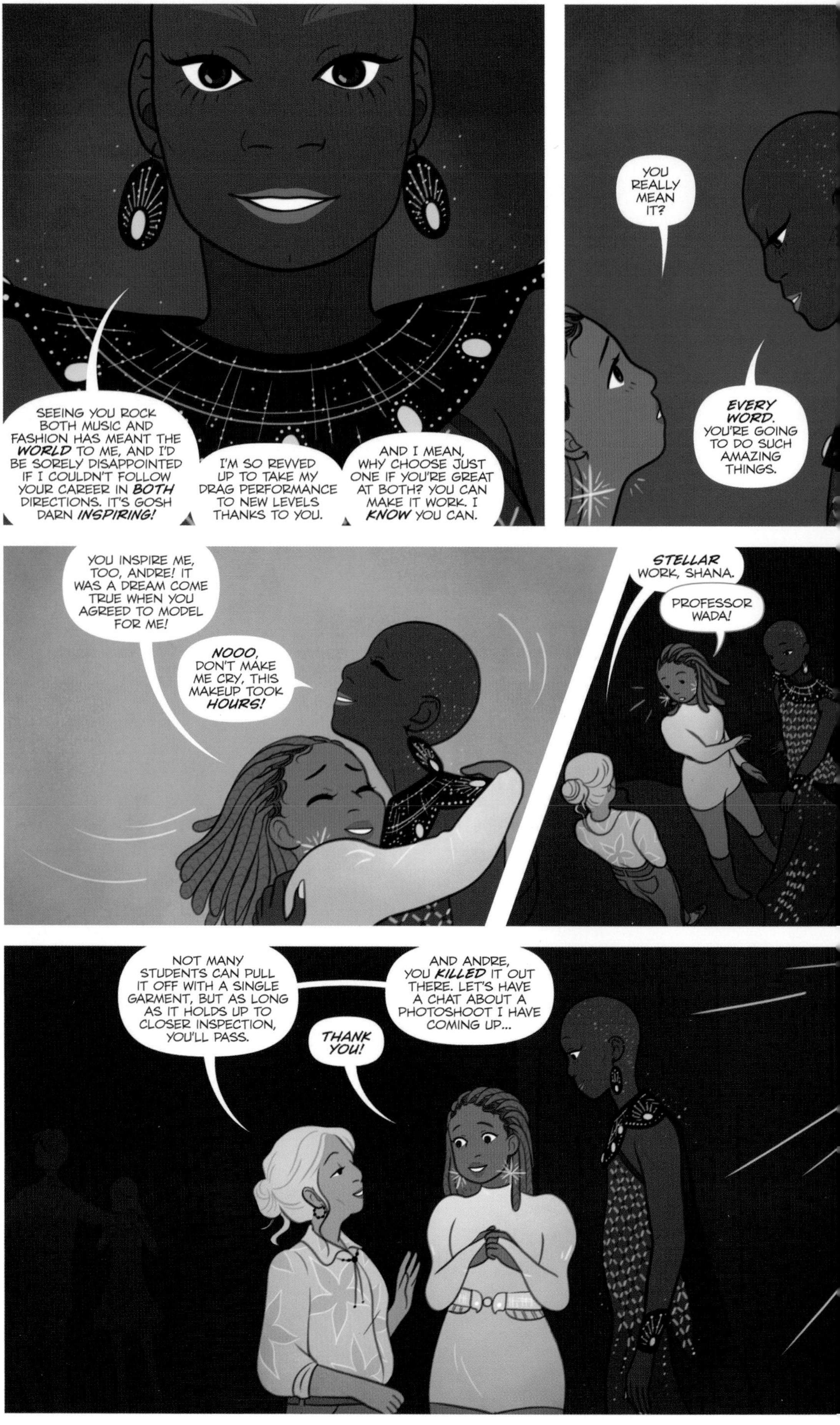
SEEING YOU ROCK BOTH MUSIC AND FASHION HAS MEANT THE *WORLD* TO ME, AND I'D BE SORELY DISAPPOINTED IF I COULDN'T FOLLOW YOUR CAREER IN *BOTH* DIRECTIONS. IT'S GOSH DARN *INSPIRING!*
I'M SO REVVED UP TO TAKE MY DRAG PERFORMANCE TO NEW LEVELS THANKS TO YOU.
AND I MEAN, WHY CHOOSE JUST ONE IF YOU'RE GREAT AT BOTH? YOU CAN MAKE IT WORK. I *KNOW* YOU CAN.
YOU REALLY MEAN IT?
EVERY WORD. YOU'RE GOING TO DO SUCH AMAZING THINGS.
YOU INSPIRE ME, TOO, ANDRE! IT WAS A DREAM COME TRUE WHEN YOU AGREED TO MODEL FOR ME!
NOOO, DON'T MAKE ME CRY, THIS MAKEUP TOOK *HOURS!*
STELLAR WORK, SHANA.
PROFESSOR WADA!
NOT MANY STUDENTS CAN PULL IT OFF WITH A SINGLE GARMENT, BUT AS LONG AS IT HOLDS UP TO CLOSER INSPECTION, YOU'LL PASS.
THANK YOU!
AND ANDRE, YOU *KILLED* IT OUT THERE. LET'S HAVE A CHAT ABOUT A PHOTOSHOOT I HAVE COMING UP...

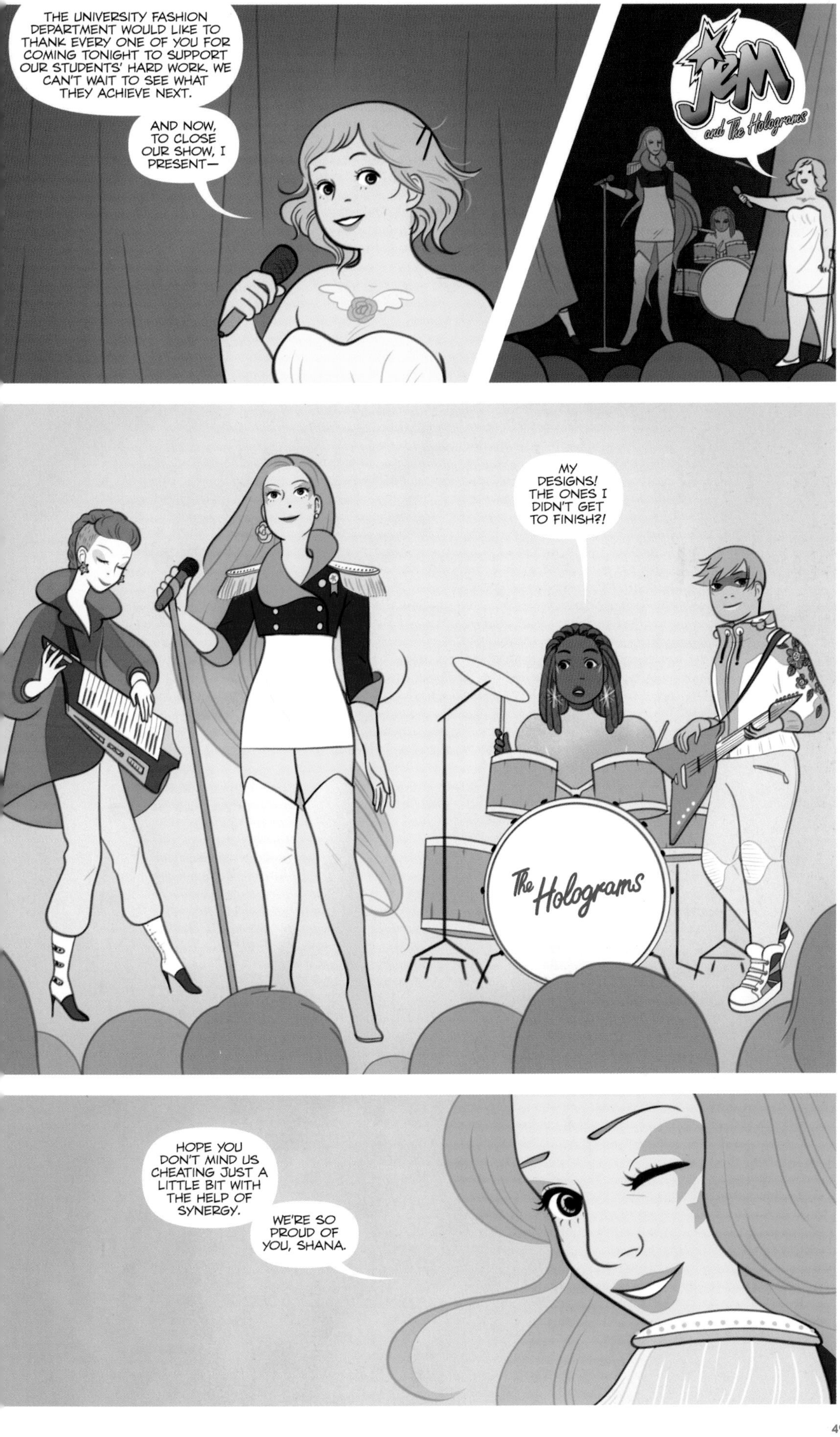
THE UNIVERSITY FASHION DEPARTMENT WOULD LIKE TO THANK EVERY ONE OF YOU FOR COMING TONIGHT TO SUPPORT OUR STUDENTS' HARD WORK. WE CAN'T WAIT TO SEE WHAT THEY ACHIEVE NEXT.
AND NOW, TO CLOSE OUR SHOW, I PRESENT—
JEM and The Holograms
MY DESIGNS! THE ONES I DIDN'T GET TO FINISH?!
The Holograms
HOPE YOU DON'T MIND US CHEATING JUST A LITTLE BIT WITH THE HELP OF SYNERGY.
WE'RE SO PROUD OF YOU, SHANA.

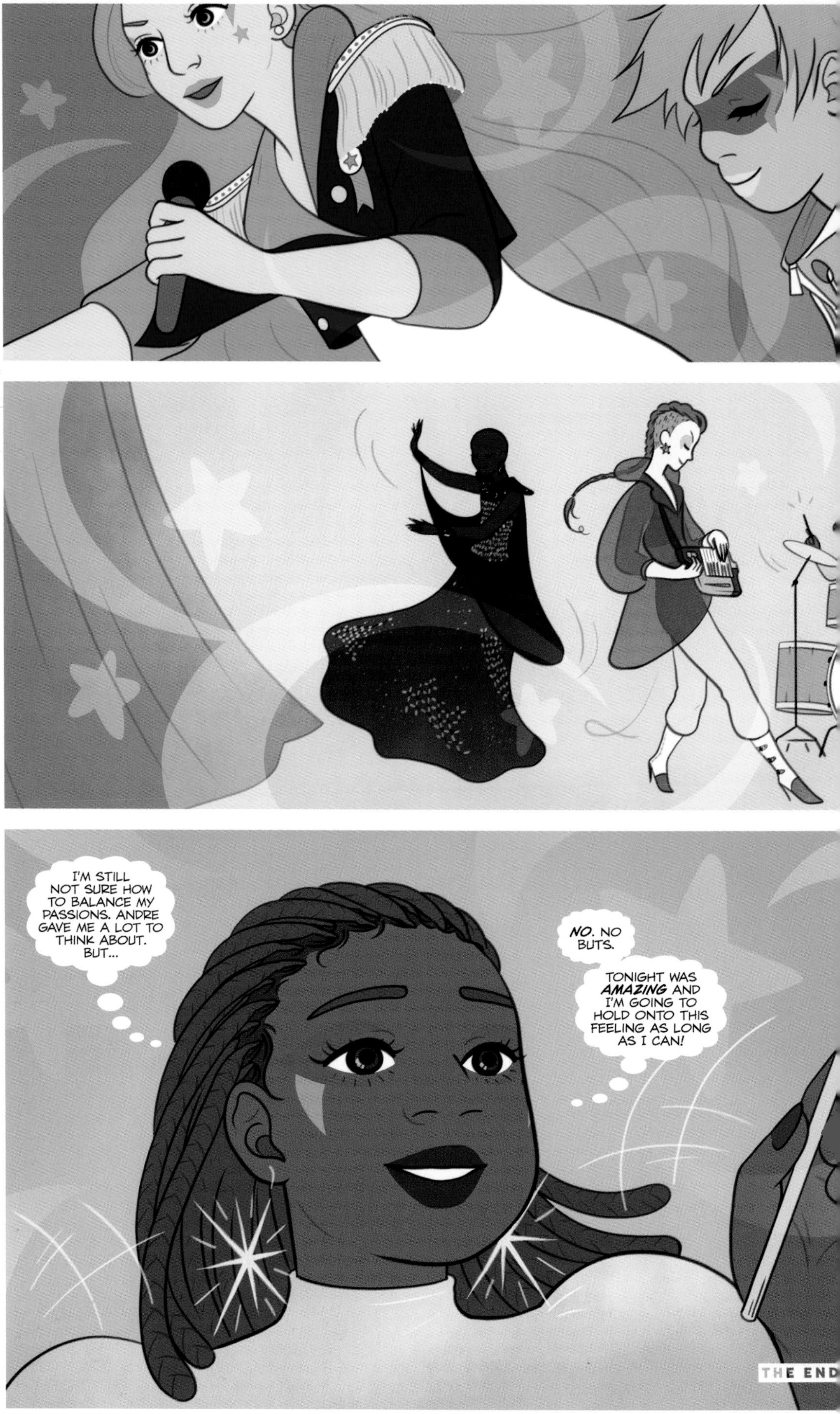
I'M STILL NOT SURE HOW TO BALANCE MY PASSIONS. ANDRE GAVE ME A LOT TO THINK ABOUT. BUT...
NO. NO BUTS.
TONIGHT WAS AMAZING AND I'M GOING TO HOLD ONTO THIS FEELING AS LONG AS I CAN!
THE END

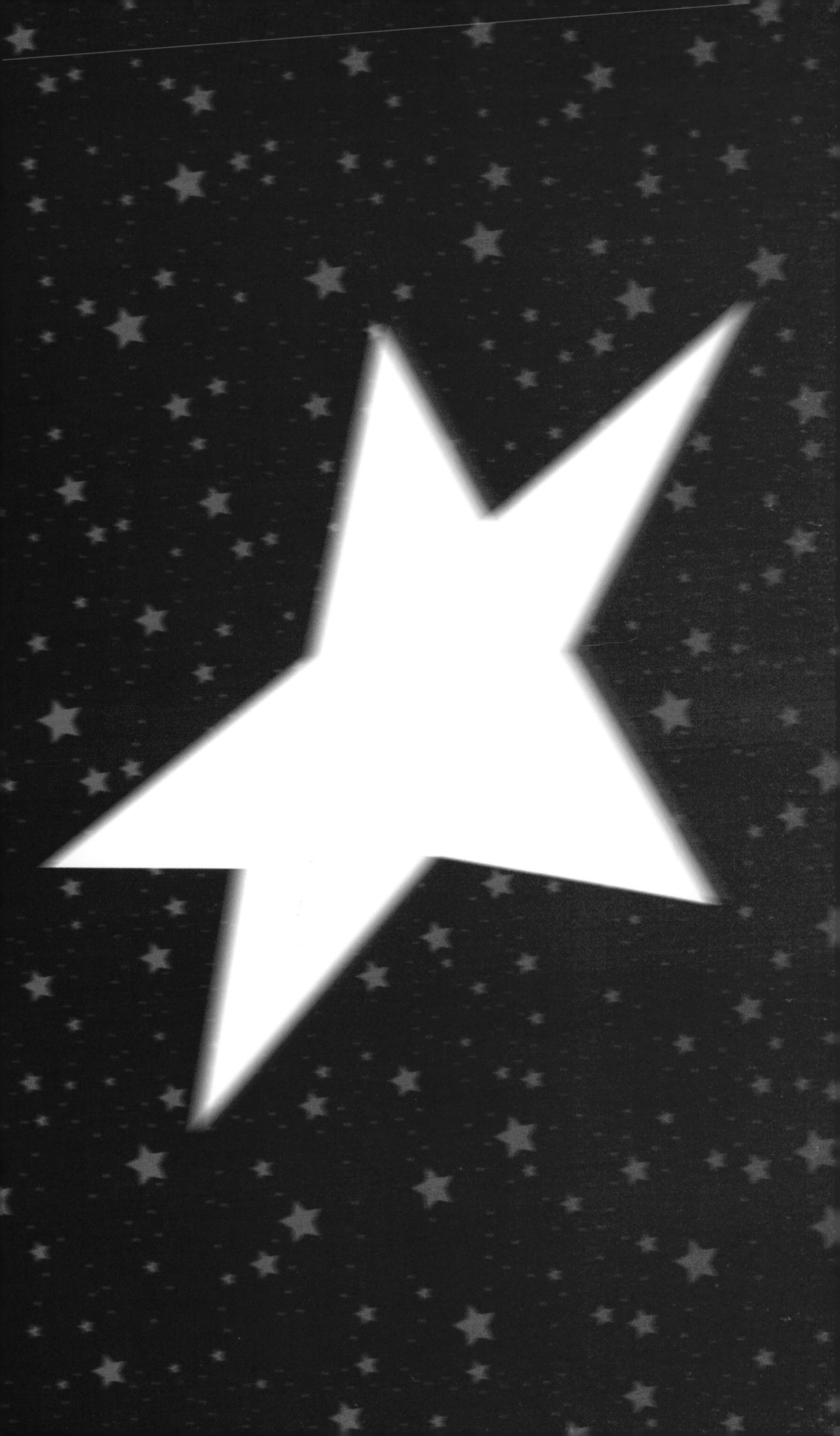

ART BY **NICOLE GOUX**

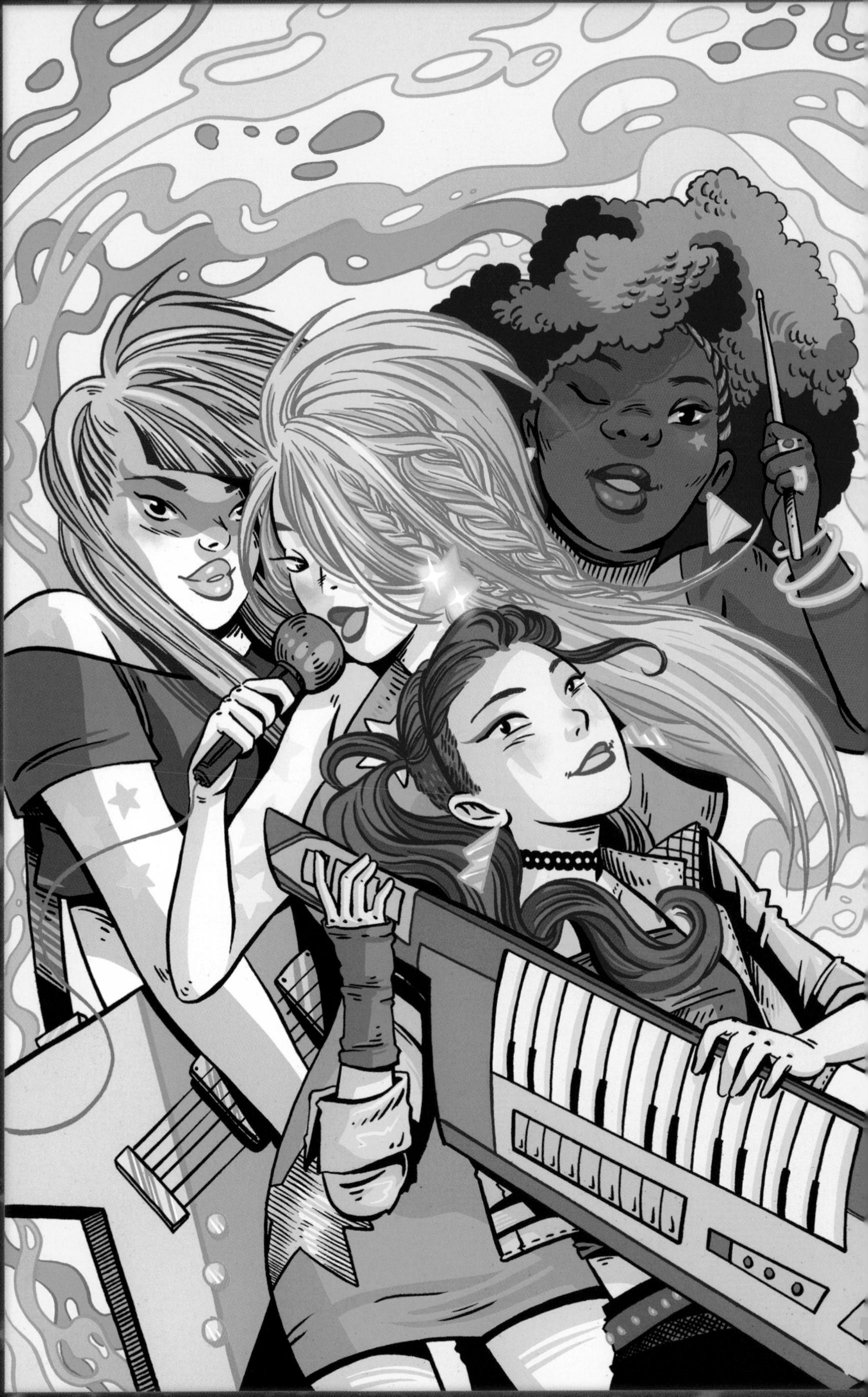

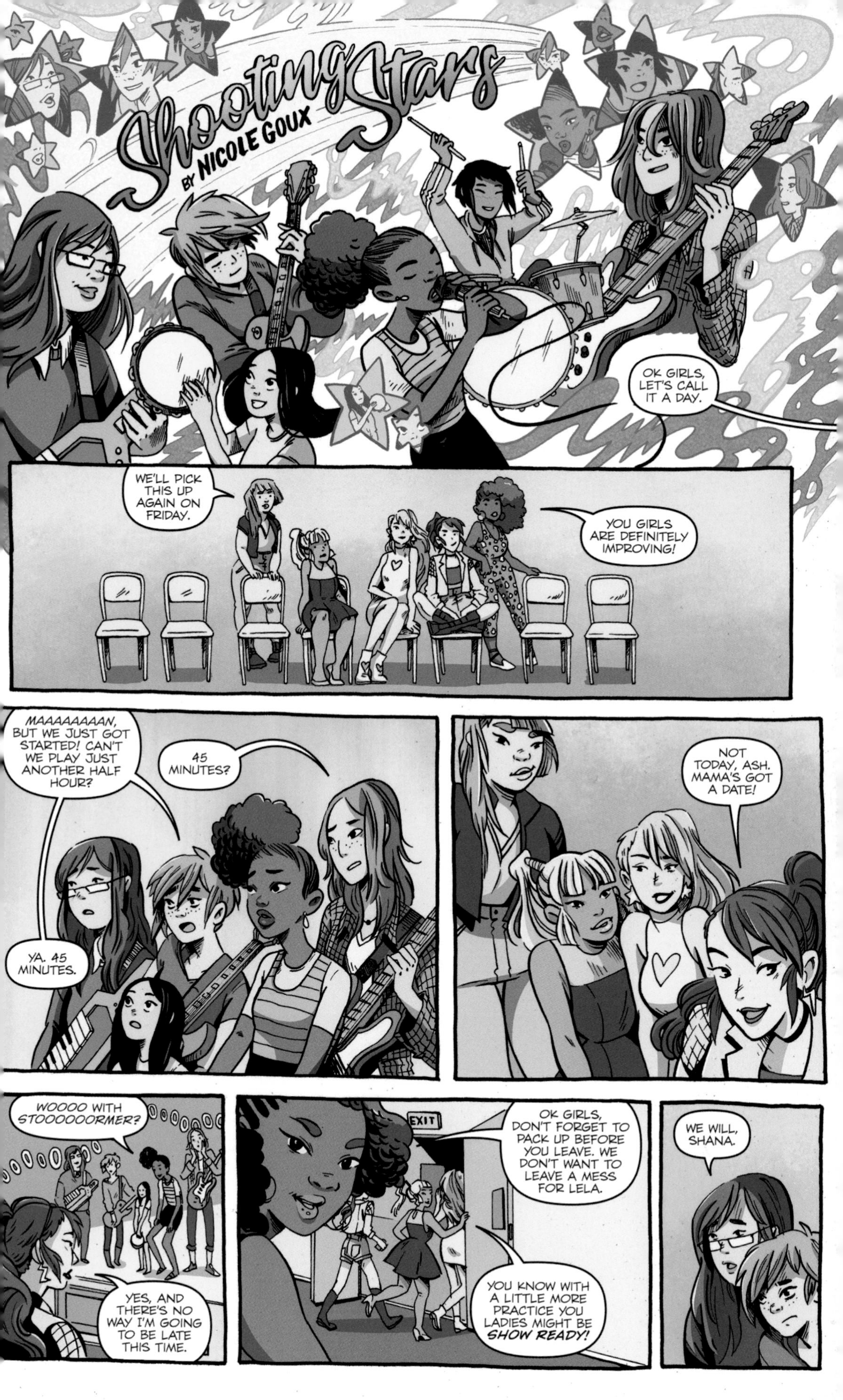
Shooting Stars
BY NICOLE GOUX
OK GIRLS, LET'S CALL IT A DAY.
WE'LL PICK THIS UP AGAIN ON FRIDAY.
YOU GIRLS ARE DEFINITELY IMPROVING!
MAAAAAAAAN, BUT WE JUST GOT STARTED! CAN'T WE PLAY JUST ANOTHER HALF HOUR?
45 MINUTES?
YA. 45 MINUTES.
NOT TODAY, ASH. MAMA'S GOT A DATE!
WOOOO WITH STOOOOOORMER?
OOOOOOOOOO
YES, AND THERE'S NO WAY I'M GOING TO BE LATE THIS TIME.
EXIT
OK GIRLS, DON'T FORGET TO PACK UP BEFORE YOU LEAVE. WE DON'T WANT TO LEAVE A MESS FOR LELA.
YOU KNOW WITH A LITTLE MORE PRACTICE YOU LADIES MIGHT BE SHOW READY!
WE WILL, SHANA.

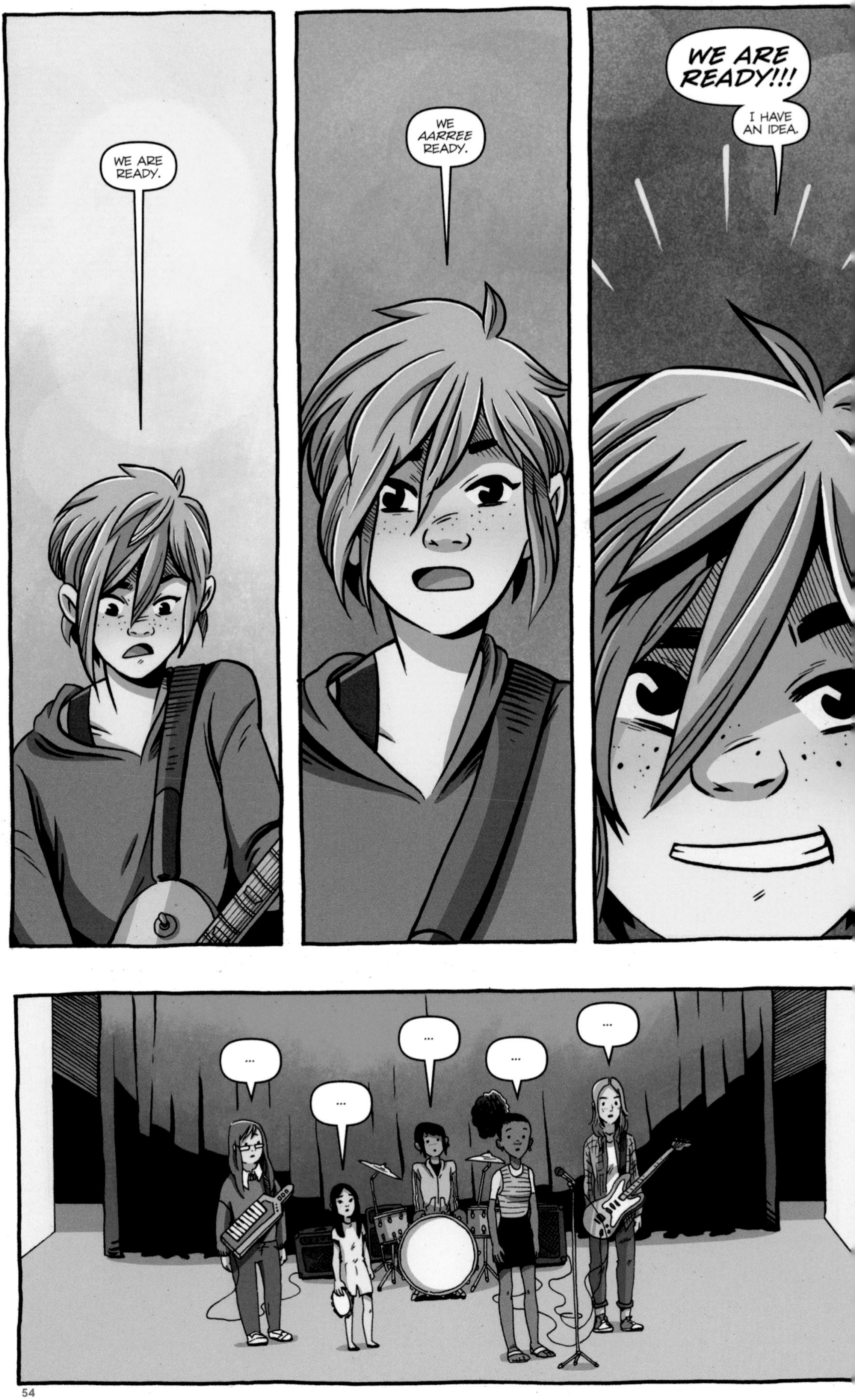
WE ARE READY.
WE AARREE READY.
WE ARE READY!!!
I HAVE AN IDEA.
...
...
...
...
...

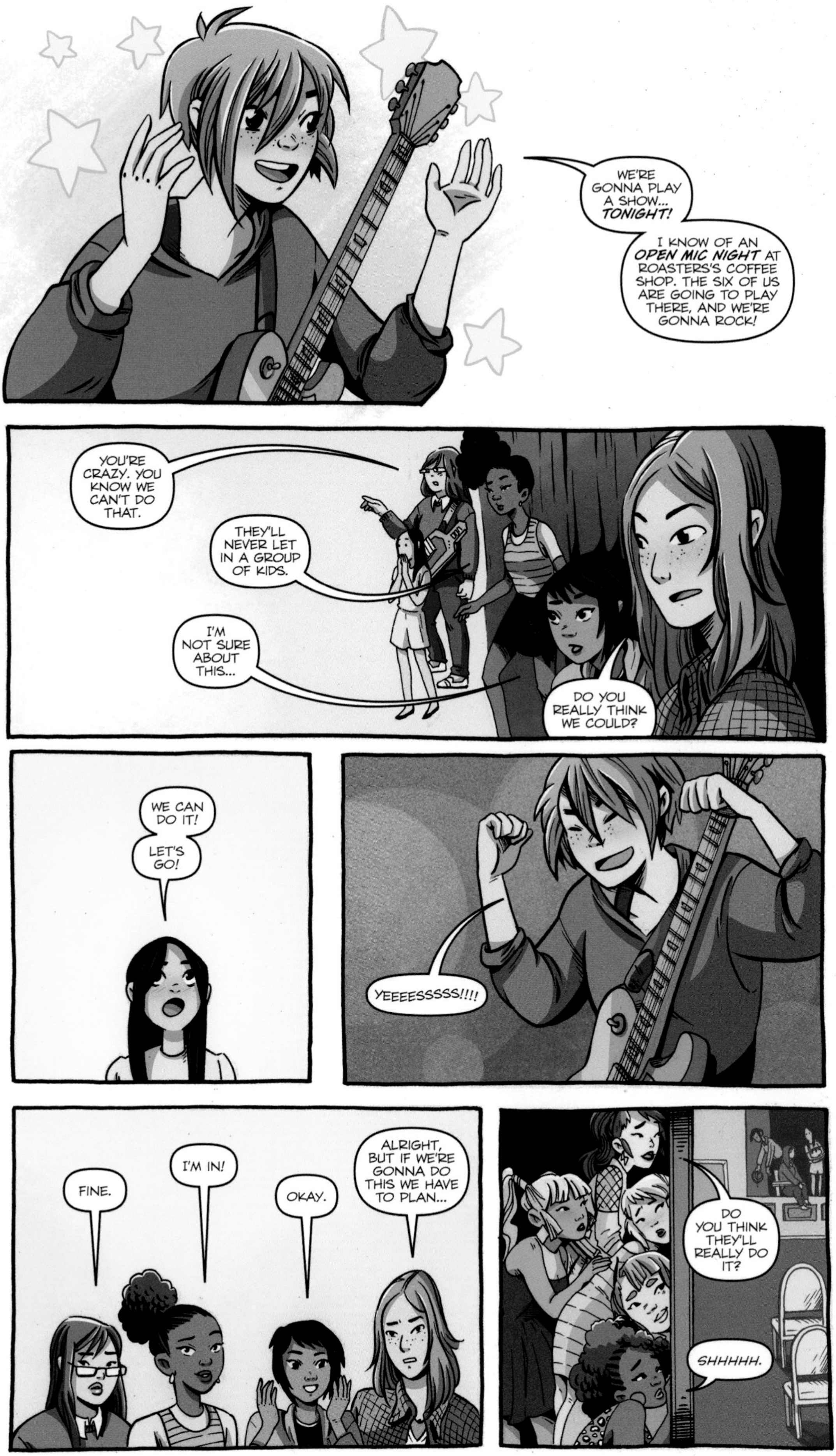

WE'RE GONNA PLAY A SHOW... TONIGHT!
I KNOW OF AN OPEN MIC NIGHT AT ROASTERS'S COFFEE SHOP. THE SIX OF US ARE GOING TO PLAY THERE, AND WE'RE GONNA ROCK!
YOU'RE CRAZY. YOU KNOW WE CAN'T DO THAT.
THEY'LL NEVER LET IN A GROUP OF KIDS.
I'M NOT SURE ABOUT THIS...
DO YOU REALLY THINK WE COULD?
WE CAN DO IT!
LET'S GO!
YEEEESSSSS!!!!
FINE.
I'M IN!
OKAY.
ALRIGHT, BUT IF WE'RE GONNA DO THIS WE HAVE TO PLAN...
DO YOU THINK THEY'LL REALLY DO IT?
SHHHHH.

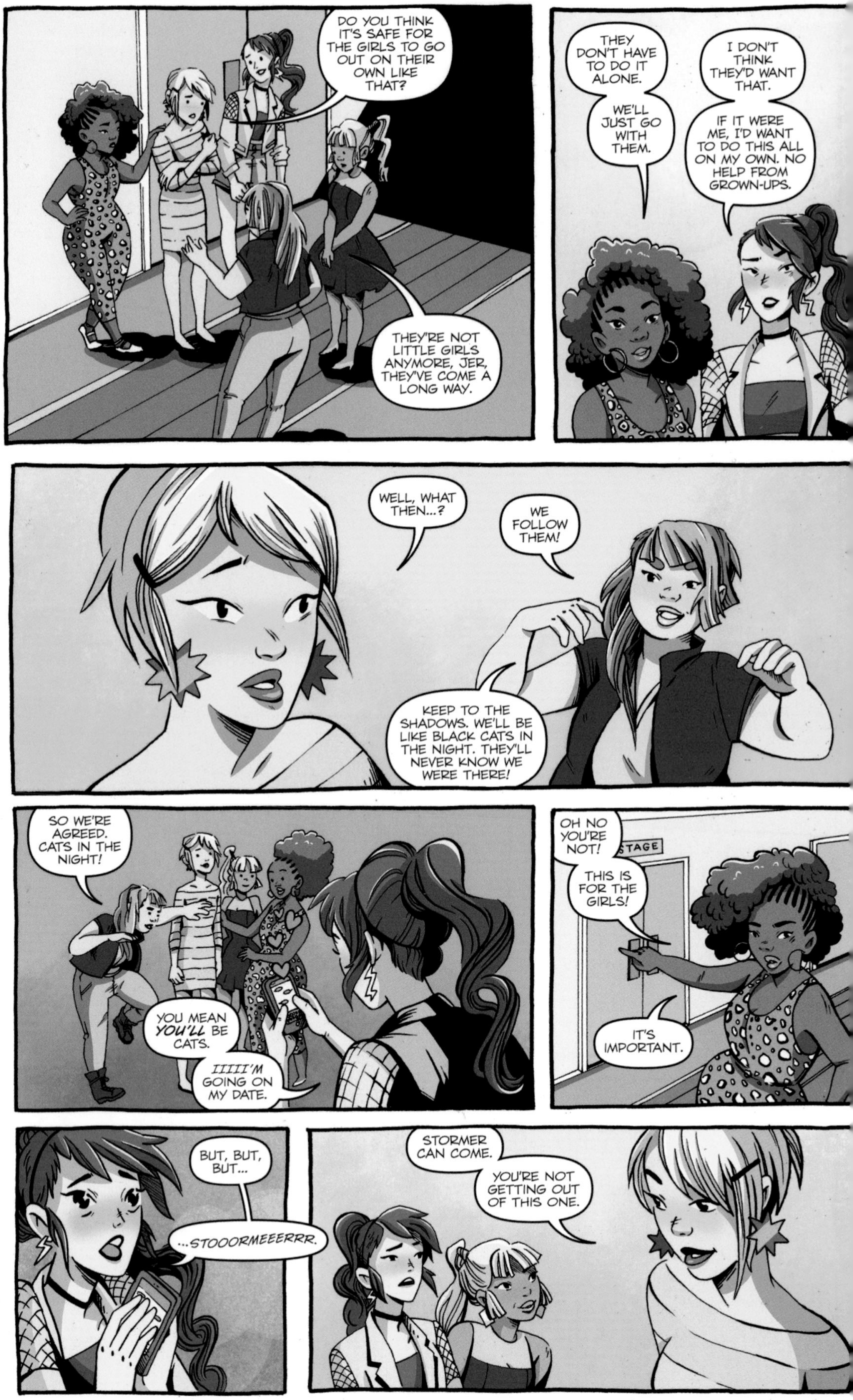
DO YOU THINK IT'S SAFE FOR THE GIRLS TO GO OUT ON THEIR OWN LIKE THAT?
THEY'RE NOT LITTLE GIRLS ANYMORE, JER, THEY'VE COME A LONG WAY.
THEY DON'T HAVE TO DO IT ALONE.
WE'LL JUST GO WITH THEM.
I DON'T THINK THEY'D WANT THAT.
IF IT WERE ME, I'D WANT TO DO THIS ALL ON MY OWN. NO HELP FROM GROWN-UPS.
WELL, WHAT THEN...?
WE FOLLOW THEM!
KEEP TO THE SHADOWS. WE'LL BE LIKE BLACK CATS IN THE NIGHT. THEY'LL NEVER KNOW WE WERE THERE!
SO WE'RE AGREED. CATS IN THE NIGHT!
YOU MEAN *YOU'LL* BE CATS.
IIIII'M GOING ON MY DATE.
OH NO YOU'RE NOT!
STAGE
THIS IS FOR THE GIRLS!
IT'S IMPORTANT.
BUT, BUT, BUT...
...*STOOORMEEERRR.*
STORMER CAN COME.
YOU'RE NOT GETTING OUT OF THIS ONE.

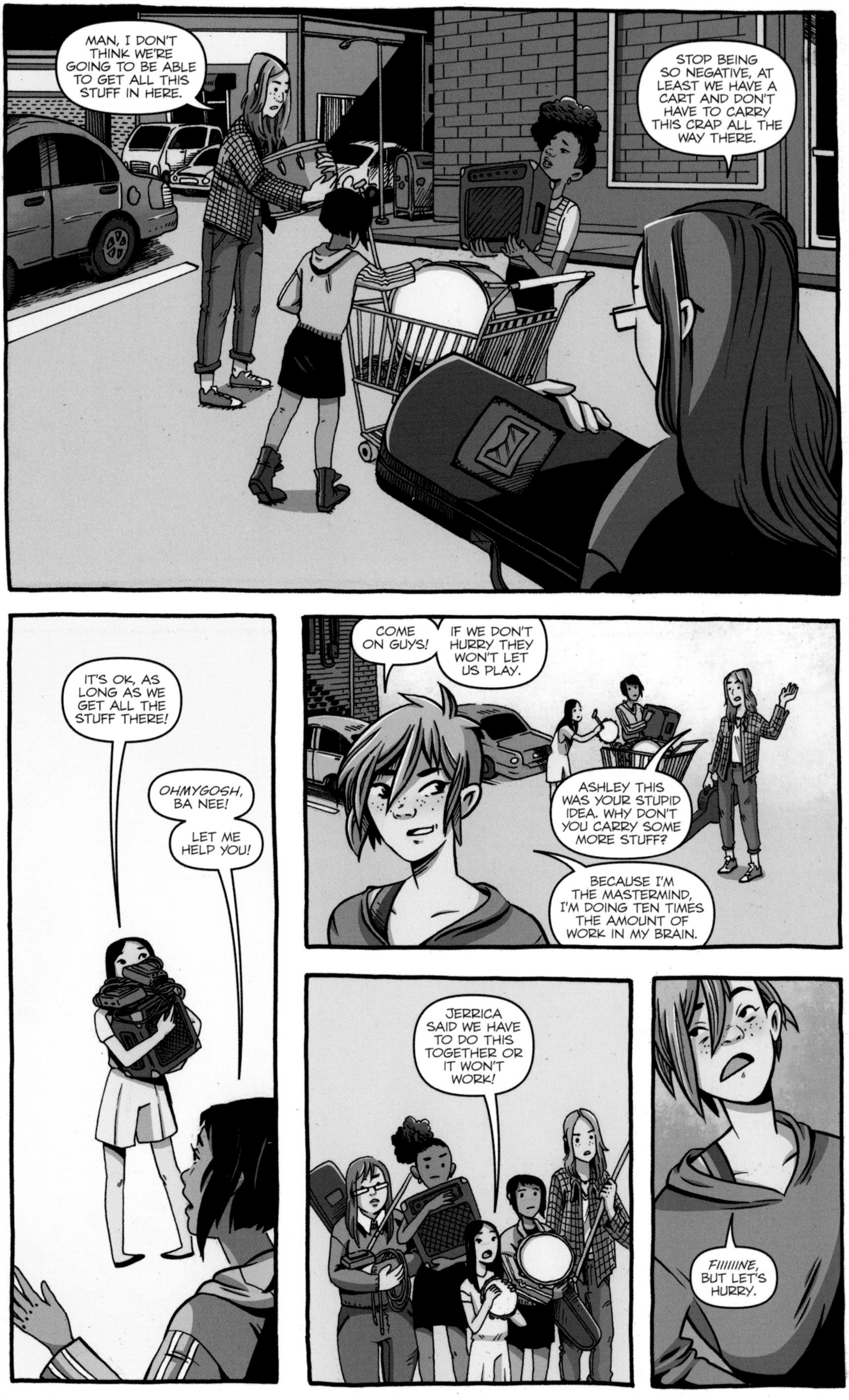
MAN, I DON'T THINK WE'RE GOING TO BE ABLE TO GET ALL THIS STUFF IN HERE.
STOP BEING SO NEGATIVE, AT LEAST WE HAVE A CART AND DON'T HAVE TO CARRY THIS CRAP ALL THE WAY THERE.
IT'S OK, AS LONG AS WE GET ALL THE STUFF THERE!
OHMYGOSH, BA NEE!
LET ME HELP YOU!
COME ON GUYS!
IF WE DON'T HURRY THEY WON'T LET US PLAY.
ASHLEY THIS WAS YOUR STUPID IDEA. WHY DON'T YOU CARRY SOME MORE STUFF?
BECAUSE I'M THE MASTERMIND, I'M DOING TEN TIMES THE AMOUNT OF WORK IN MY BRAIN.
JERRICA SAID WE HAVE TO DO THIS TOGETHER OR IT WON'T WORK!
FIIIIINE, BUT LET'S HURRY.

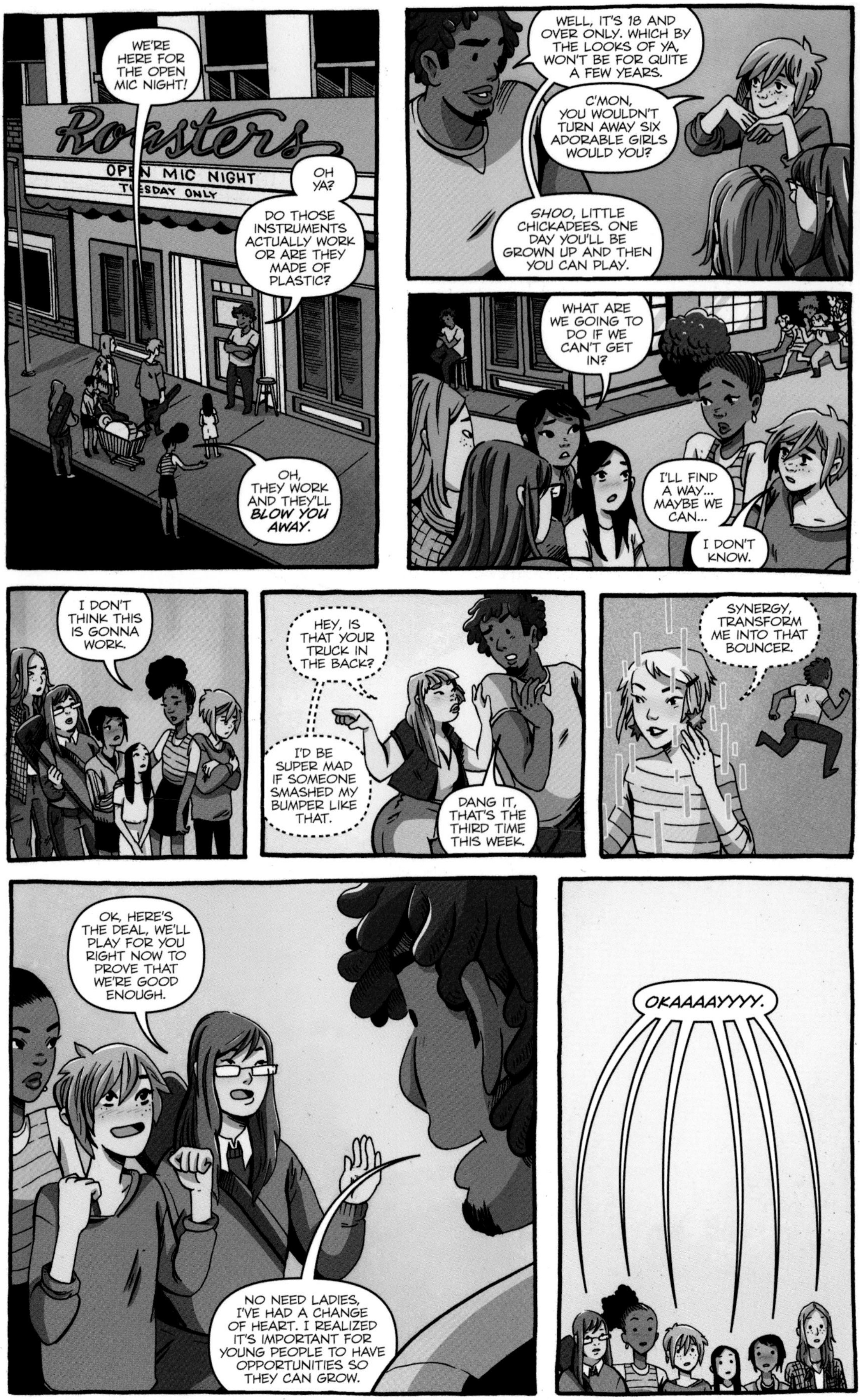
WE'RE HERE FOR THE OPEN MIC NIGHT!
Roasters
OPEN MIC NIGHT
TUESDAY ONLY
OH YA?
DO THOSE INSTRUMENTS ACTUALLY WORK OR ARE THEY MADE OF PLASTIC?
OH, THEY WORK AND THEY'LL BLOW YOU AWAY.
WELL, IT'S 18 AND OVER ONLY. WHICH BY THE LOOKS OF YA, WON'T BE FOR QUITE A FEW YEARS.
C'MON, YOU WOULDN'T TURN AWAY SIX ADORABLE GIRLS WOULD YOU?
SHOO, LITTLE CHICKADEES. ONE DAY YOU'LL BE GROWN UP AND THEN YOU CAN PLAY.
WHAT ARE WE GOING TO DO IF WE CAN'T GET IN?
I'LL FIND A WAY... MAYBE WE CAN...
I DON'T KNOW.
I DON'T THINK THIS IS GONNA WORK.
HEY, IS THAT YOUR TRUCK IN THE BACK?
I'D BE SUPER MAD IF SOMEONE SMASHED MY BUMPER LIKE THAT.
DANG IT, THAT'S THE THIRD TIME THIS WEEK.
SYNERGY, TRANSFORM ME INTO THAT BOUNCER.
OK, HERE'S THE DEAL, WE'LL PLAY FOR YOU RIGHT NOW TO PROVE THAT WE'RE GOOD ENOUGH.
NO NEED LADIES, I'VE HAD A CHANGE OF HEART. I REALIZED IT'S IMPORTANT FOR YOUNG PEOPLE TO HAVE OPPORTUNITIES SO THEY CAN GROW.
OKAAAAYYYY.

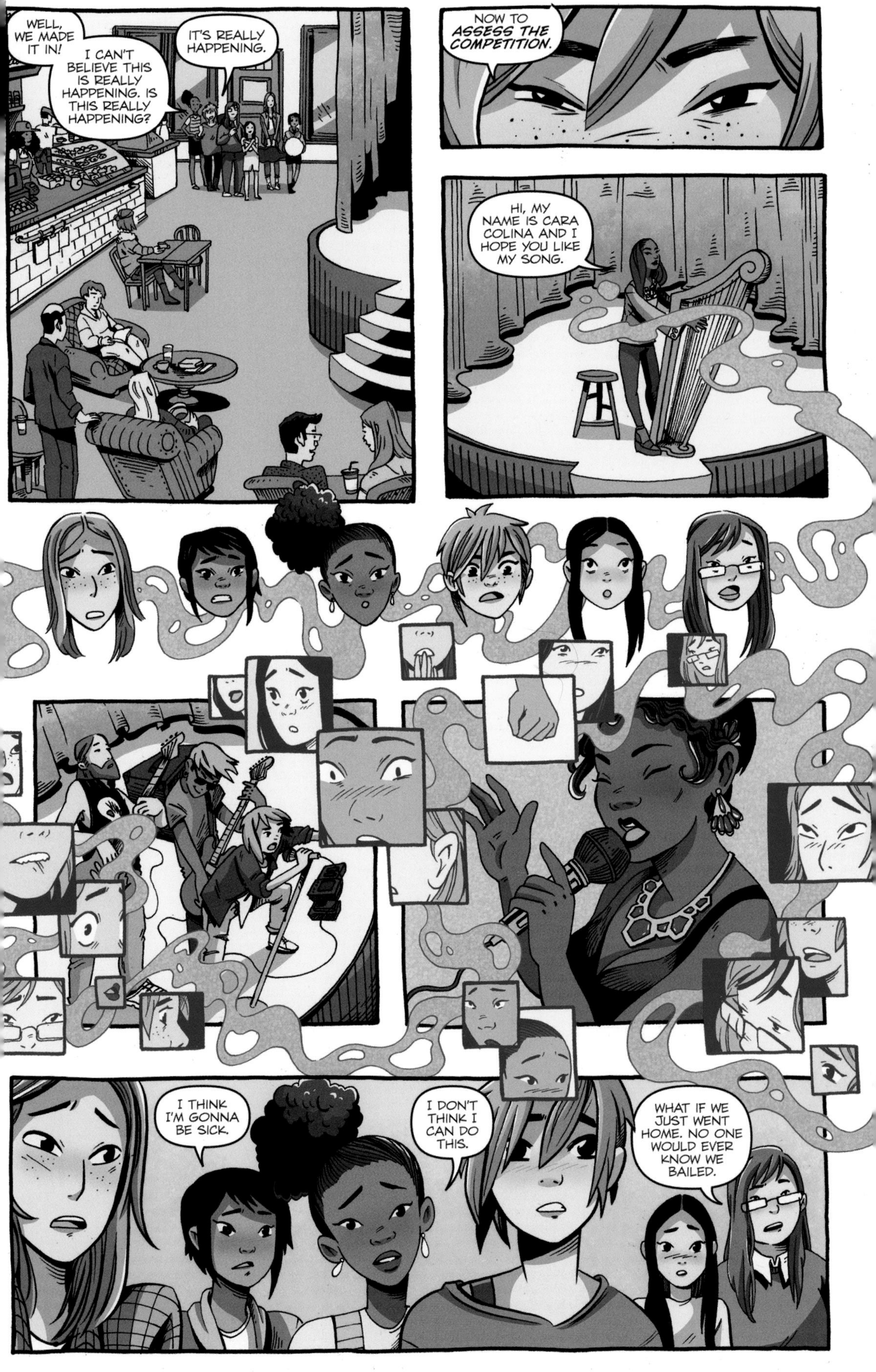
WELL, WE MADE IT IN!
I CAN'T BELIEVE THIS IS REALLY HAPPENING. IS THIS REALLY HAPPENING?
IT'S REALLY HAPPENING.
NOW TO ASSESS THE COMPETITION.
HI, MY NAME IS CARA COLINA AND I HOPE YOU LIKE MY SONG.
I THINK I'M GONNA BE SICK.
I DON'T THINK I CAN DO THIS.
WHAT IF WE JUST WENT HOME. NO ONE WOULD EVER KNOW WE BAILED.

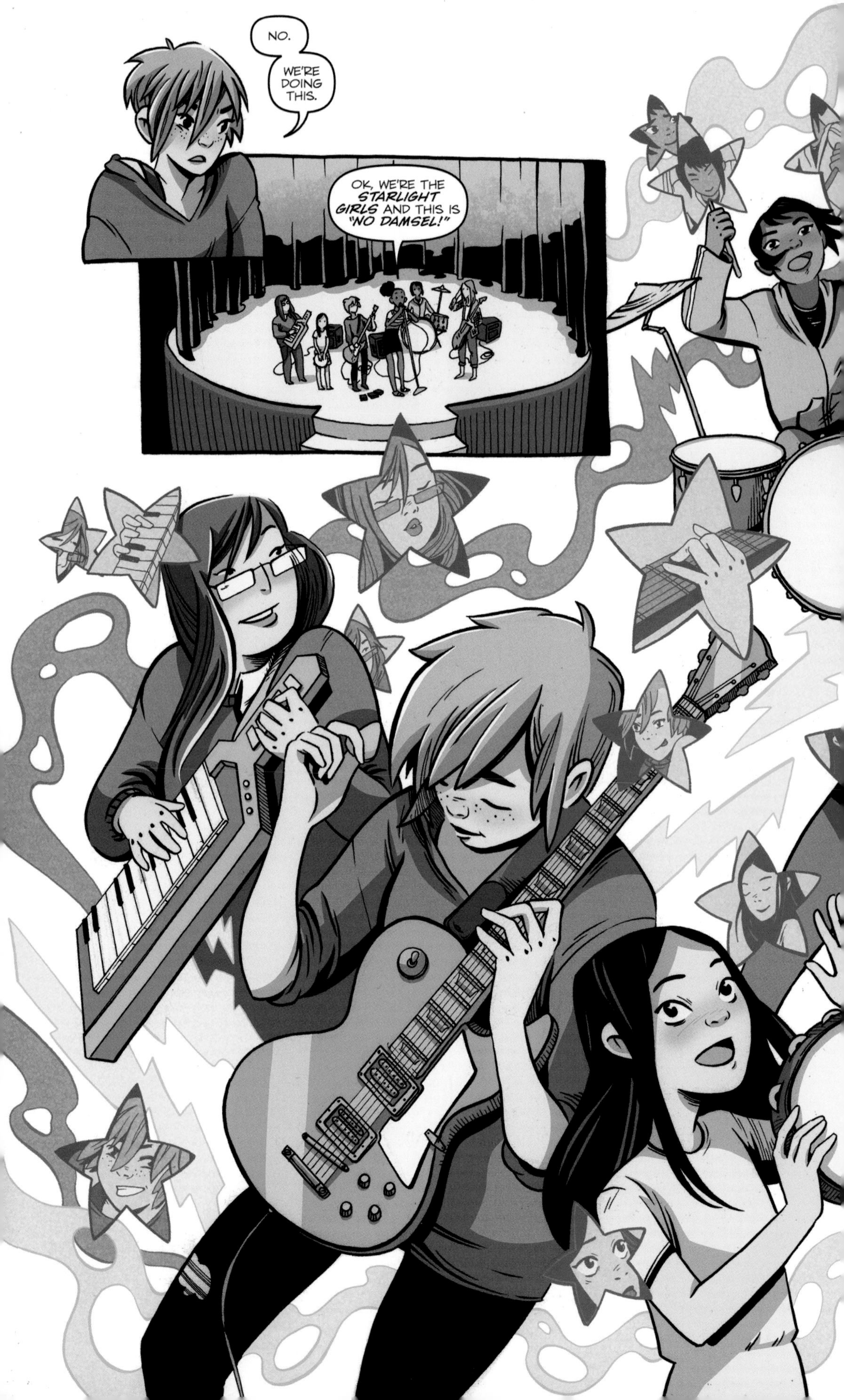
NO.
WE'RE DOING THIS.
OK, WE'RE THE **STARLIGHT GIRLS** AND THIS IS **"NO DAMSEL!"**

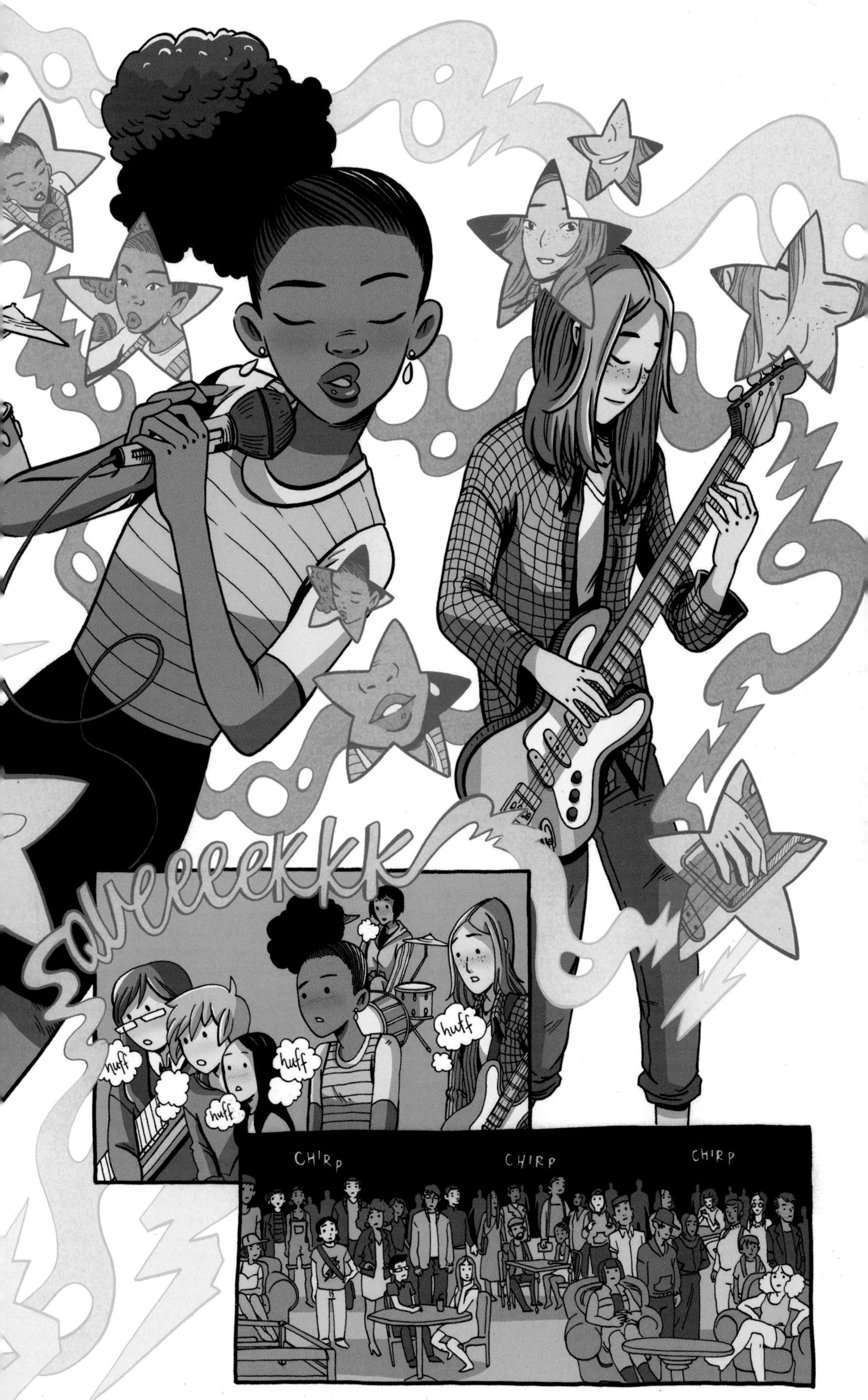
SQUEEEEKKK
huff
huff
huff
huff
CHIRP
CHIRP
CHIRP

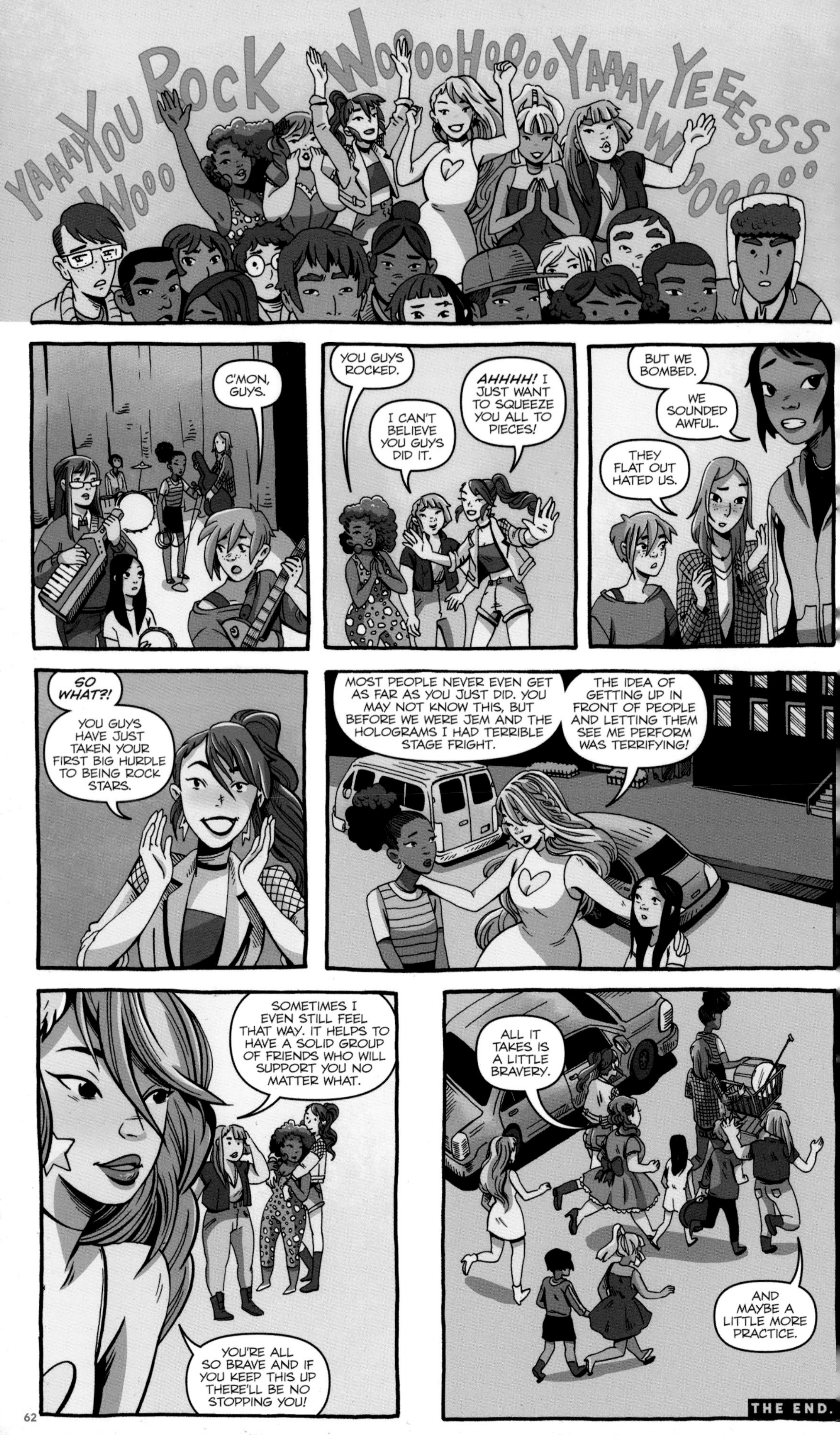
YAAAY YOU ROCK WOOOOHOOOOOYAAAY YEEESSS WOOO WOOOOOOO
C'MON, GUYS.
YOU GUYS ROCKED.
I CAN'T BELIEVE YOU GUYS DID IT.
AHHHH! I JUST WANT TO SQUEEZE YOU ALL TO PIECES!
BUT WE BOMBED.
WE SOUNDED AWFUL.
THEY FLAT OUT HATED US.
SO WHAT?!
YOU GUYS HAVE JUST TAKEN YOUR FIRST BIG HURDLE TO BEING ROCK STARS.
MOST PEOPLE NEVER EVEN GET AS FAR AS YOU JUST DID. YOU MAY NOT KNOW THIS, BUT BEFORE WE WERE JEM AND THE HOLOGRAMS I HAD TERRIBLE STAGE FRIGHT.
THE IDEA OF GETTING UP IN FRONT OF PEOPLE AND LETTING THEM SEE ME PERFORM WAS TERRIFYING!
SOMETIMES I EVEN STILL FEEL THAT WAY. IT HELPS TO HAVE A SOLID GROUP OF FRIENDS WHO WILL SUPPORT YOU NO MATTER WHAT.
YOU'RE ALL SO BRAVE AND IF YOU KEEP THIS UP THERE'LL BE NO STOPPING YOU!
ALL IT TAKES IS A LITTLE BRAVERY.
AND MAYBE A LITTLE MORE PRACTICE.
THE END.

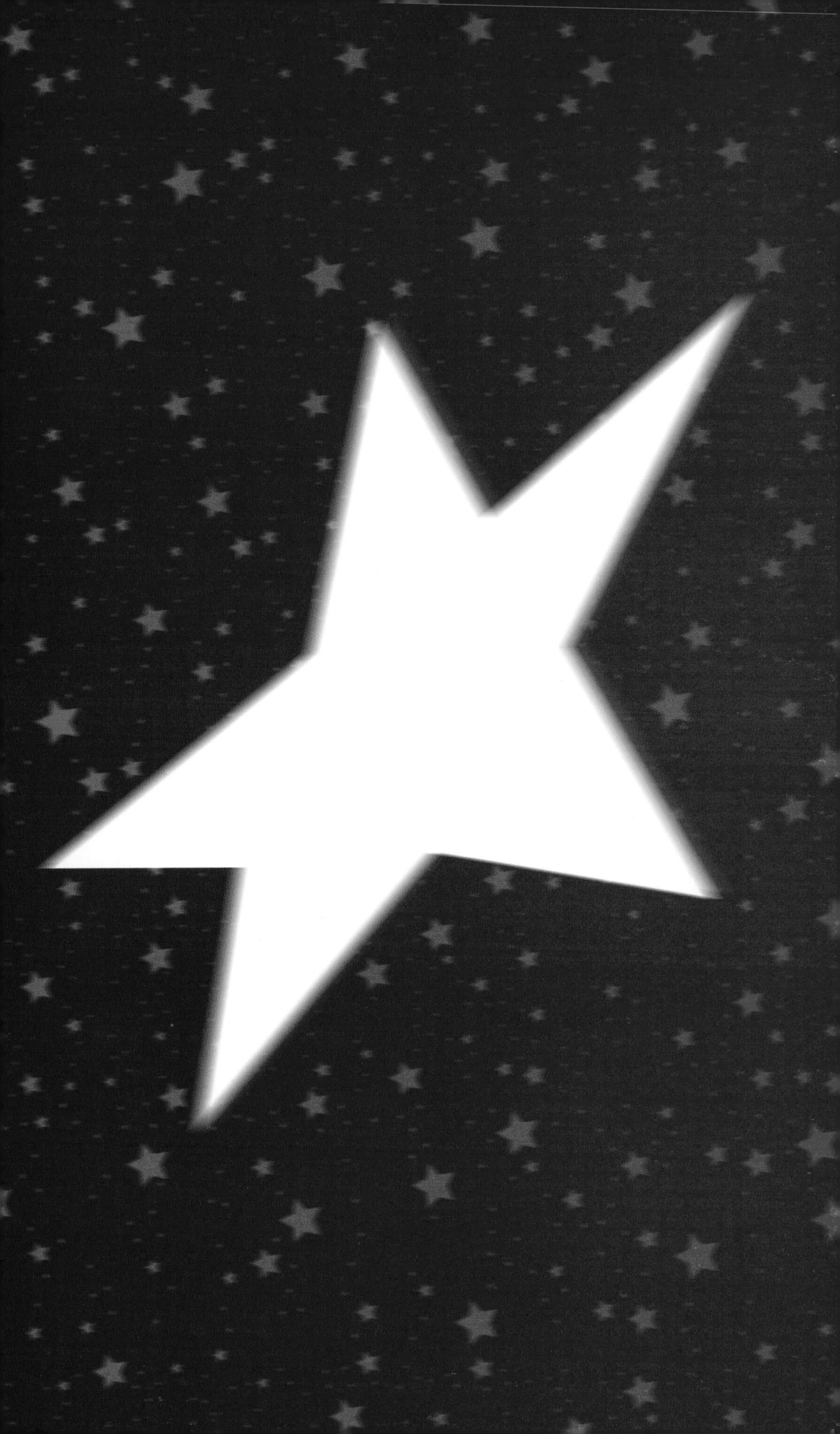

ART BY **RACHAEL STOTT**

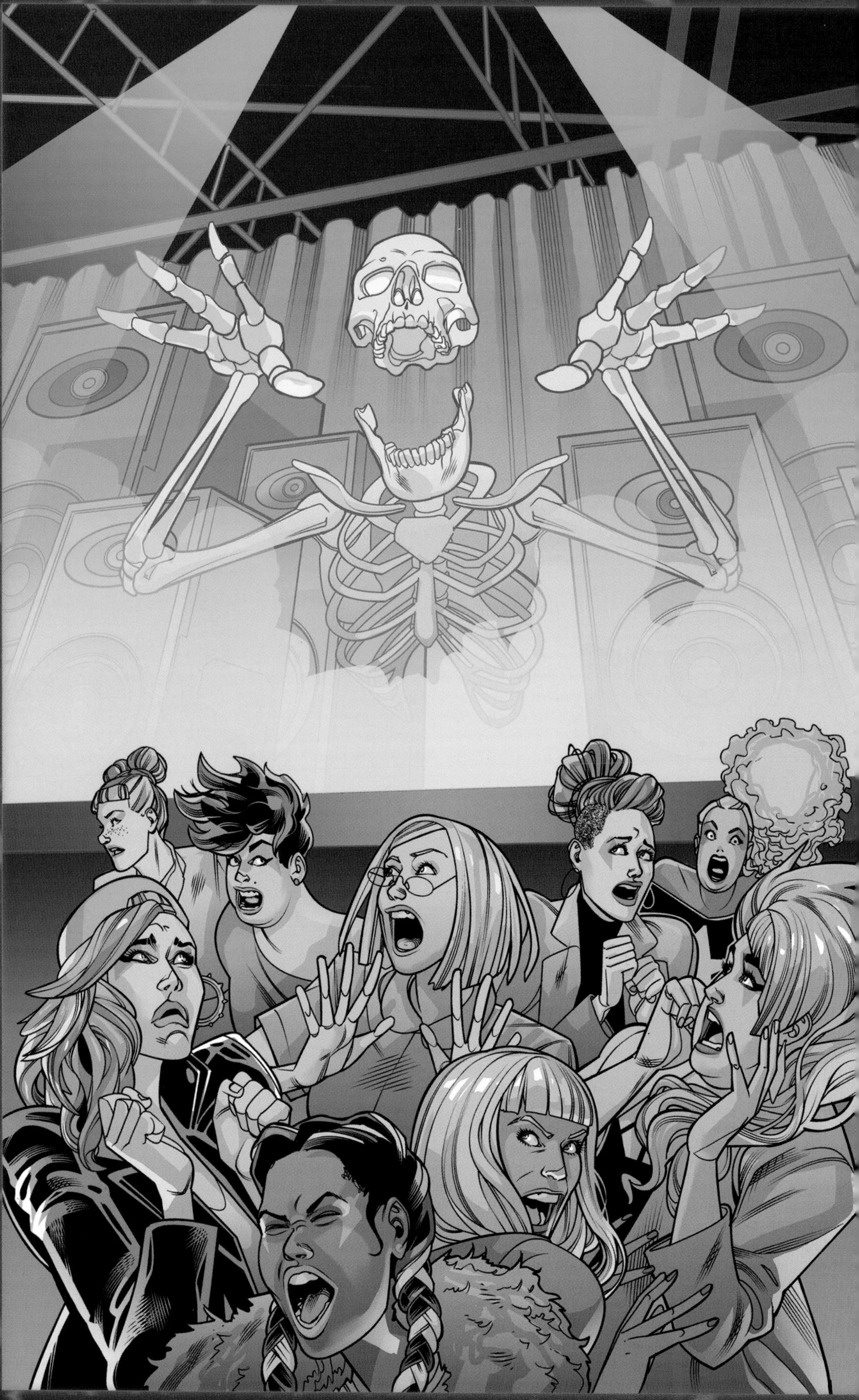

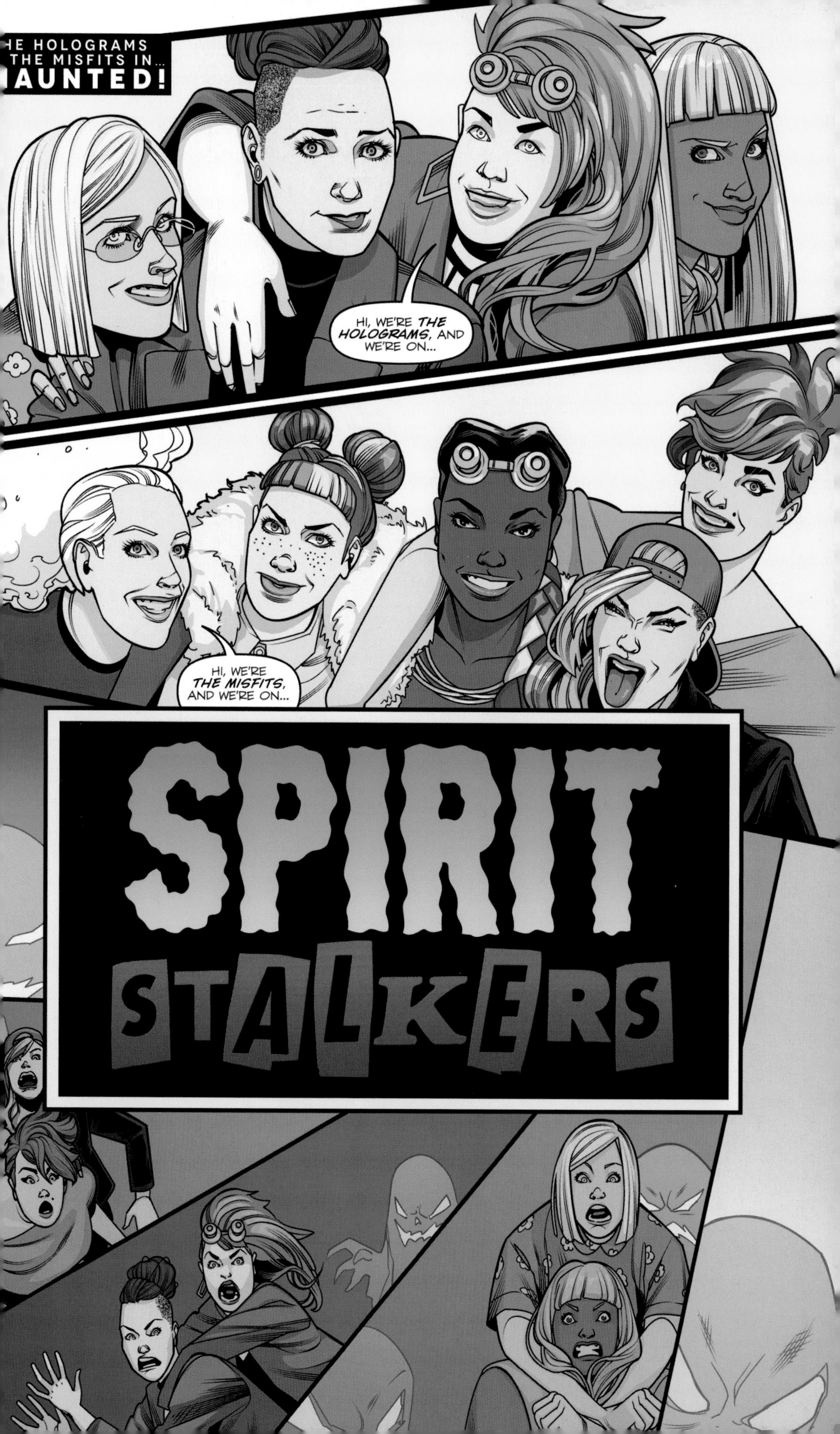

HE HOLOGRAMS
THE MISFITS IN...
AUNTED!
HI, WE'RE THE HOLOGRAMS, AND WE'RE ON...
HI, WE'RE THE MISFITS, AND WE'RE ON...
SPIRIT STALKERS

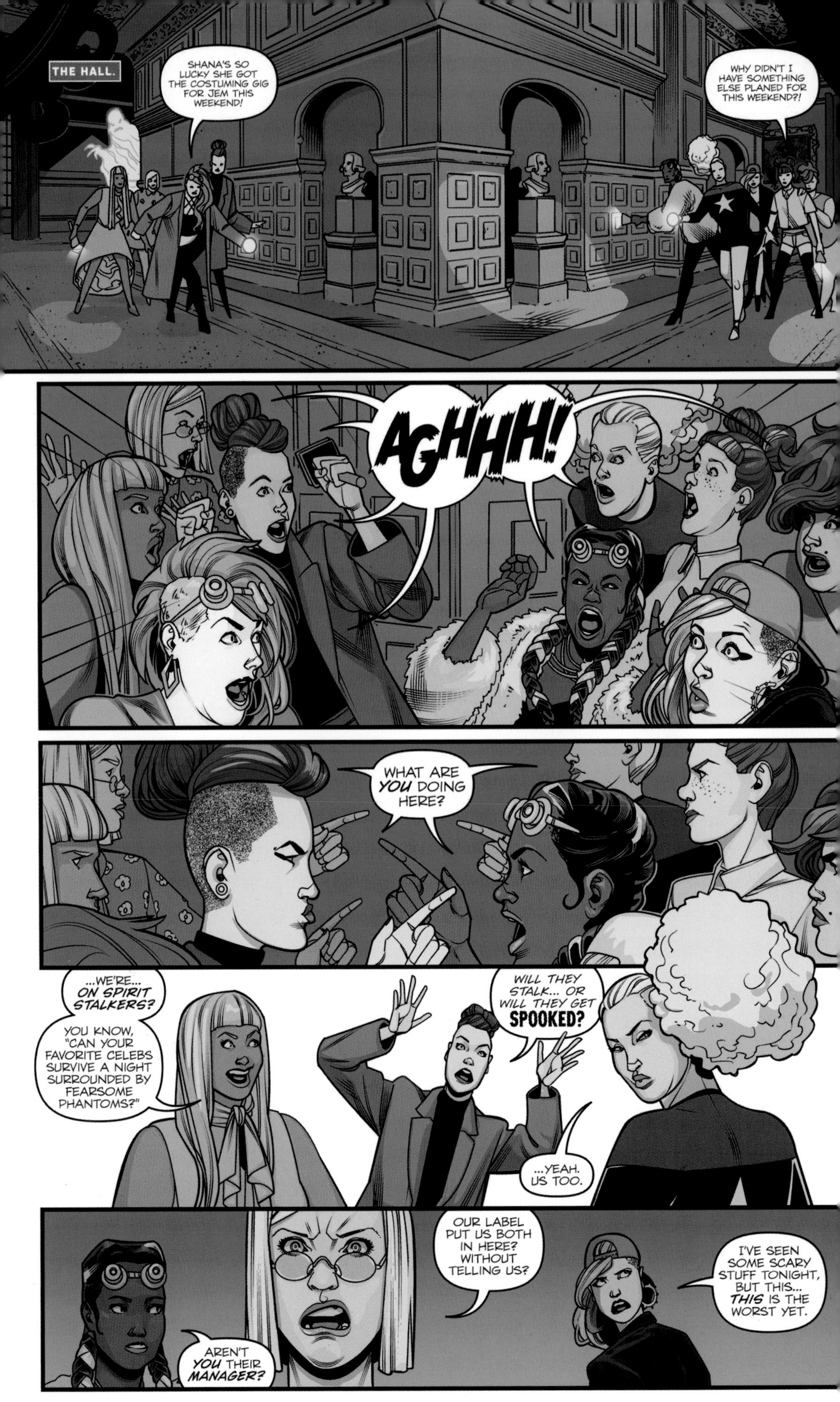
THE HALL.
SHANA'S SO LUCKY SHE GOT THE COSTUMING GIG FOR JEM THIS WEEKEND!
WHY DIDN'T I HAVE SOMETHING ELSE PLANED FOR THIS WEEKEND?!
AGHHH!
WHAT ARE *YOU* DOING HERE?
...WE'RE... *ON SPIRIT STALKERS?*
YOU KNOW, "CAN YOUR FAVORITE CELEBS SURVIVE A NIGHT SURROUNDED BY FEARSOME PHANTOMS?"
WILL THEY STALK... OR WILL THEY GET **SPOOKED?**
...YEAH. US TOO.
OUR LABEL PUT US BOTH IN HERE? WITHOUT TELLING US?
AREN'T *YOU* THEIR *MANAGER?*
I'VE SEEN SOME SCARY STUFF TONIGHT, BUT THIS... *THIS* IS THE WORST YET.

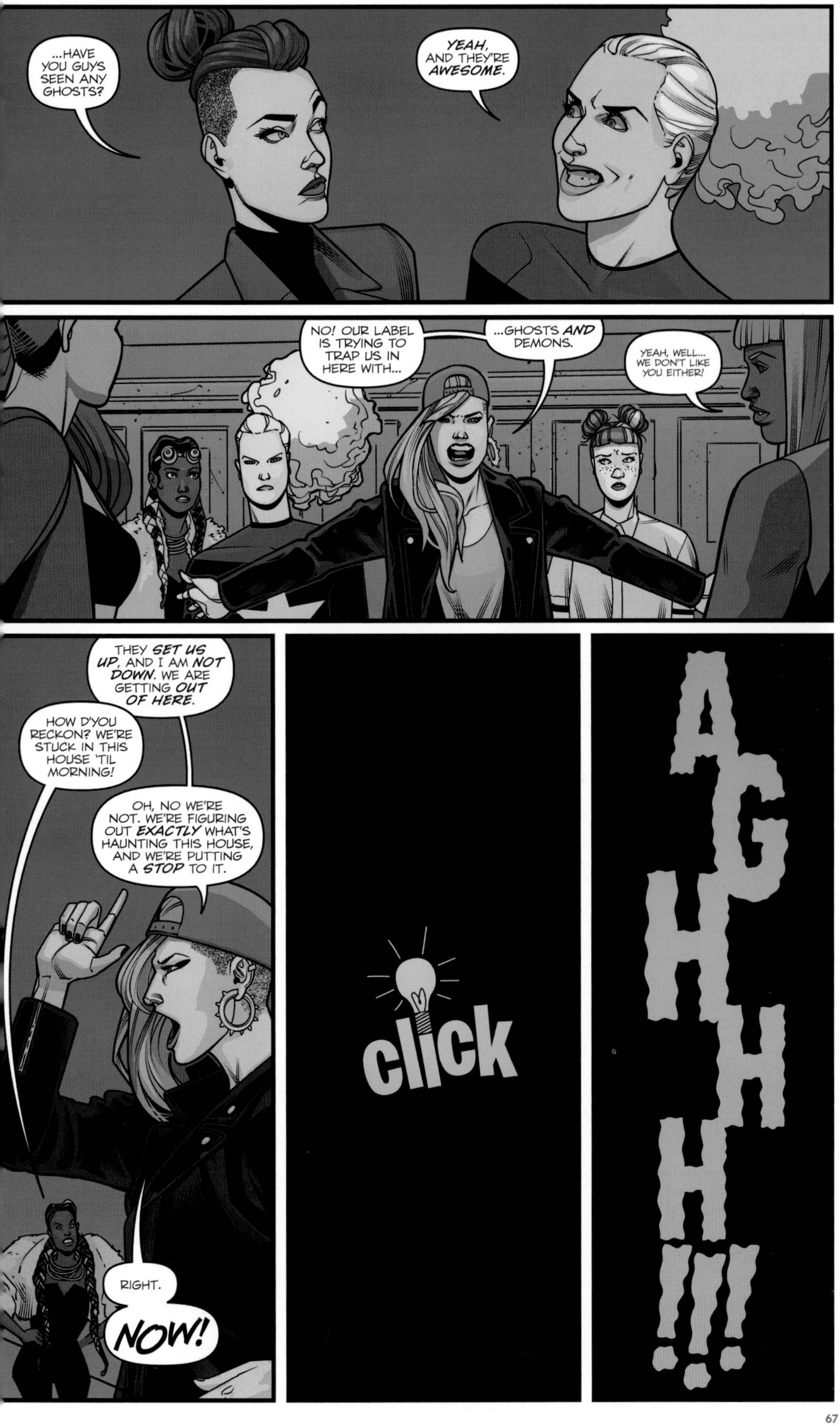
...HAVE YOU GUYS SEEN ANY GHOSTS?
YEAH, AND THEY'RE AWESOME.
NO! OUR LABEL IS TRYING TO TRAP US IN HERE WITH...
...GHOSTS AND DEMONS.
YEAH, WELL... WE DON'T LIKE YOU EITHER!
THEY SET US UP, AND I AM NOT DOWN. WE ARE GETTING OUT OF HERE.
HOW D'YOU RECKON? WE'RE STUCK IN THIS HOUSE 'TIL MORNING!
OH, NO WE'RE NOT. WE'RE FIGURING OUT EXACTLY WHAT'S HAUNTING THIS HOUSE, AND WE'RE PUTTING A STOP TO IT.
RIGHT.
NOW!
click
AGHHHH!!!

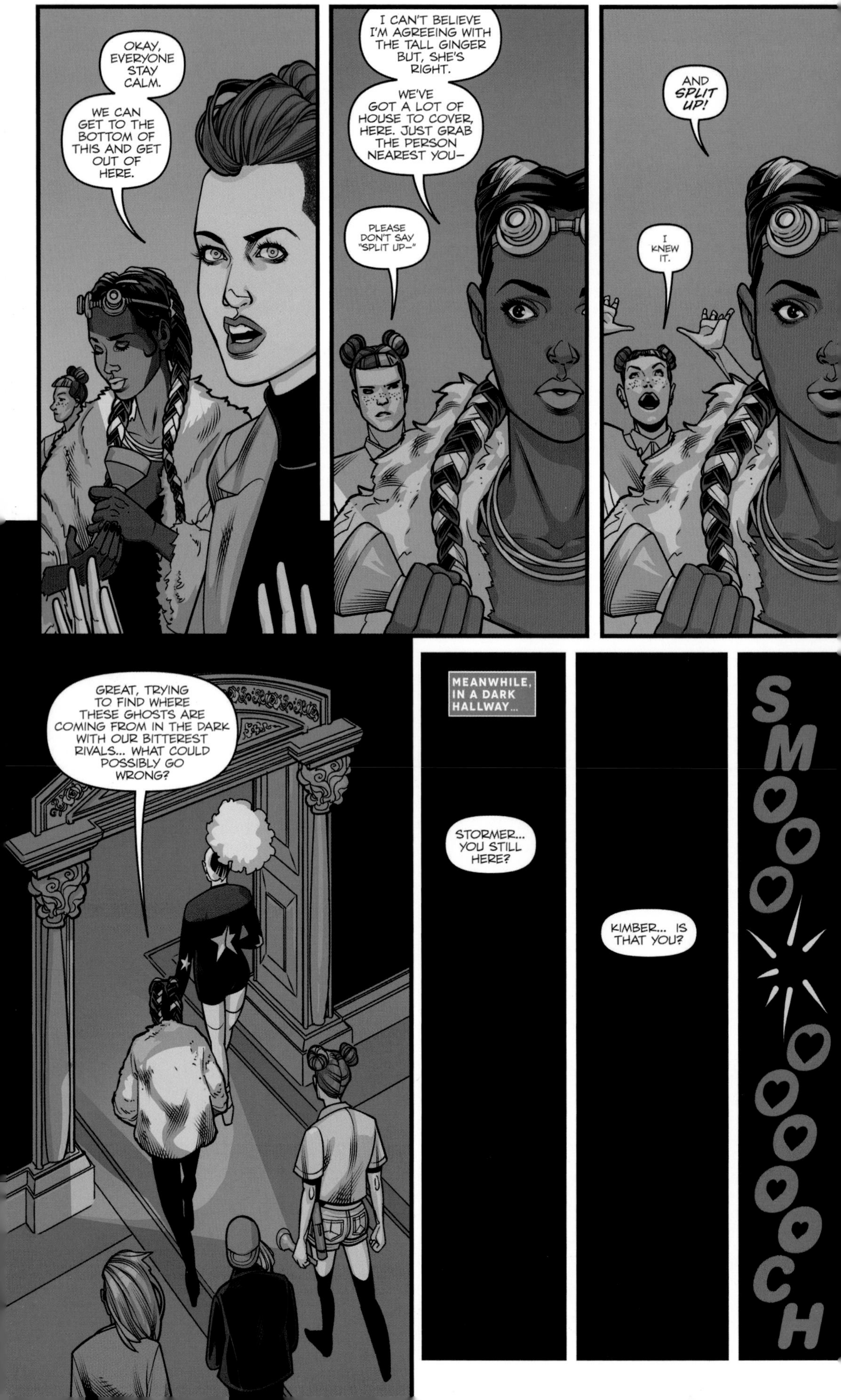
OKAY, EVERYONE STAY CALM.
WE CAN GET TO THE BOTTOM OF THIS AND GET OUT OF HERE.
I CAN'T BELIEVE I'M AGREEING WITH THE TALL GINGER BUT, SHE'S RIGHT.
WE'VE GOT A LOT OF HOUSE TO COVER, HERE. JUST GRAB THE PERSON NEAREST YOU–
PLEASE DON'T SAY "SPLIT UP–"
AND SPLIT UP!
I KNEW IT.
GREAT, TRYING TO FIND WHERE THESE GHOSTS ARE COMING FROM IN THE DARK WITH OUR BITTEREST RIVALS... WHAT COULD POSSIBLY GO WRONG?
MEANWHILE, IN A DARK HALLWAY...
STORMER... YOU STILL HERE?
KIMBER... IS THAT YOU?
SMOOOOOOOOOCH

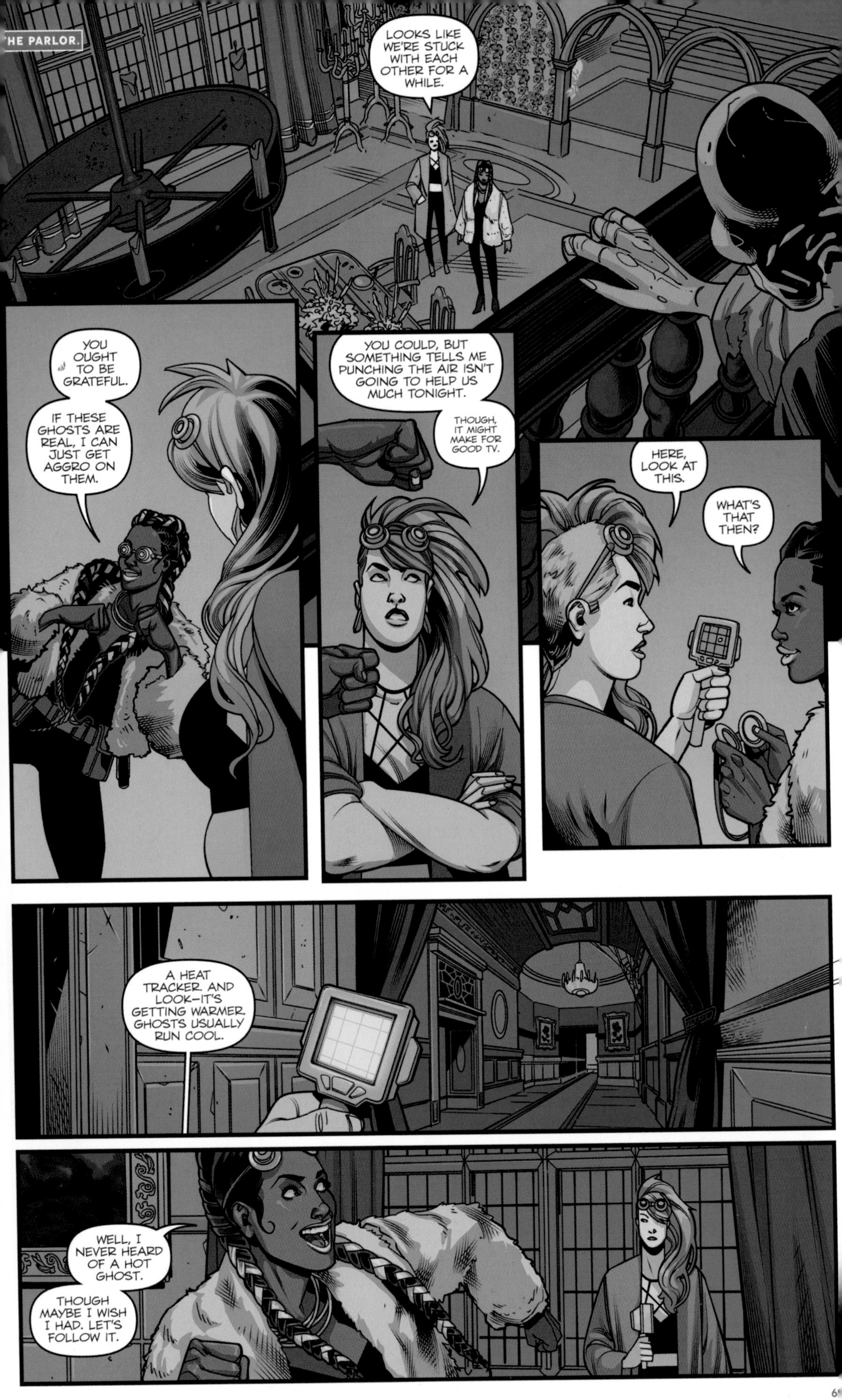

HE PARLOR.
LOOKS LIKE WE'RE STUCK WITH EACH OTHER FOR A WHILE.
YOU OUGHT TO BE GRATEFUL.
IF THESE GHOSTS ARE REAL, I CAN JUST GET AGGRO ON THEM.
YOU COULD, BUT SOMETHING TELLS ME PUNCHING THE AIR ISN'T GOING TO HELP US MUCH TONIGHT.
THOUGH, IT MIGHT MAKE FOR GOOD TV.
HERE, LOOK AT THIS.
WHAT'S THAT THEN?
A HEAT TRACKER. AND LOOK—IT'S GETTING WARMER. GHOSTS USUALLY RUN COOL.
WELL, I NEVER HEARD OF A HOT GHOST.
THOUGH MAYBE I WISH I HAD. LET'S FOLLOW IT.

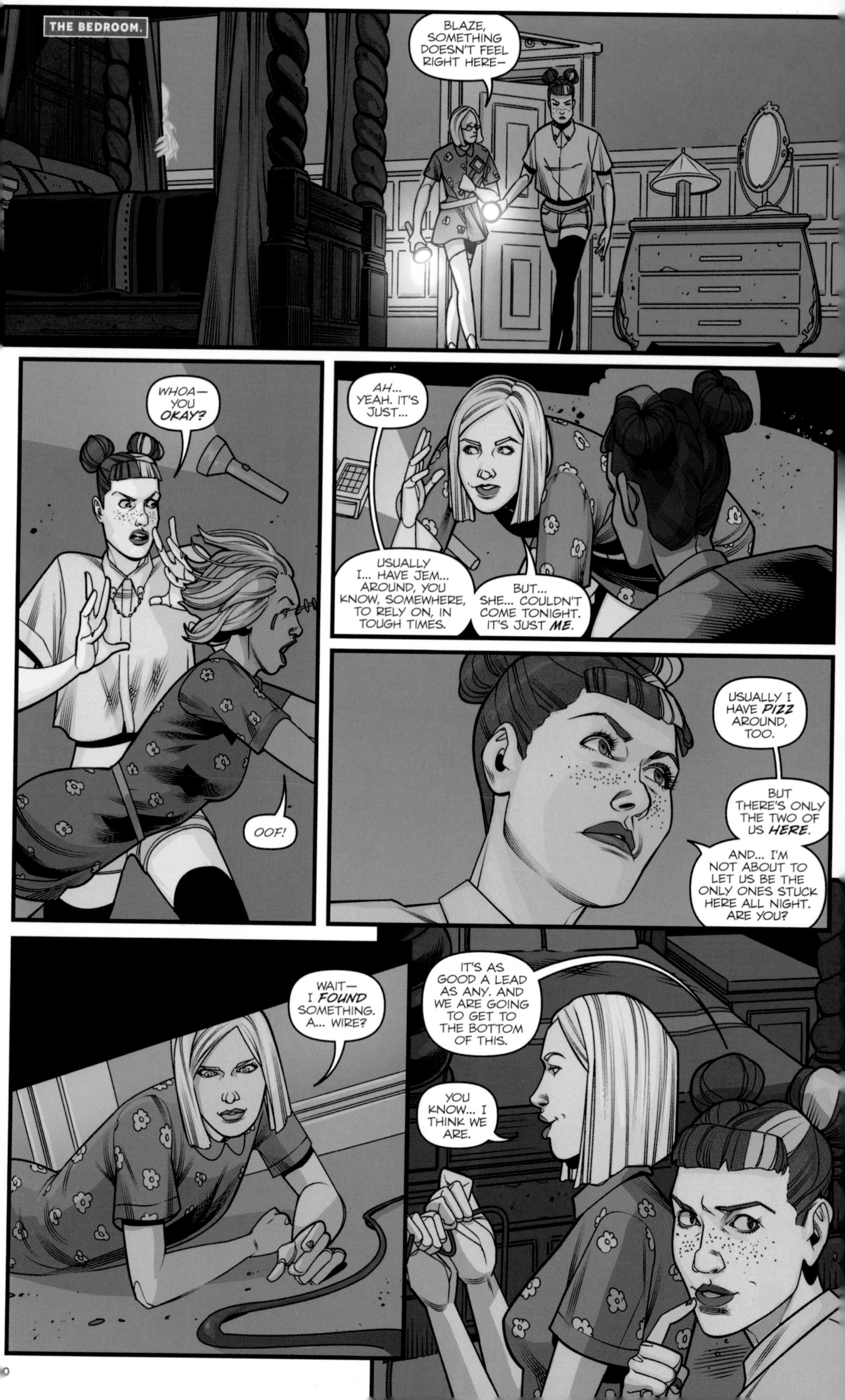
THE BEDROOM.
BLAZE, SOMETHING DOESN'T FEEL RIGHT HERE—
WHOA— YOU OKAY?
OOF!
AH... YEAH. IT'S JUST...
USUALLY I... HAVE JEM... AROUND, YOU KNOW, SOMEWHERE, TO RELY ON, IN TOUGH TIMES.
BUT... SHE... COULDN'T COME TONIGHT. IT'S JUST ME.
USUALLY I HAVE PIZZ AROUND, TOO.
BUT THERE'S ONLY THE TWO OF US HERE.
AND... I'M NOT ABOUT TO LET US BE THE ONLY ONES STUCK HERE ALL NIGHT. ARE YOU?
WAIT— I FOUND SOMETHING. A... WIRE?
IT'S AS GOOD A LEAD AS ANY. AND WE ARE GOING TO GET TO THE BOTTOM OF THIS.
YOU KNOW... I THINK WE ARE.

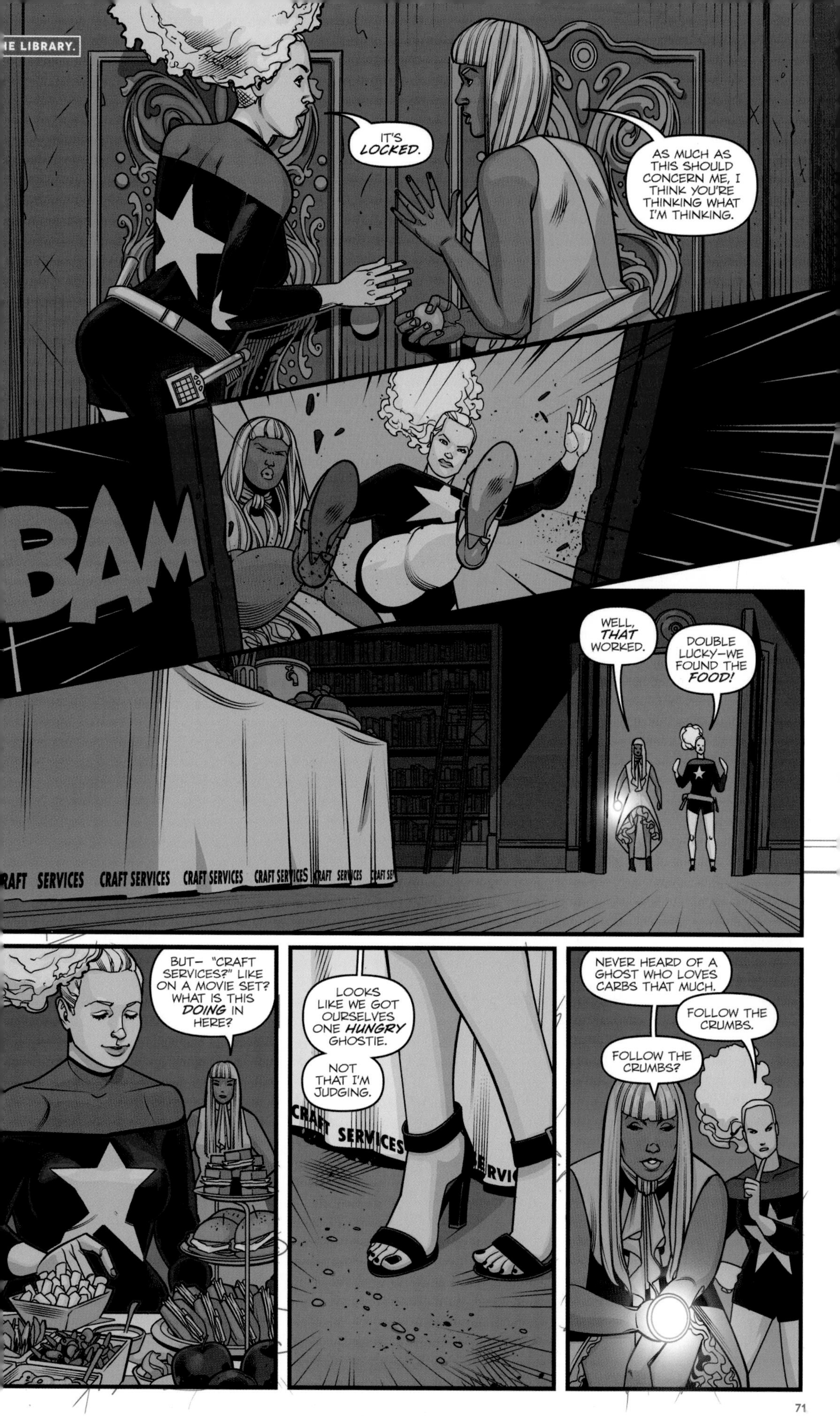
HE LIBRARY.
IT'S LOCKED.
AS MUCH AS THIS SHOULD CONCERN ME, I THINK YOU'RE THINKING WHAT I'M THINKING.
BAM
WELL, THAT WORKED.
DOUBLE LUCKY—WE FOUND THE FOOD!
RAFT SERVICES CRAFT SERVICES CRAFT SERVICES CRAFT SERVICES
BUT– "CRAFT SERVICES?" LIKE ON A MOVIE SET? WHAT IS THIS DOING IN HERE?
LOOKS LIKE WE GOT OURSELVES ONE HUNGRY GHOSTIE.
NOT THAT I'M JUDGING.
CRAFT SERVICES
NEVER HEARD OF A GHOST WHO LOVES CARBS THAT MUCH.
FOLLOW THE CRUMBS.
FOLLOW THE CRUMBS?

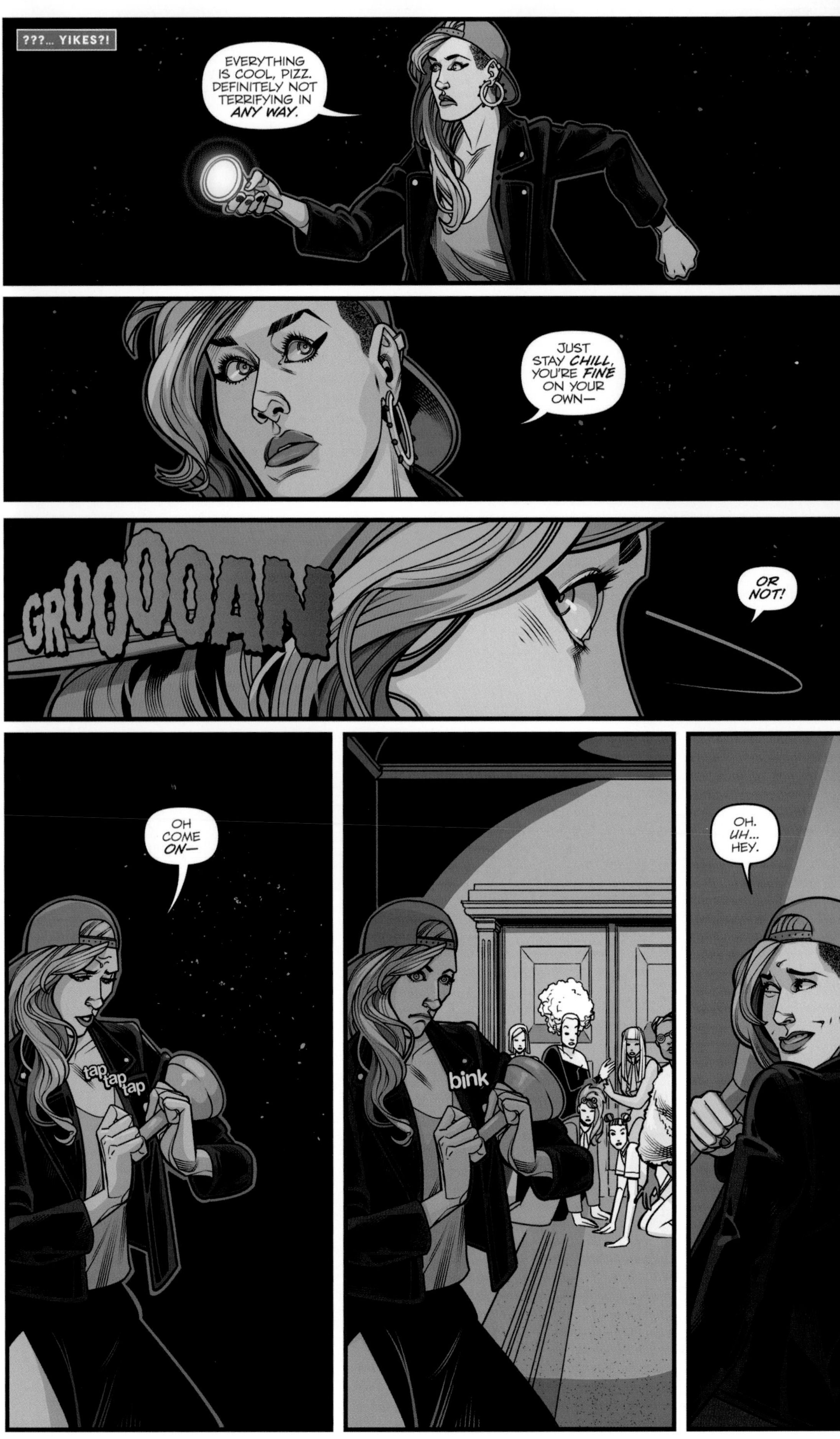
???... YIKES?!
EVERYTHING IS COOL, PIZZ. DEFINITELY NOT TERRIFYING IN ANY WAY.
JUST STAY CHILL, YOU'RE FINE ON YOUR OWN—
GROOOOAN
OR NOT!
OH COME ON—
tap tap tap
bink
OH. UH... HEY.

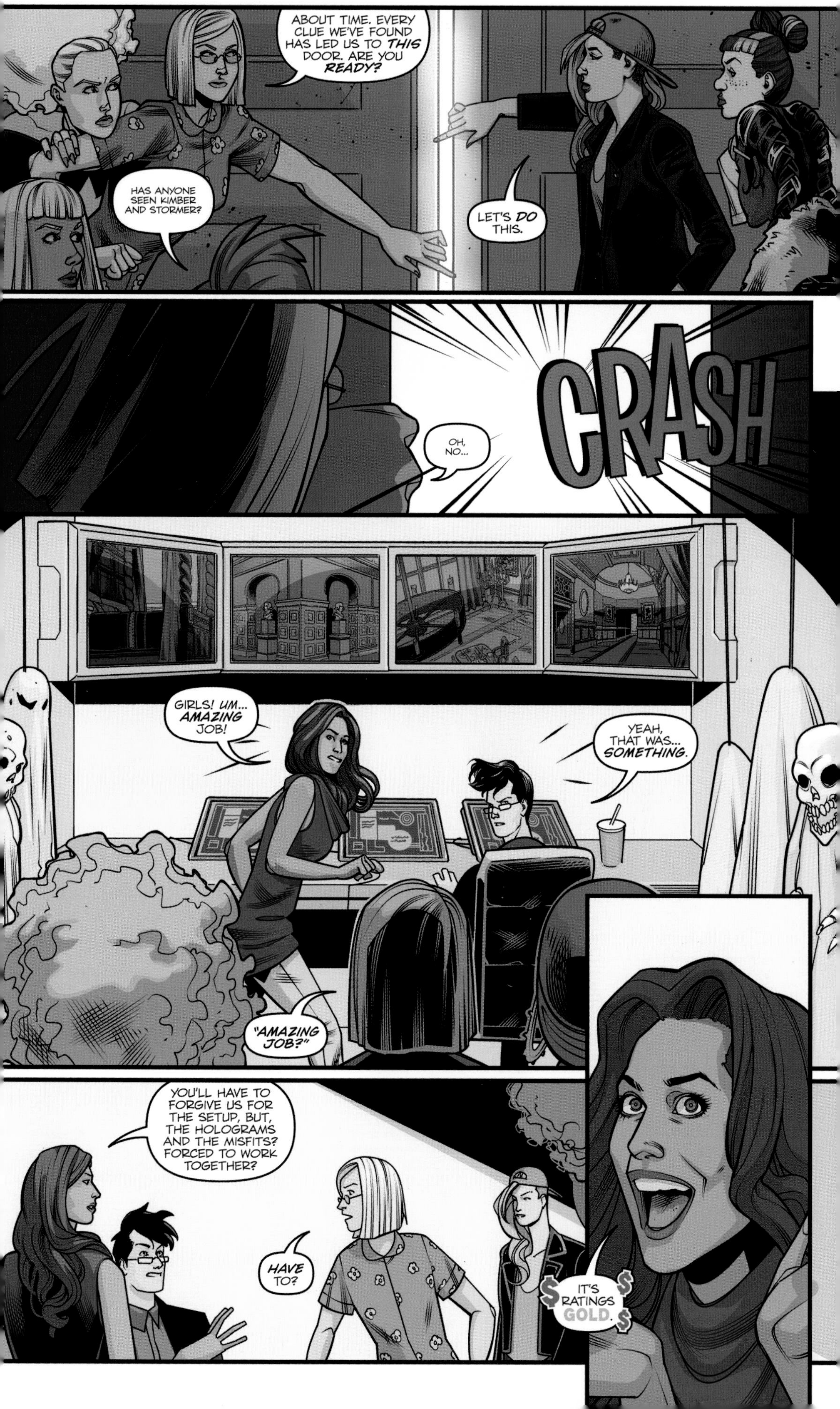
ABOUT TIME. EVERY CLUE WE'VE FOUND HAS LED US TO THIS DOOR. ARE YOU READY?
HAS ANYONE SEEN KIMBER AND STORMER?
LET'S DO THIS.
OH, NO...
CRASH
GIRLS! UM... AMAZING JOB!
YEAH, THAT WAS... SOMETHING.
"AMAZING JOB?"
YOU'LL HAVE TO FORGIVE US FOR THE SETUP, BUT, THE HOLOGRAMS AND THE MISFITS? FORCED TO WORK TOGETHER?
HAVE TO?
IT'S RATINGS GOLD.

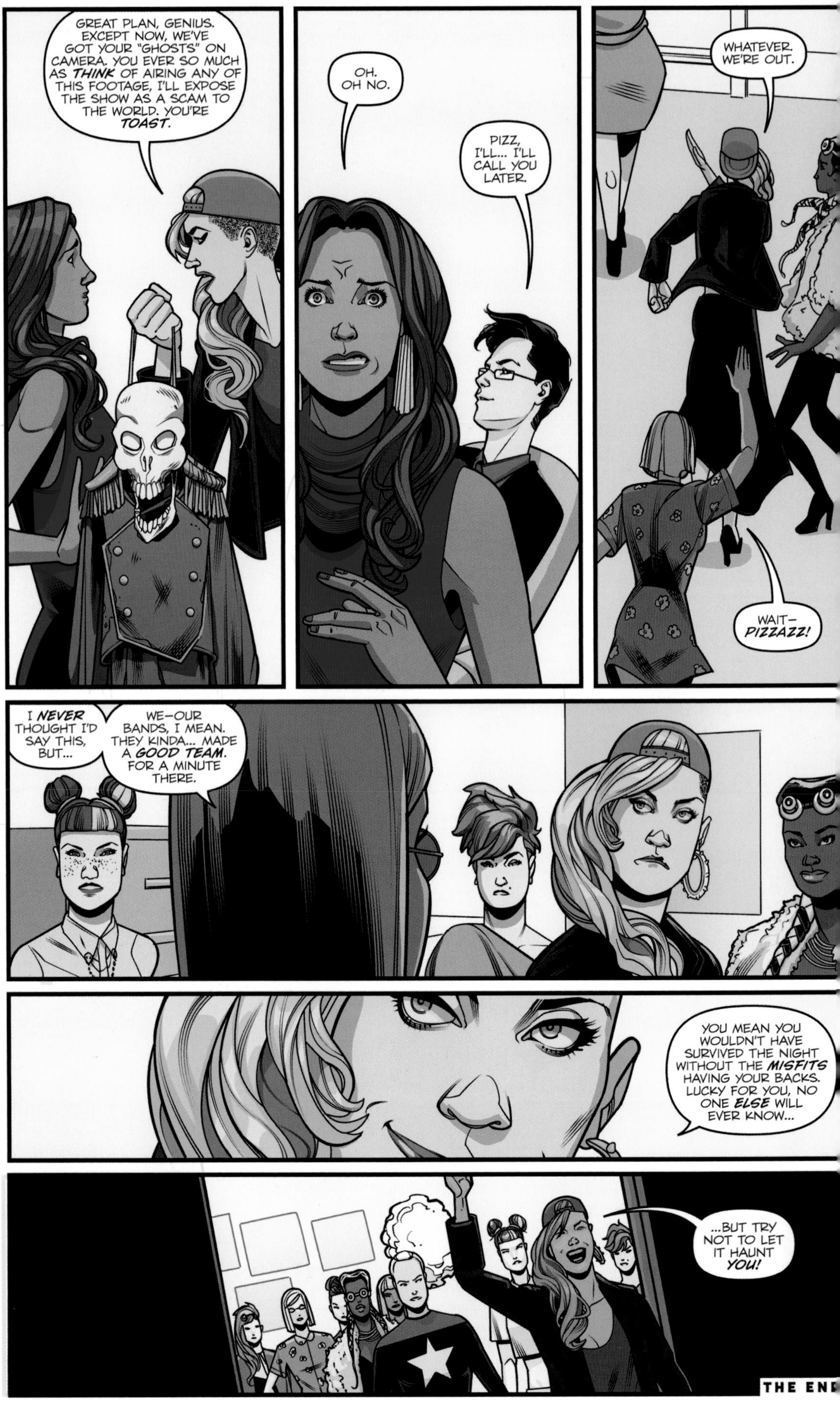

GREAT PLAN, GENIUS. EXCEPT NOW, WE'VE GOT YOUR "GHOSTS" ON CAMERA. YOU EVER SO MUCH AS *THINK* OF AIRING ANY OF THIS FOOTAGE, I'LL EXPOSE THE SHOW AS A SCAM TO THE WORLD. YOU'RE *TOAST*.
OH. OH NO.
PIZZ, I'LL... I'LL CALL YOU LATER.
WHATEVER. WE'RE OUT.
WAIT— *PIZZAZZ!*
I *NEVER* THOUGHT I'D SAY THIS, BUT...
WE—OUR BANDS, I MEAN. THEY KINDA... MADE A *GOOD TEAM*. FOR A MINUTE THERE.
YOU MEAN YOU WOULDN'T HAVE SURVIVED THE NIGHT WITHOUT THE *MISFITS* HAVING YOUR BACKS. LUCKY FOR YOU, NO ONE *ELSE* WILL EVER KNOW...
...BUT TRY NOT TO LET IT HAUNT *YOU!*
THE END

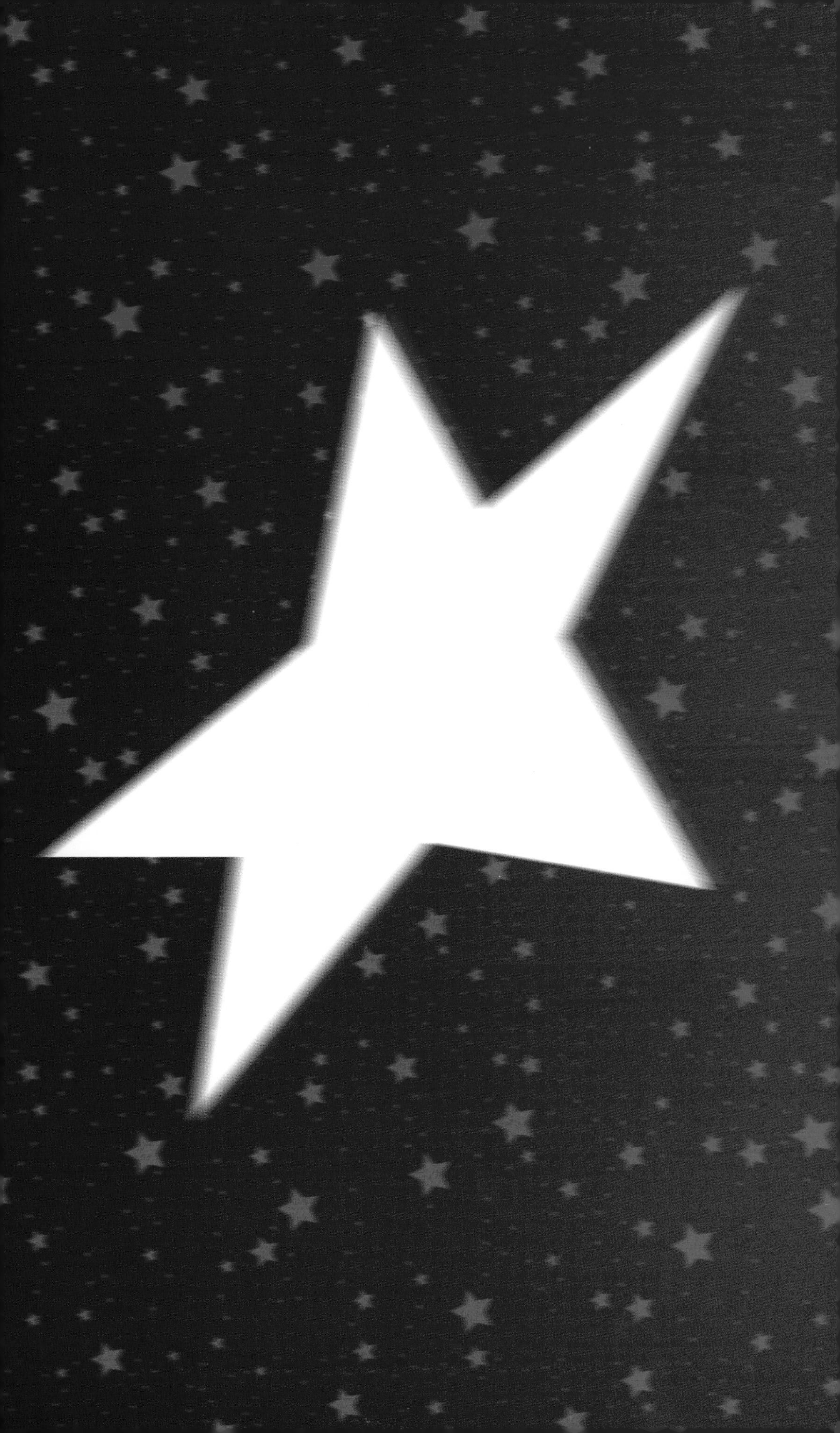

ART BY **HANNAH TEMPLER**

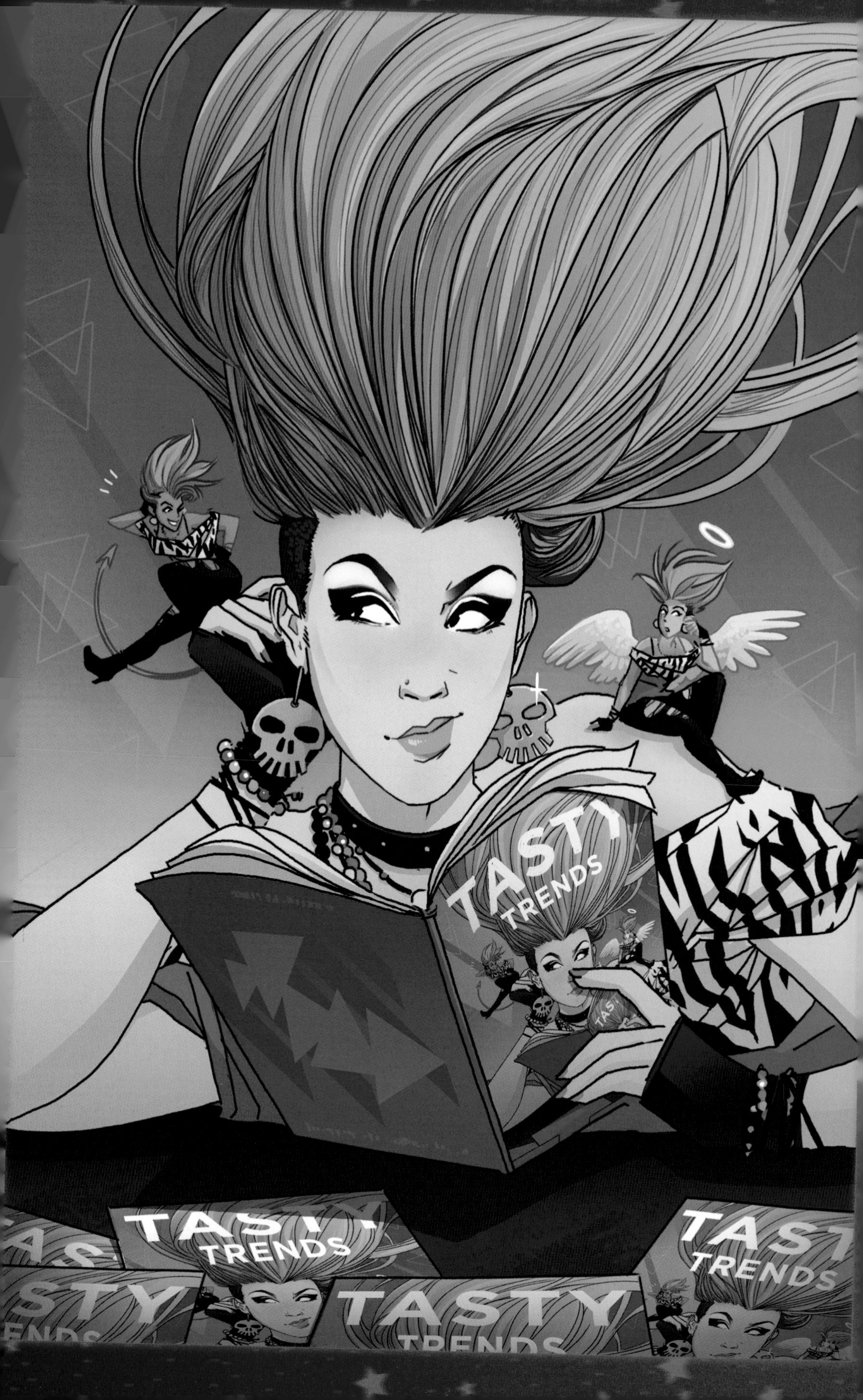

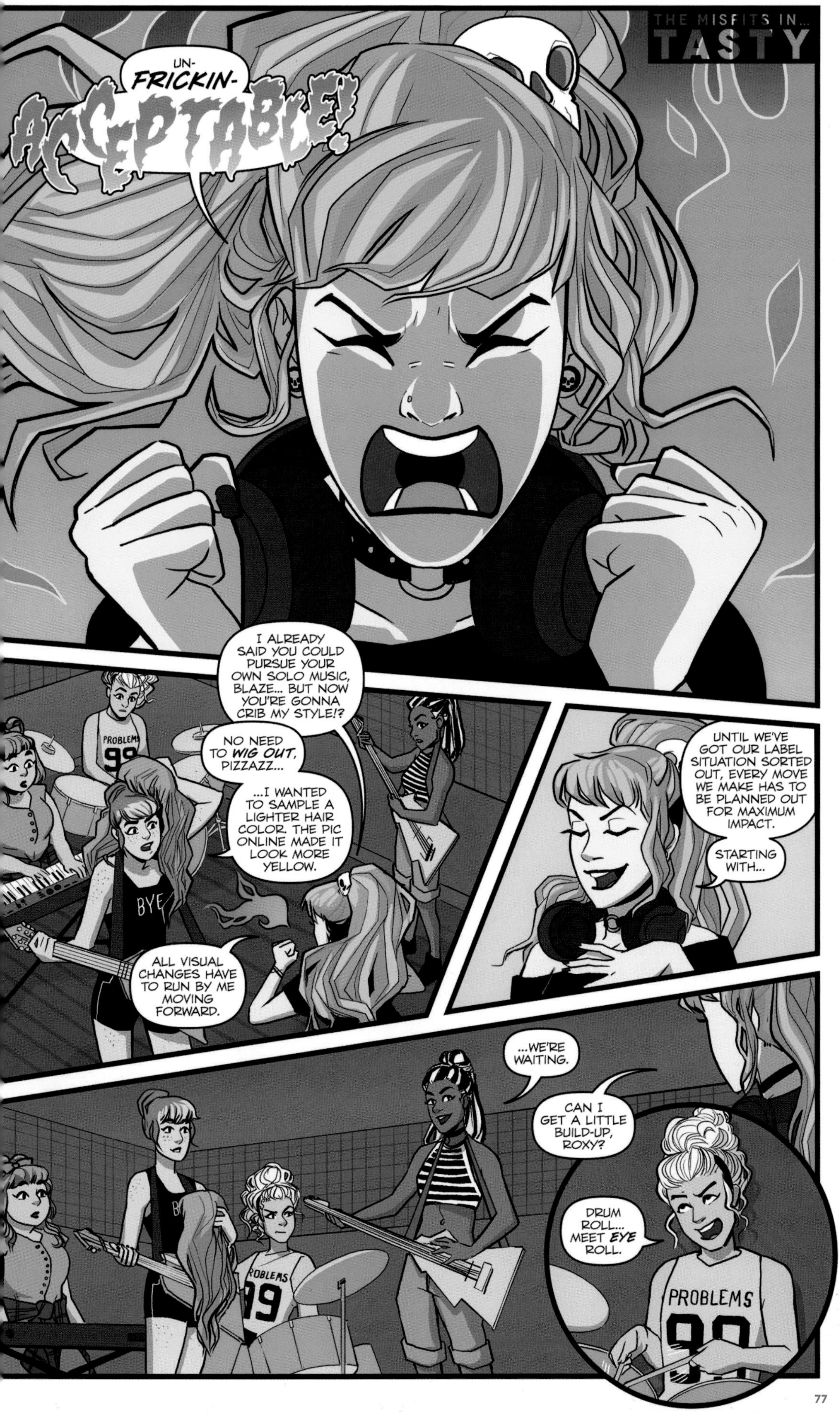
THE MISFITS IN...
TASTY
UN-FRICKIN-ACCEPTABLE!
I ALREADY SAID YOU COULD PURSUE YOUR OWN SOLO MUSIC, BLAZE... BUT NOW YOU'RE GONNA CRIB MY STYLE!?
NO NEED TO WIG OUT, PIZZAZZ...
...I WANTED TO SAMPLE A LIGHTER HAIR COLOR. THE PIC ONLINE MADE IT LOOK MORE YELLOW.
ALL VISUAL CHANGES HAVE TO RUN BY ME MOVING FORWARD.
UNTIL WE'VE GOT OUR LABEL SITUATION SORTED OUT, EVERY MOVE WE MAKE HAS TO BE PLANNED OUT FOR MAXIMUM IMPACT.
STARTING WITH...
...WE'RE WAITING.
CAN I GET A LITTLE BUILD-UP, ROXY?
DRUM ROLL... MEET EYE ROLL.

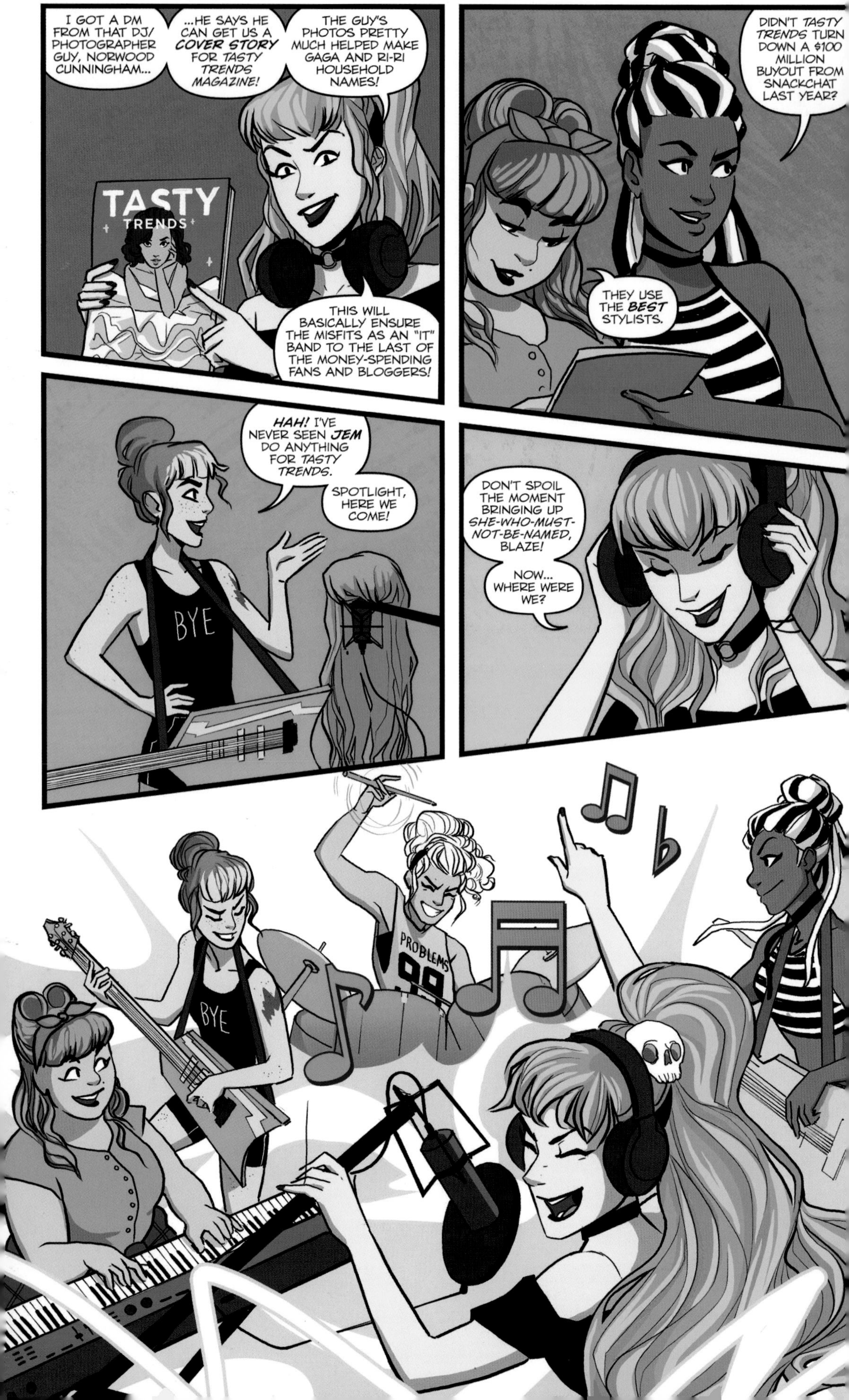

I GOT A DM FROM THAT DJ/ PHOTOGRAPHER GUY, NORWOOD CUNNINGHAM...
...HE SAYS HE CAN GET US A *COVER STORY* FOR *TASTY TRENDS MAGAZINE!*
THE GUY'S PHOTOS PRETTY MUCH HELPED MAKE GAGA AND RI-RI HOUSEHOLD NAMES!
TASTY TRENDS
THIS WILL BASICALLY ENSURE THE MISFITS AS AN "IT" BAND TO THE LAST OF THE MONEY-SPENDING FANS AND BLOGGERS!
DIDN'T *TASTY TRENDS* TURN DOWN A $100 MILLION BUYOUT FROM SNACKCHAT LAST YEAR?
THEY USE THE *BEST* STYLISTS.
HAH! I'VE NEVER SEEN *JEM* DO ANYTHING FOR *TASTY TRENDS.*
SPOTLIGHT, HERE WE COME!
BYE
DON'T SPOIL THE MOMENT BRINGING UP *SHE-WHO-MUST-NOT-BE-NAMED,* BLAZE!
NOW... WHERE WERE WE?
PROBLEMS 99
BYE

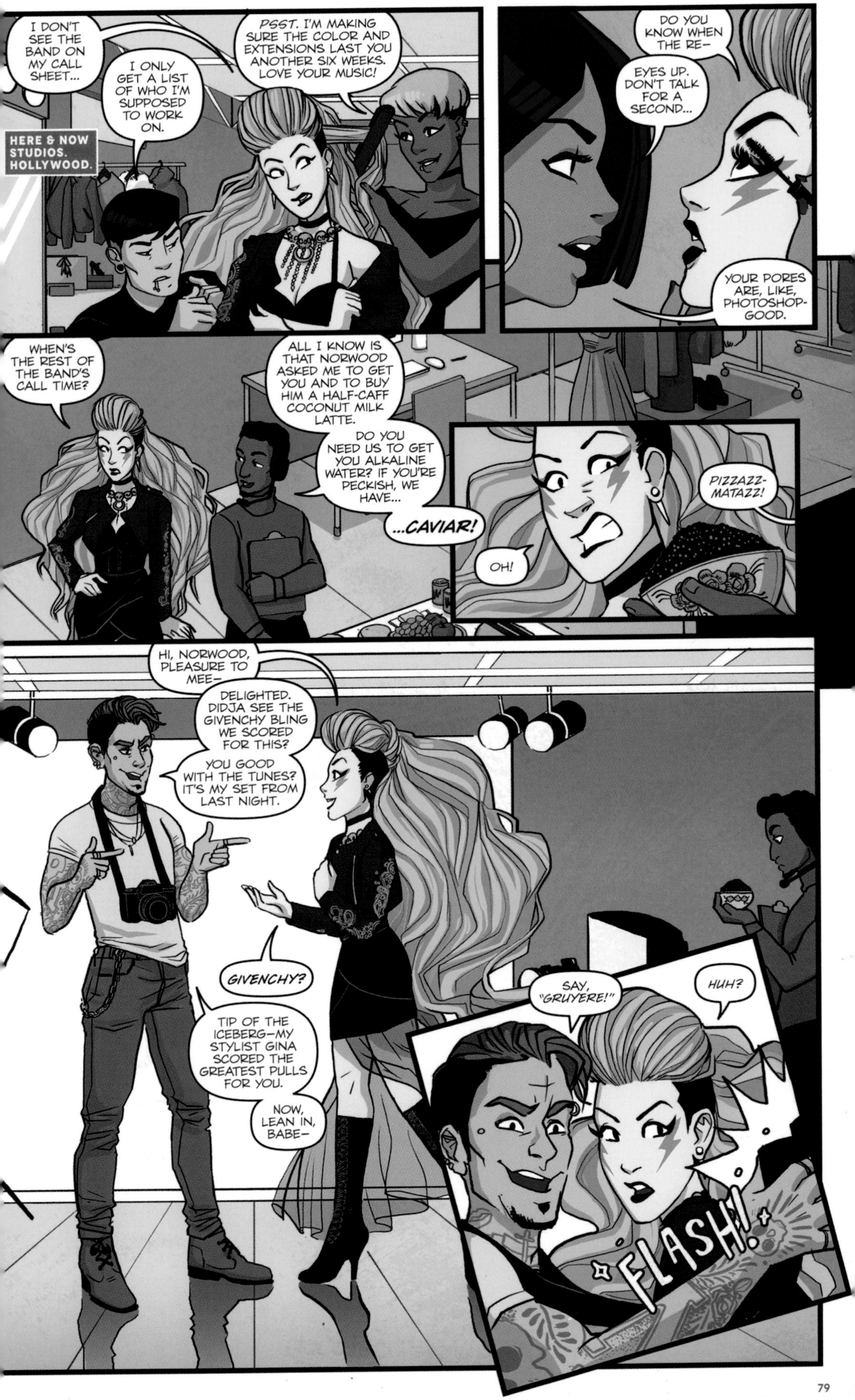

HERE & NOW STUDIOS. HOLLYWOOD.
I DON'T SEE THE BAND ON MY CALL SHEET...
I ONLY GET A LIST OF WHO I'M SUPPOSED TO WORK ON.
PSST. I'M MAKING SURE THE COLOR AND EXTENSIONS LAST YOU ANOTHER SIX WEEKS. LOVE YOUR MUSIC!
DO YOU KNOW WHEN THE RE–
EYES UP. DON'T TALK FOR A SECOND...
YOUR PORES ARE, LIKE, PHOTOSHOP-GOOD.
WHEN'S THE REST OF THE BAND'S CALL TIME?
ALL I KNOW IS THAT NORWOOD ASKED ME TO GET YOU AND TO BUY HIM A HALF-CAFF COCONUT MILK LATTE.
DO YOU NEED US TO GET YOU ALKALINE WATER? IF YOU'RE PECKISH, WE HAVE...
...CAVIAR!
PIZZAZZ-MATAZZ!
OH!
HI, NORWOOD, PLEASURE TO MEE–
DELIGHTED. DIDJA SEE THE GIVENCHY BLING WE SCORED FOR THIS?
YOU GOOD WITH THE TUNES? IT'S MY SET FROM LAST NIGHT.
GIVENCHY?
TIP OF THE ICEBERG—MY STYLIST GINA SCORED THE GREATEST PULLS FOR YOU.
NOW, LEAN IN, BABE–
SAY, "GRUYÈRE!"
HUH?
FLASH!

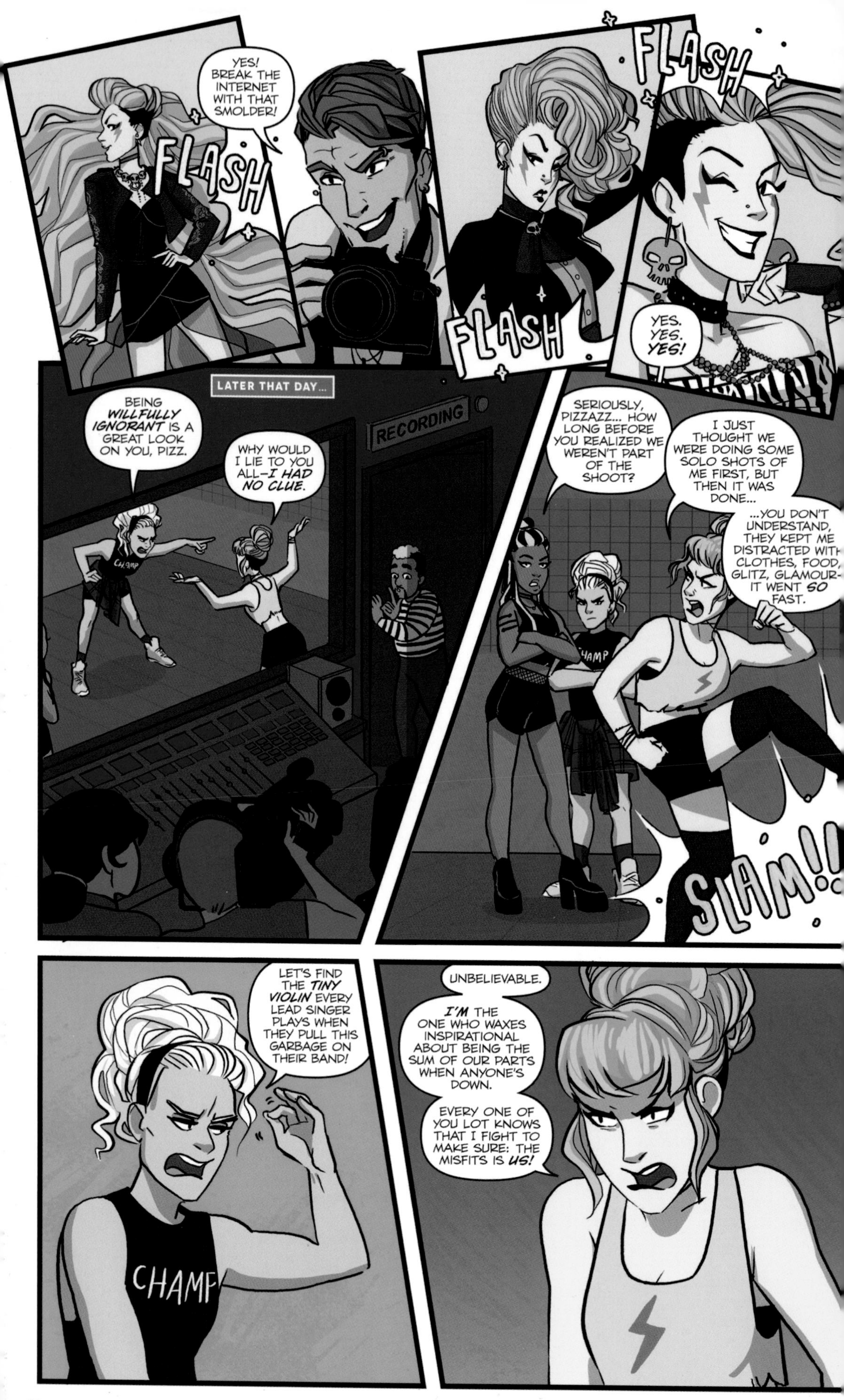
YES! BREAK THE INTERNET WITH THAT SMOLDER!
FLASH
FLASH
FLASH
YES. YES. YES!
LATER THAT DAY...
BEING WILLFULLY IGNORANT IS A GREAT LOOK ON YOU, PIZZ.
WHY WOULD I LIE TO YOU ALL—I HAD NO CLUE.
RECORDING
CHAMP
SERIOUSLY, PIZZAZZ... HOW LONG BEFORE YOU REALIZED WE WEREN'T PART OF THE SHOOT?
I JUST THOUGHT WE WERE DOING SOME SOLO SHOTS OF ME FIRST, BUT THEN IT WAS DONE...
...YOU DON'T UNDERSTAND, THEY KEPT ME DISTRACTED WITH CLOTHES, FOOD, GLITZ, GLAMOUR- IT WENT SO FAST.
SLAM!!
LET'S FIND THE TINY VIOLIN EVERY LEAD SINGER PLAYS WHEN THEY PULL THIS GARBAGE ON THEIR BAND!
CHAMP
UNBELIEVABLE.
I'M THE ONE WHO WAXES INSPIRATIONAL ABOUT BEING THE SUM OF OUR PARTS WHEN ANYONE'S DOWN.
EVERY ONE OF YOU LOT KNOWS THAT I FIGHT TO MAKE SURE: THE MISFITS IS US!

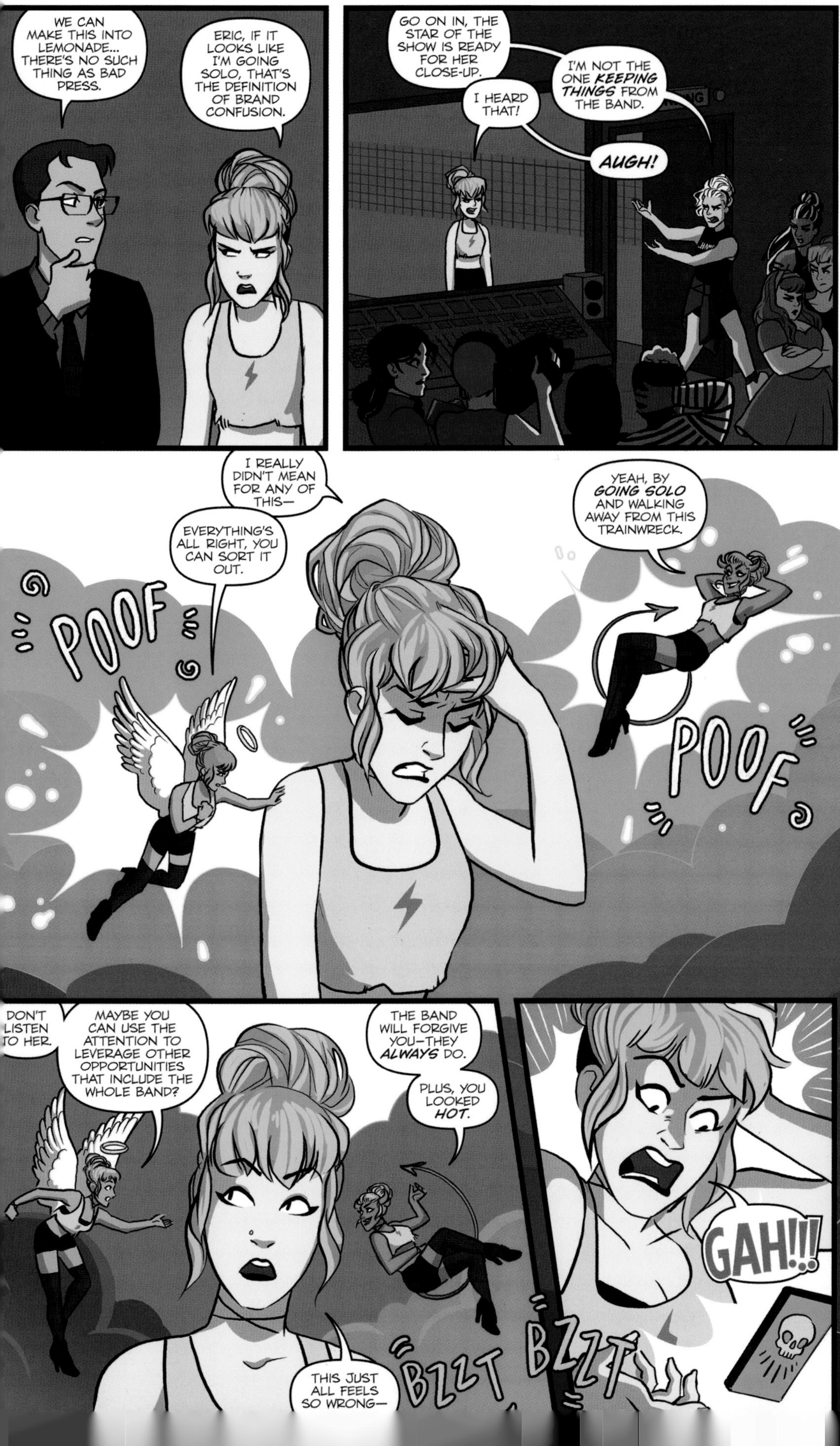
WE CAN MAKE THIS INTO LEMONADE... THERE'S NO SUCH THING AS BAD PRESS.
ERIC, IF IT LOOKS LIKE I'M GOING SOLO, THAT'S THE DEFINITION OF BRAND CONFUSION.
GO ON IN, THE STAR OF THE SHOW IS READY FOR HER CLOSE-UP.
I'M NOT THE ONE KEEPING THINGS FROM THE BAND.
I HEARD THAT!
AUGH!
I REALLY DIDN'T MEAN FOR ANY OF THIS—
EVERYTHING'S ALL RIGHT, YOU CAN SORT IT OUT.
POOF
YEAH, BY GOING SOLO AND WALKING AWAY FROM THIS TRAINWRECK.
POOF
DON'T LISTEN TO HER.
MAYBE YOU CAN USE THE ATTENTION TO LEVERAGE OTHER OPPORTUNITIES THAT INCLUDE THE WHOLE BAND?
THE BAND WILL FORGIVE YOU—THEY ALWAYS DO.
PLUS, YOU LOOKED HOT.
THIS JUST ALL FEELS SO WRONG—
BZZT BZZT
GAH!!!

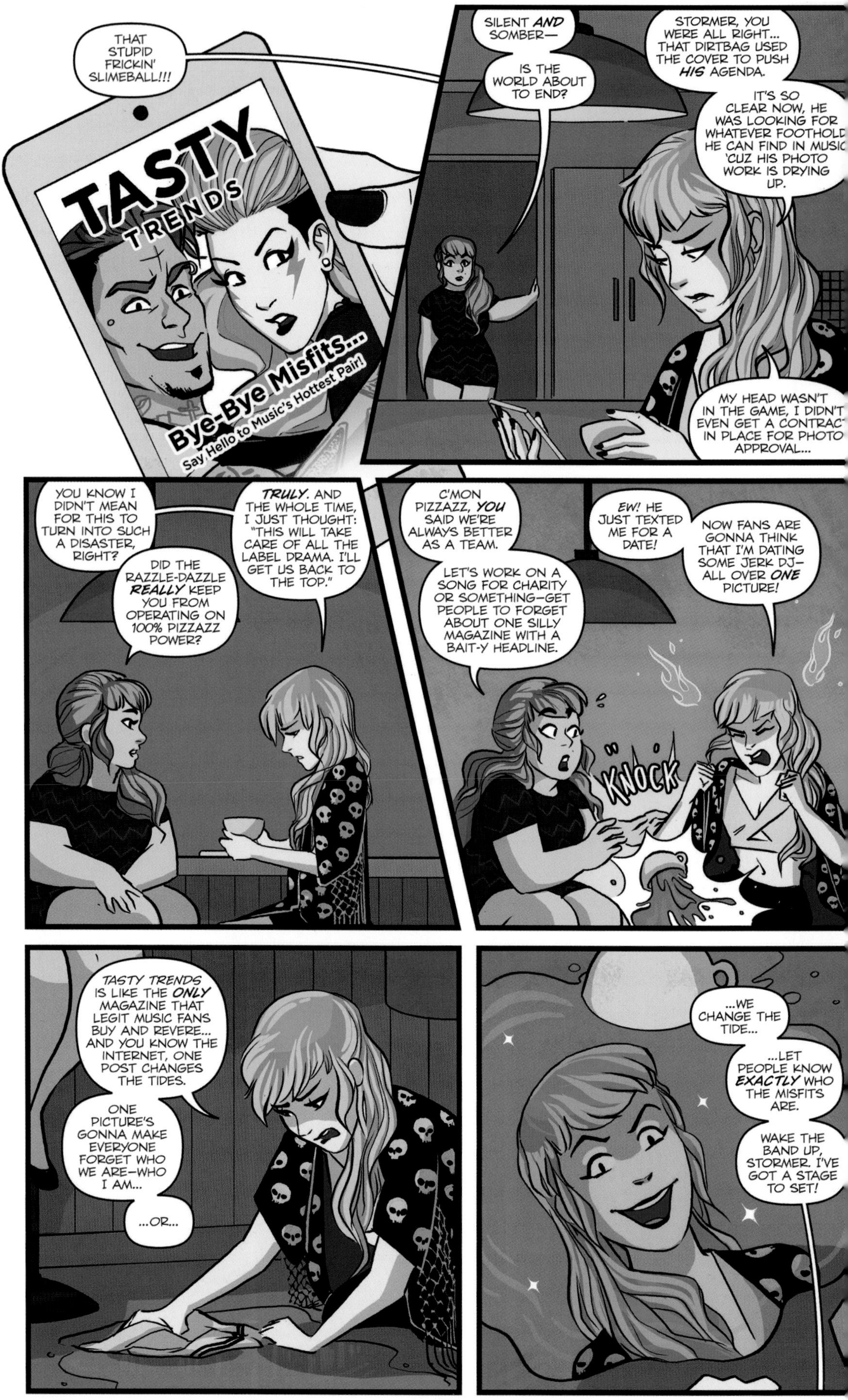
THAT STUPID FRICKIN' SLIMEBALL!!!
TASTY TRENDS
Bye-Bye Misfits...
Say Hello to Music's Hottest Pair!
SILENT AND SOMBER—
IS THE WORLD ABOUT TO END?
STORMER, YOU WERE ALL RIGHT... THAT DIRTBAG USED THE COVER TO PUSH HIS AGENDA.
IT'S SO CLEAR NOW, HE WAS LOOKING FOR WHATEVER FOOTHOLD HE CAN FIND IN MUSIC 'CUZ HIS PHOTO WORK IS DRYING UP.
MY HEAD WASN'T IN THE GAME, I DIDN'T EVEN GET A CONTRACT IN PLACE FOR PHOTO APPROVAL...
YOU KNOW I DIDN'T MEAN FOR THIS TO TURN INTO SUCH A DISASTER, RIGHT?
TRULY. AND THE WHOLE TIME, I JUST THOUGHT: "THIS WILL TAKE CARE OF ALL THE LABEL DRAMA. I'LL GET US BACK TO THE TOP."
DID THE RAZZLE-DAZZLE REALLY KEEP YOU FROM OPERATING ON 100% PIZZAZZ POWER?
C'MON PIZZAZZ, YOU SAID WE'RE ALWAYS BETTER AS A TEAM.
LET'S WORK ON A SONG FOR CHARITY OR SOMETHING—GET PEOPLE TO FORGET ABOUT ONE SILLY MAGAZINE WITH A BAIT-Y HEADLINE.
EW! HE JUST TEXTED ME FOR A DATE!
NOW FANS ARE GONNA THINK THAT I'M DATING SOME JERK DJ—ALL OVER ONE PICTURE!
KNOCK
TASTY TRENDS IS LIKE THE ONLY MAGAZINE THAT LEGIT MUSIC FANS BUY AND REVERE... AND YOU KNOW THE INTERNET, ONE POST CHANGES THE TIDES.
ONE PICTURE'S GONNA MAKE EVERYONE FORGET WHO WE ARE—WHO I AM...
...OR...
...WE CHANGE THE TIDE...
...LET PEOPLE KNOW EXACTLY WHO THE MISFITS ARE.
WAKE THE BAND UP, STORMER. I'VE GOT A STAGE TO SET!

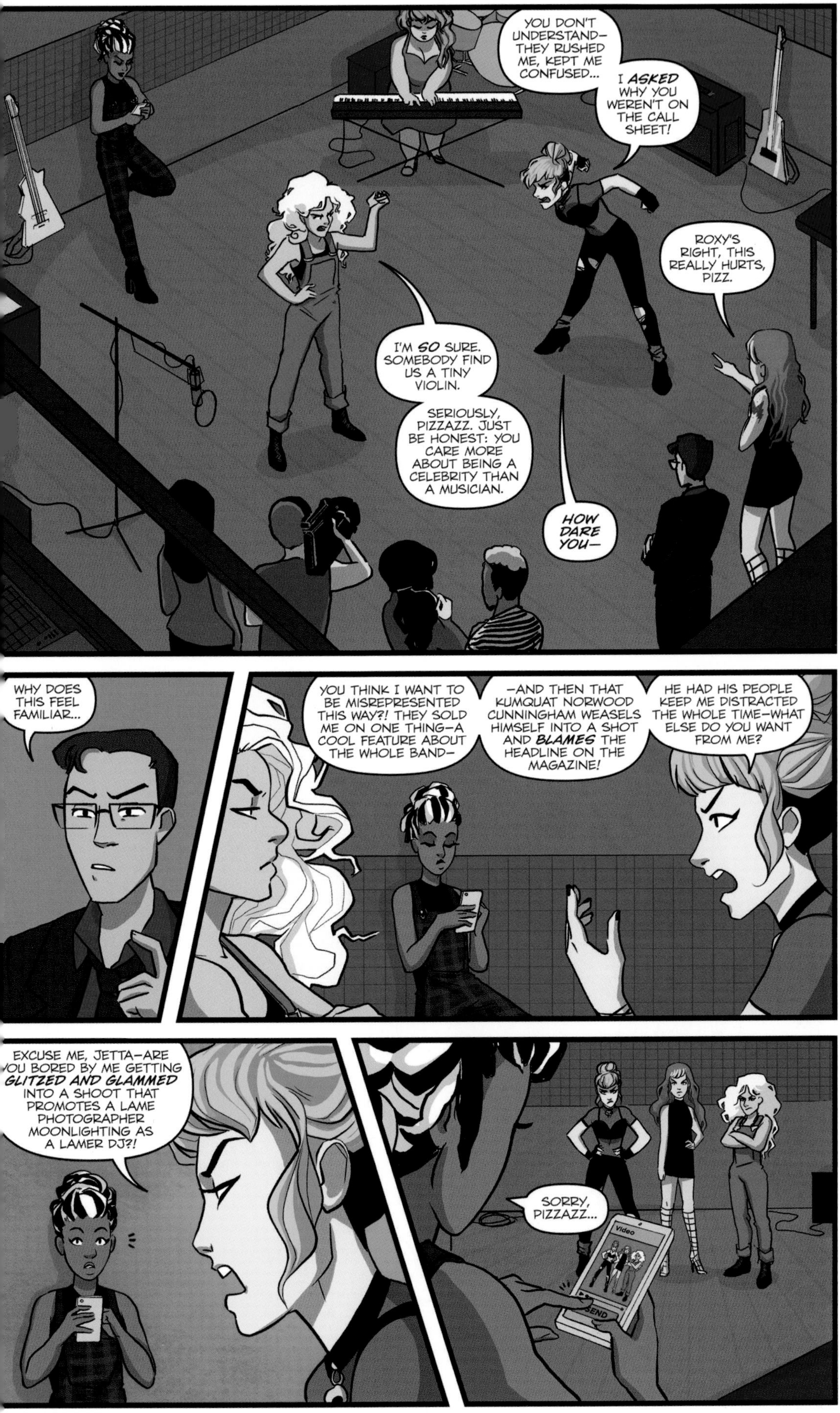
YOU DON'T UNDERSTAND—THEY RUSHED ME, KEPT ME CONFUSED...
I ASKED WHY YOU WEREN'T ON THE CALL SHEET!
ROXY'S RIGHT, THIS REALLY HURTS, PIZZ.
I'M SO SURE. SOMEBODY FIND US A TINY VIOLIN.
SERIOUSLY, PIZZAZZ. JUST BE HONEST: YOU CARE MORE ABOUT BEING A CELEBRITY THAN A MUSICIAN.
HOW DARE YOU—
WHY DOES THIS FEEL FAMILIAR...
YOU THINK I WANT TO BE MISREPRESENTED THIS WAY?! THEY SOLD ME ON ONE THING—A COOL FEATURE ABOUT THE WHOLE BAND—
—AND THEN THAT KUMQUAT NORWOOD CUNNINGHAM WEASELS HIMSELF INTO A SHOT AND BLAMES THE HEADLINE ON THE MAGAZINE!
HE HAD HIS PEOPLE KEEP ME DISTRACTED THE WHOLE TIME—WHAT ELSE DO YOU WANT FROM ME?
EXCUSE ME, JETTA—ARE YOU BORED BY ME GETTING GLITZED AND GLAMMED INTO A SHOOT THAT PROMOTES A LAME PHOTOGRAPHER MOONLIGHTING AS A LAMER DJ?!
SORRY, PIZZAZZ...
Video
SEND

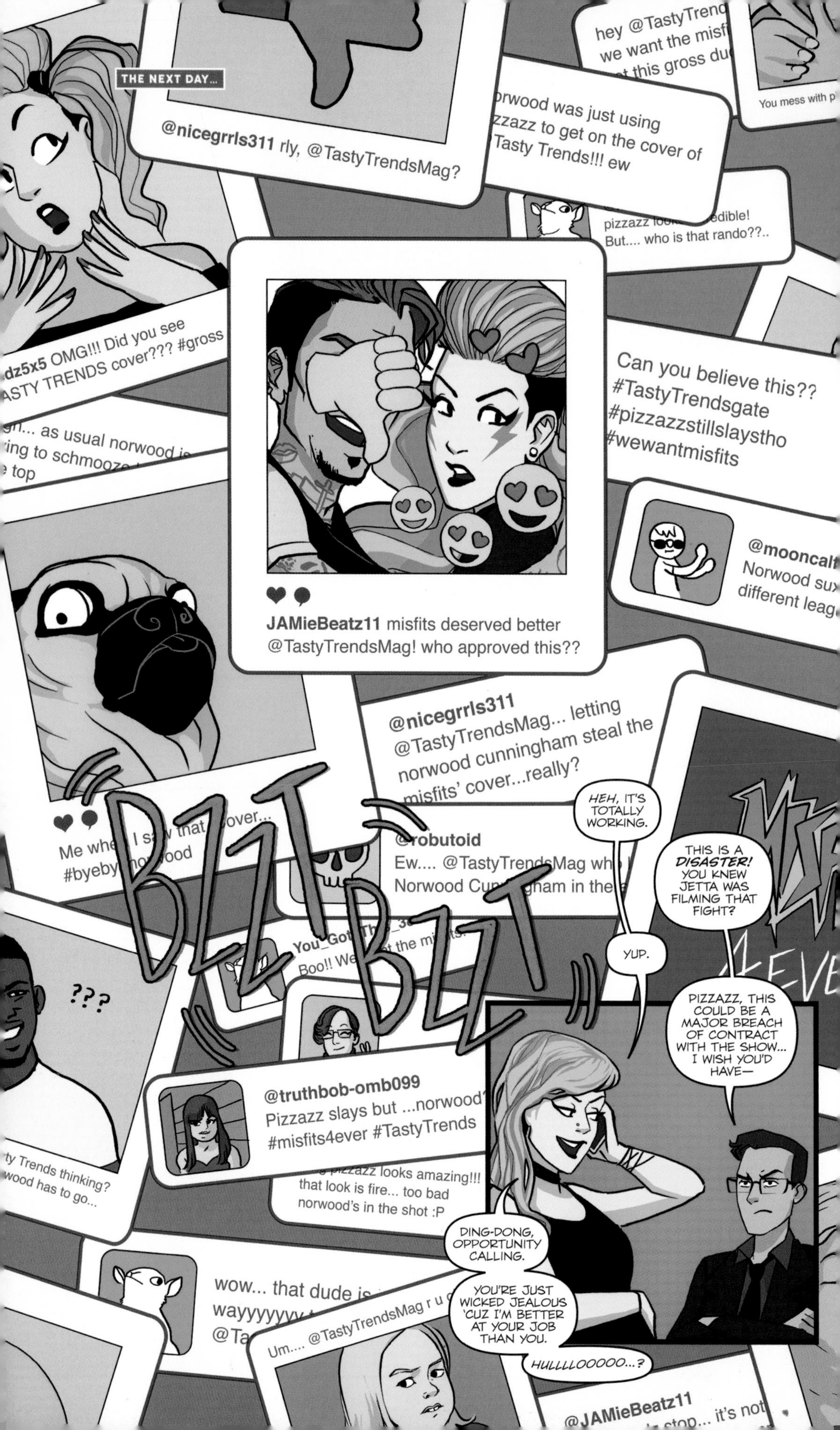
THE NEXT DAY...
@nicegrrls311 rly, @TastyTrendsMag?
hey @TastyTrend
we want the misf
this gross du
orwood was just using
zzazz to get on the cover of
Tasty Trends!!! ew
You mess with p
pizzazz looks incredible!
But.... who is that rando??..
dz5x5 OMG!!! Did you see
ASTY TRENDS cover??? #gross
... as usual norwood is
ing to schmooze
top
JAMieBeatz11 misfits deserved better
@TastyTrendsMag! who approved this??
Can you believe this??
#TastyTrendsgate
#pizzazzstillslaystho
#wewantmisfits
@mooncal
Norwood su
different leag
@nicegrrls311
@TastyTrendsMag... letting
@TastyTrendsMag... letting norwood cunningham steal the
misfits' cover...really?
Me whe I saw that cover...
#byeby norwood
@robutoid
Ew.... @TastyTrendsMag wh
Norwood Cu gham in the
BZZT BZZT
You_Got
Boo!! We the misfits.
???
HEH, IT'S TOTALLY WORKING.
THIS IS A DISASTER! YOU KNEW JETTA WAS FILMING THAT FIGHT?
YUP.
PIZZAZZ, THIS COULD BE A MAJOR BREACH OF CONTRACT WITH THE SHOW... I WISH YOU'D HAVE—
4EVE
@truthbob-omb099
Pizzazz slays but ...norwood?
#misfits4ever #TastyTrends
ty Trends thinking?
wood has to go...
pizzazz looks amazing!!!
that look is fire... too bad
norwood's in the shot :P
DING-DONG, OPPORTUNITY CALLING.
YOU'RE JUST WICKED JEALOUS 'CUZ I'M BETTER AT YOUR JOB THAN YOU.
HULLLLOOOOO...?
wow... that dude is
wayyyyyyy
@Ta
Um.... @TastyTrendsMag r u
@JAMieBeatz11
stop... it's not

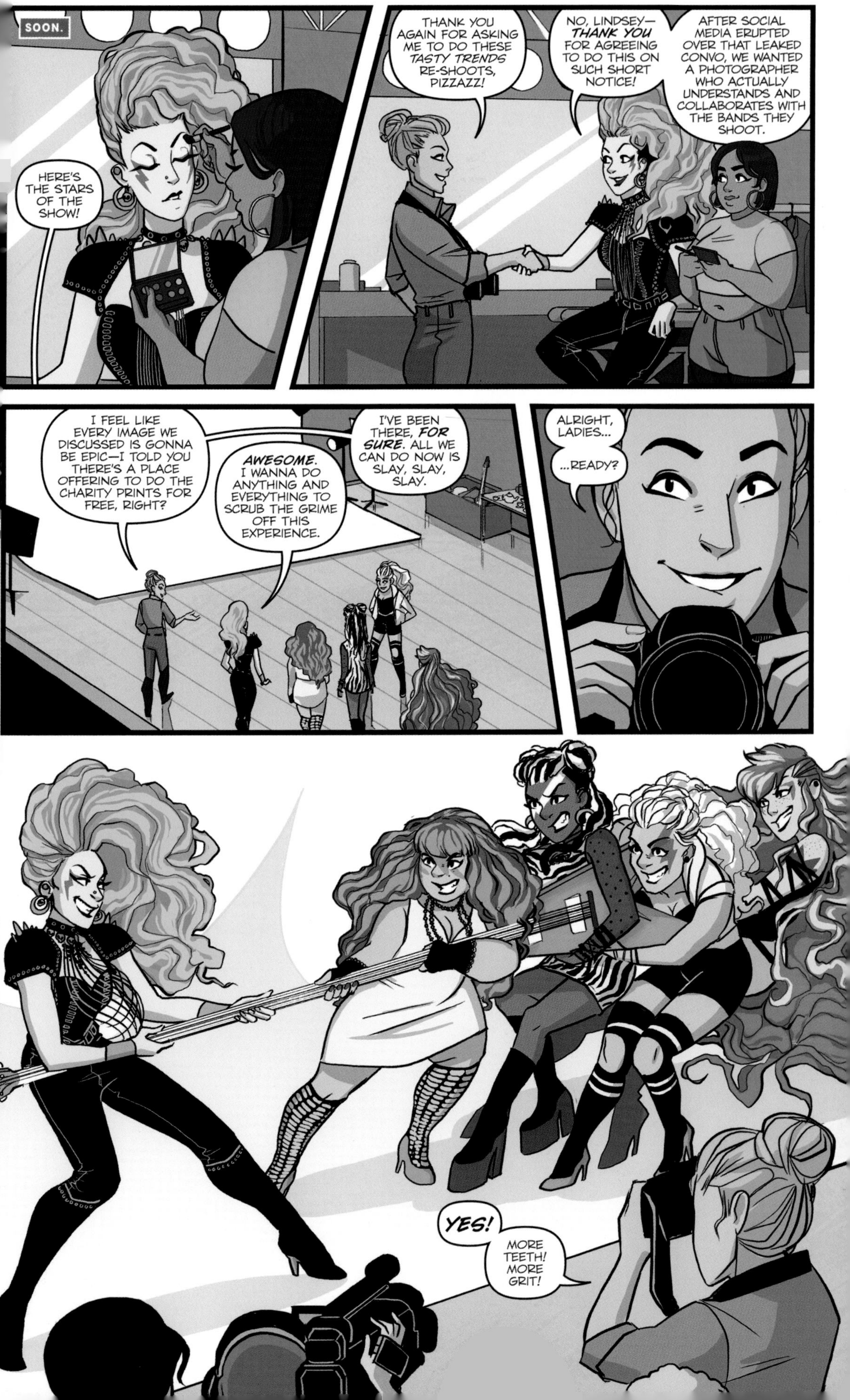
SOON.
HERE'S THE STARS OF THE SHOW!
THANK YOU AGAIN FOR ASKING ME TO DO THESE TASTY TRENDS RE-SHOOTS, PIZZAZZ!
NO, LINDSEY— THANK YOU FOR AGREEING TO DO THIS ON SUCH SHORT NOTICE!
AFTER SOCIAL MEDIA ERUPTED OVER THAT LEAKED CONVO, WE WANTED A PHOTOGRAPHER WHO ACTUALLY UNDERSTANDS AND COLLABORATES WITH THE BANDS THEY SHOOT.
I FEEL LIKE EVERY IMAGE WE DISCUSSED IS GONNA BE EPIC—I TOLD YOU THERE'S A PLACE OFFERING TO DO THE CHARITY PRINTS FOR FREE, RIGHT?
AWESOME. I WANNA DO ANYTHING AND EVERYTHING TO SCRUB THE GRIME OFF THIS EXPERIENCE.
I'VE BEEN THERE, FOR SURE. ALL WE CAN DO NOW IS SLAY, SLAY, SLAY.
ALRIGHT, LADIES...
...READY?
YES!
MORE TEETH! MORE GRIT!

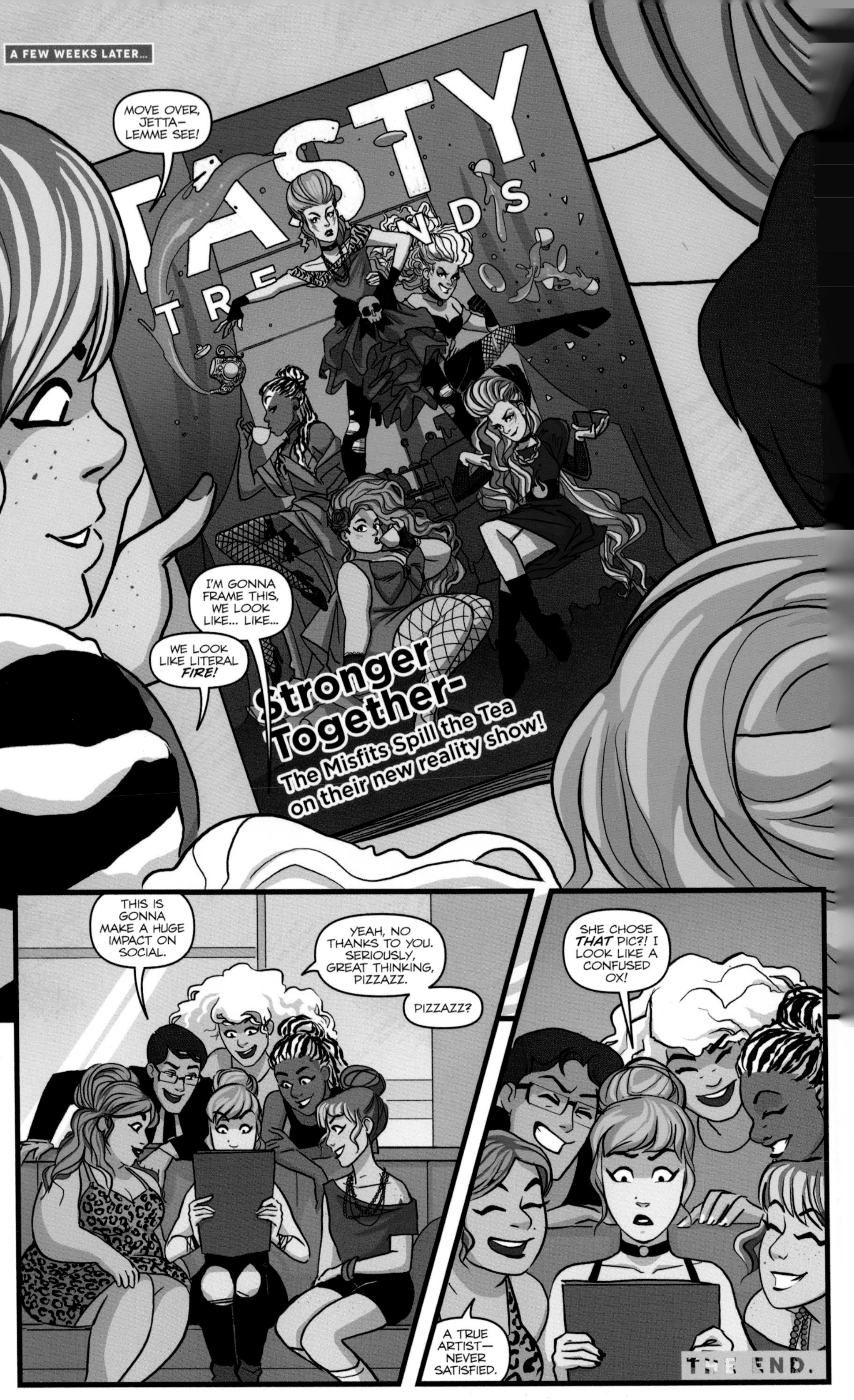

A FEW WEEKS LATER...
MOVE OVER, JETTA— LEMME SEE!
TASTY TRENDS
I'M GONNA FRAME THIS, WE LOOK LIKE... LIKE...
WE LOOK LIKE LITERAL *FIRE!*
Stronger Together-
The Misfits Spill the Tea on their new reality show!
THIS IS GONNA MAKE A HUGE IMPACT ON SOCIAL.
YEAH, NO THANKS TO YOU. SERIOUSLY, GREAT THINKING, PIZZAZZ.
PIZZAZZ?
SHE CHOSE *THAT* PIC?! I LOOK LIKE A CONFUSED OX!
A TRUE ARTIST— NEVER SATISFIED.
THE END.

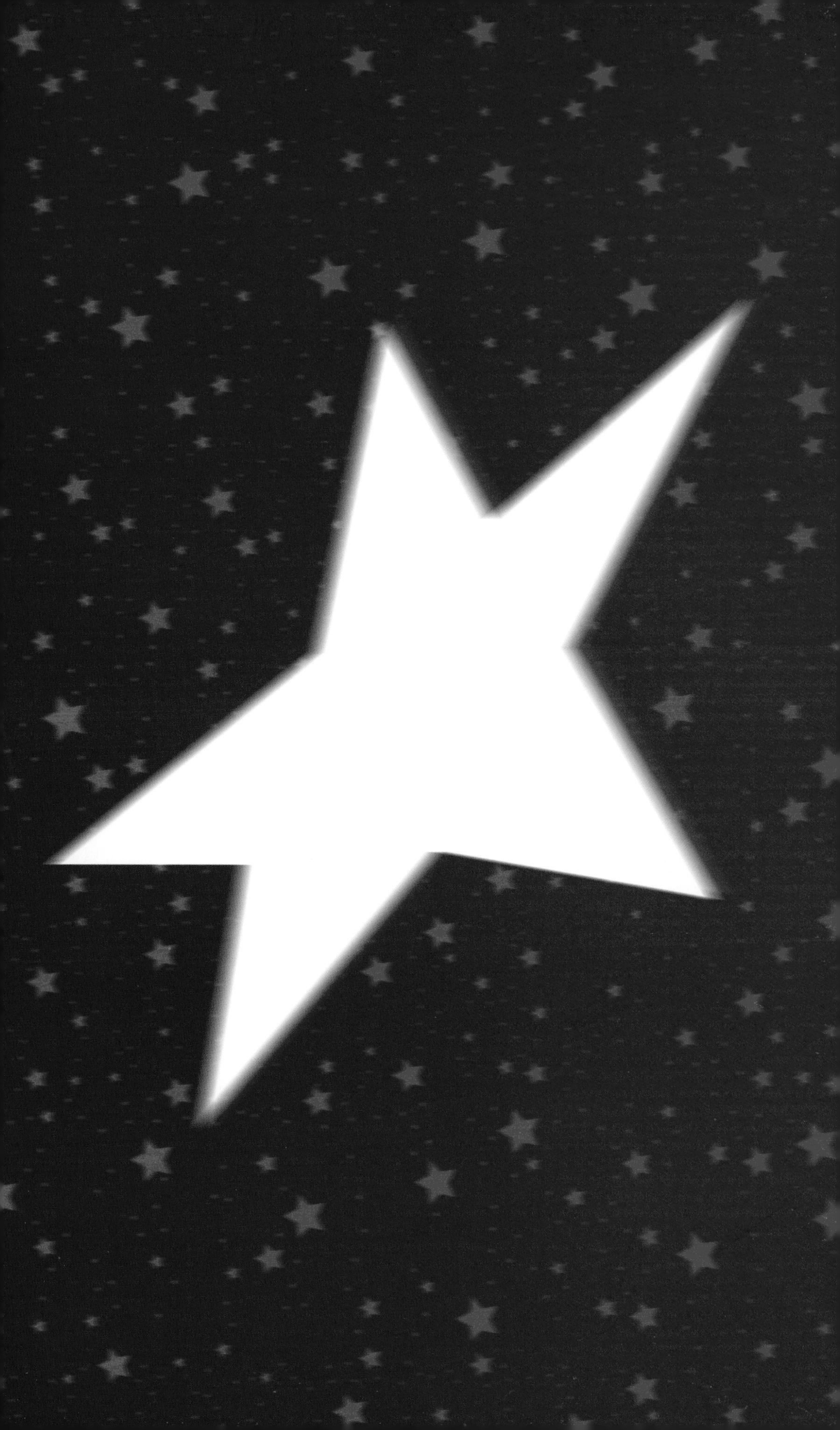

ART BY **ABBY BOEH**

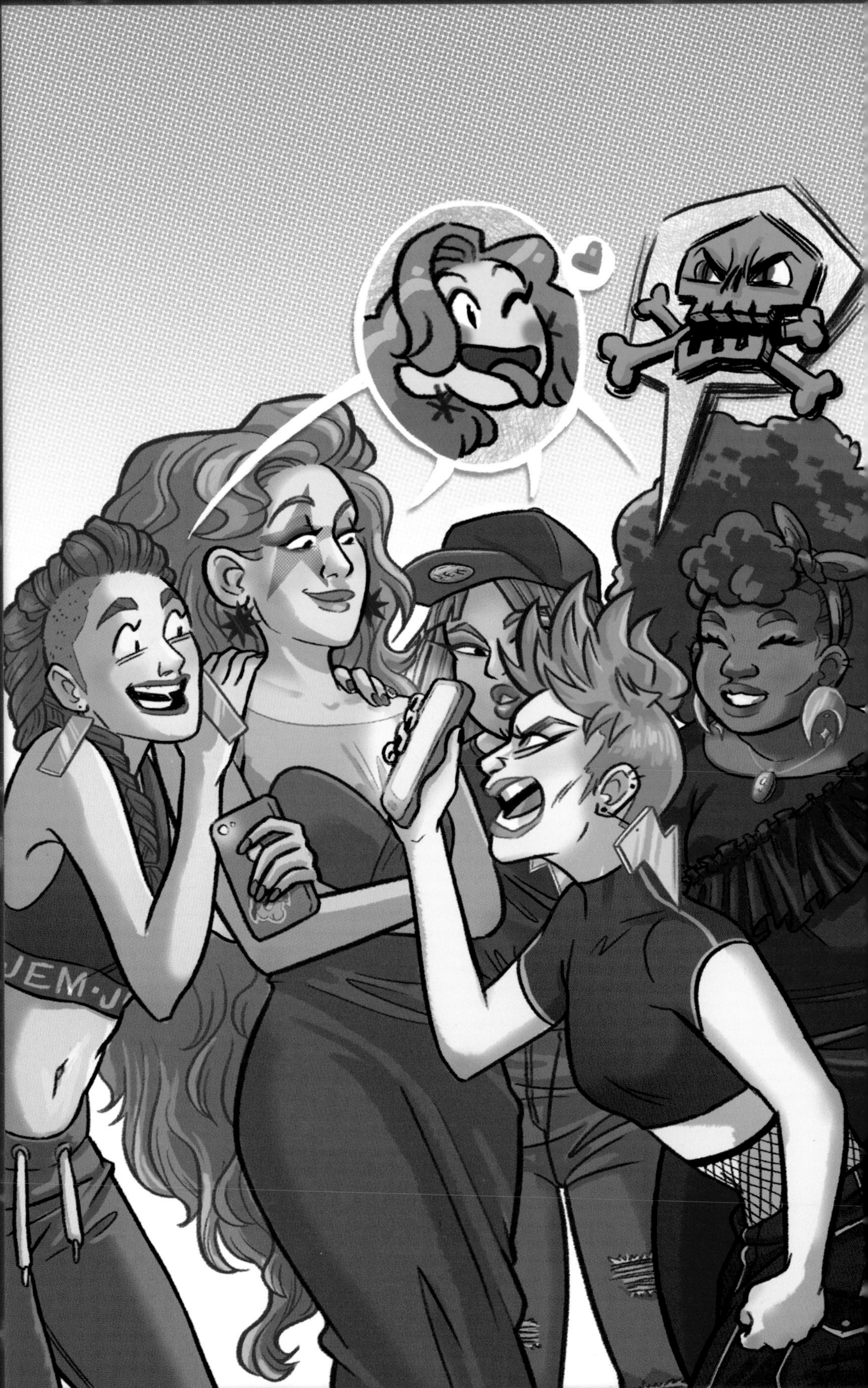
JEM·J

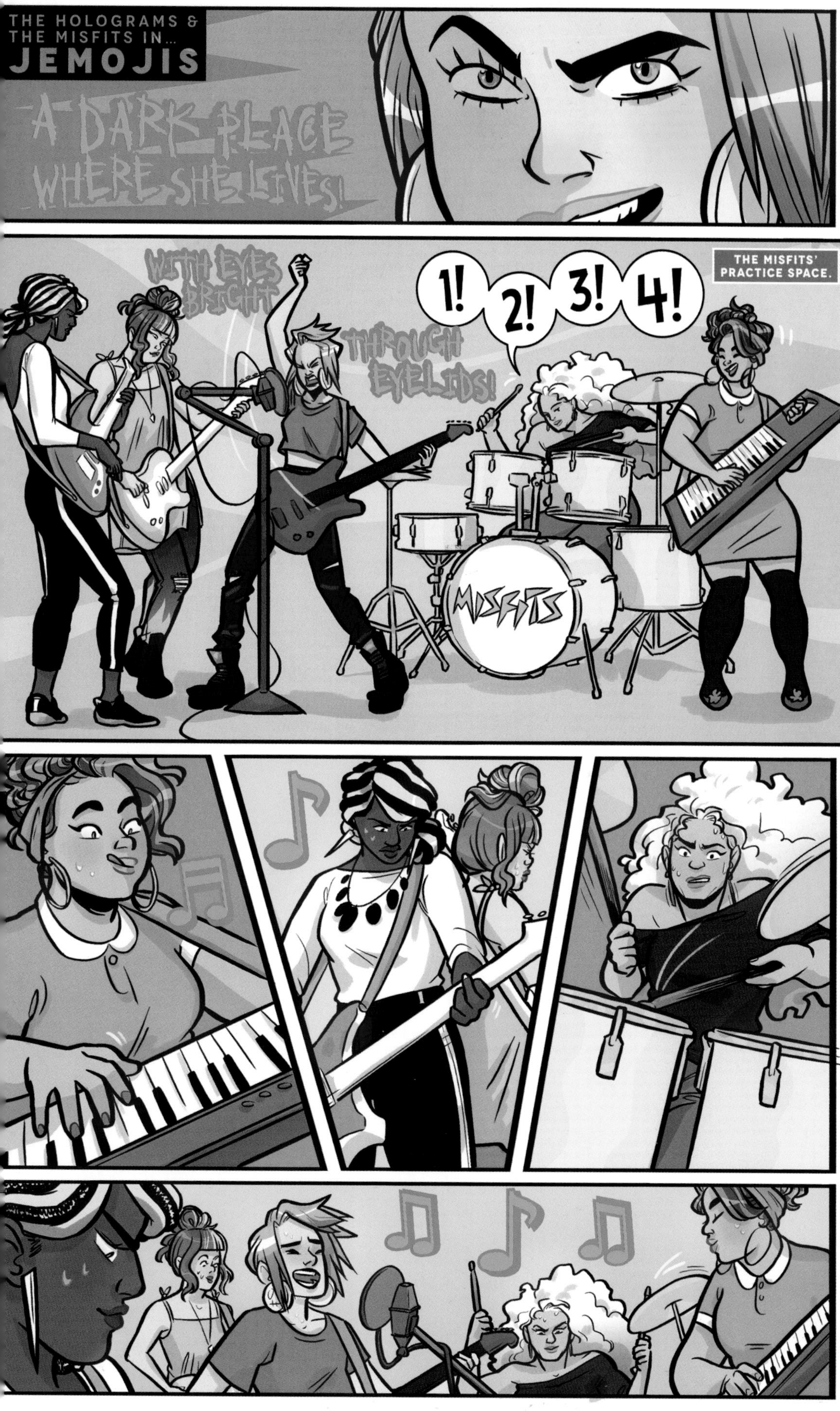
THE HOLOGRAMS & THE MISFITS IN…
JEMOJIS
A DARK PLACE WHERE SHE LIVES!
WITH EYES BRIGHT
THROUGH EYELIDS!
THE MISFITS' PRACTICE SPACE.
1! 2! 3! 4!
MISFITS

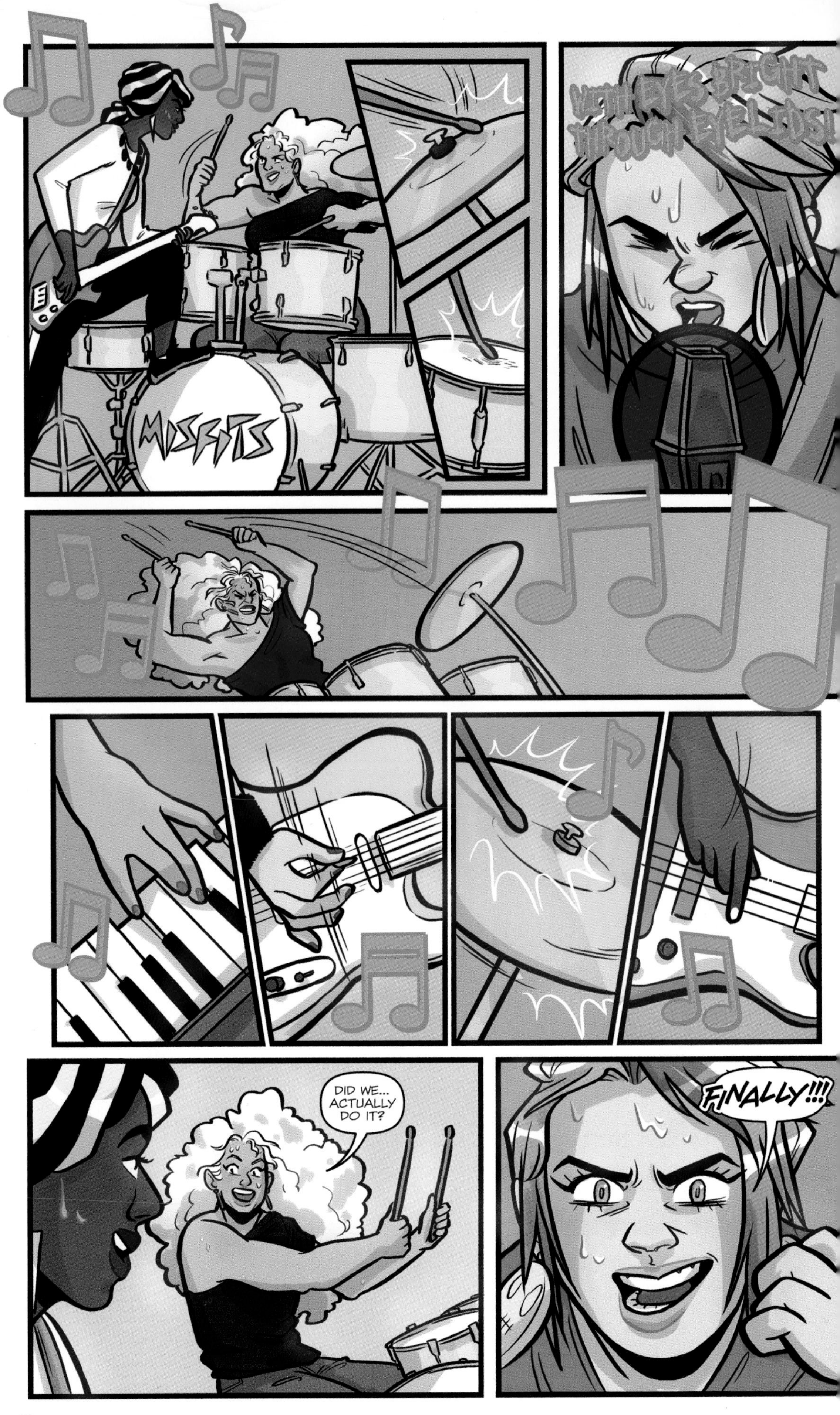
MISFITS
WITH EYES BRIGHT THROUGH EYELIDS!
DID WE... ACTUALLY DO IT?
FINALLY!!!

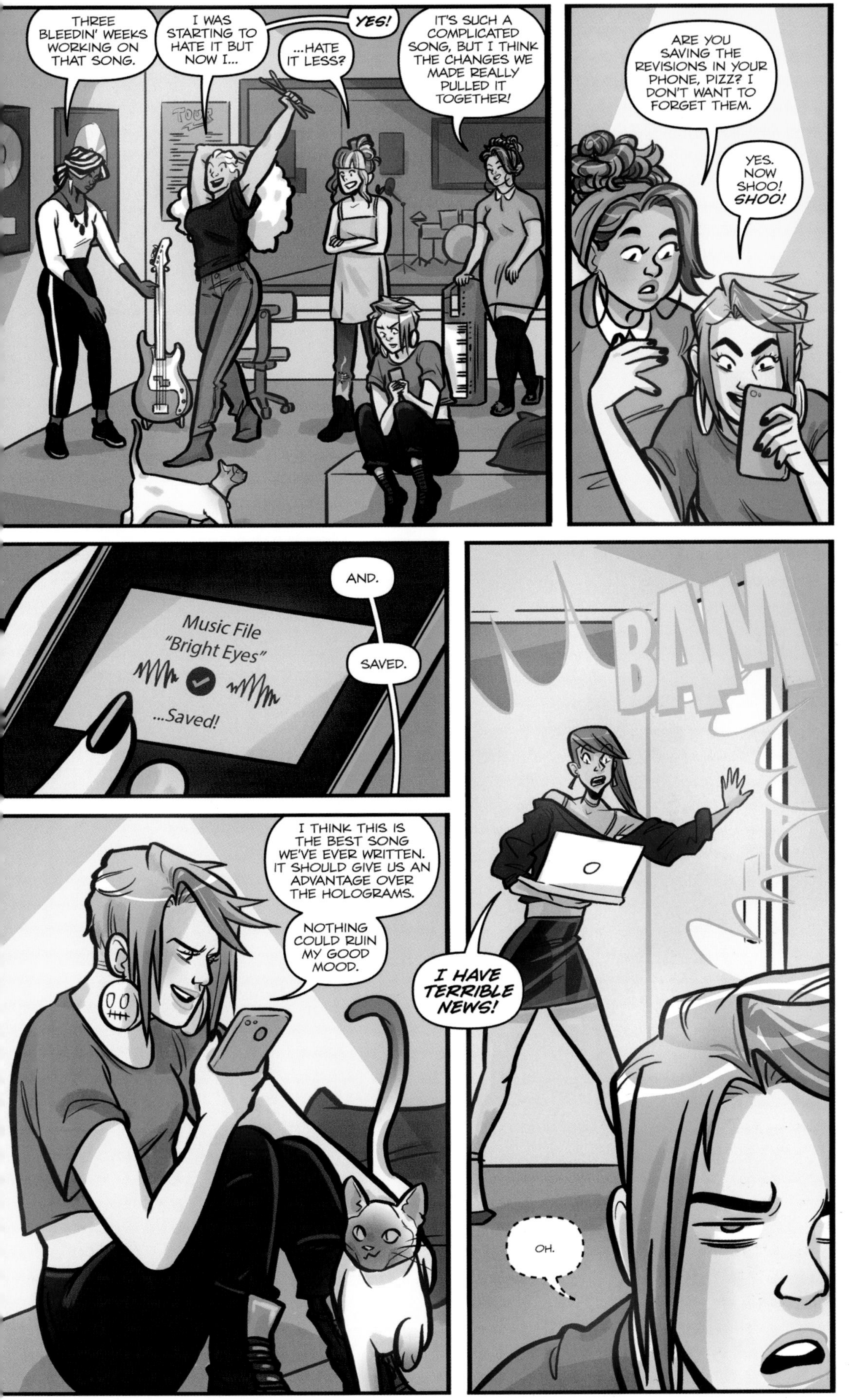
THREE BLEEDIN' WEEKS WORKING ON THAT SONG.
I WAS STARTING TO HATE IT BUT NOW I...
YES!
...HATE IT LESS?
IT'S SUCH A COMPLICATED SONG, BUT I THINK THE CHANGES WE MADE REALLY PULLED IT TOGETHER!
TOUR
ARE YOU SAVING THE REVISIONS IN YOUR PHONE, PIZZ? I DON'T WANT TO FORGET THEM.
YES. NOW SHOO! SHOO!
Music File
"Bright Eyes"
...Saved!
AND.
SAVED.
I THINK THIS IS THE BEST SONG WE'VE EVER WRITTEN. IT SHOULD GIVE US AN ADVANTAGE OVER THE HOLOGRAMS.
NOTHING COULD RUIN MY GOOD MOOD.
BAM
I HAVE TERRIBLE NEWS!
OH.

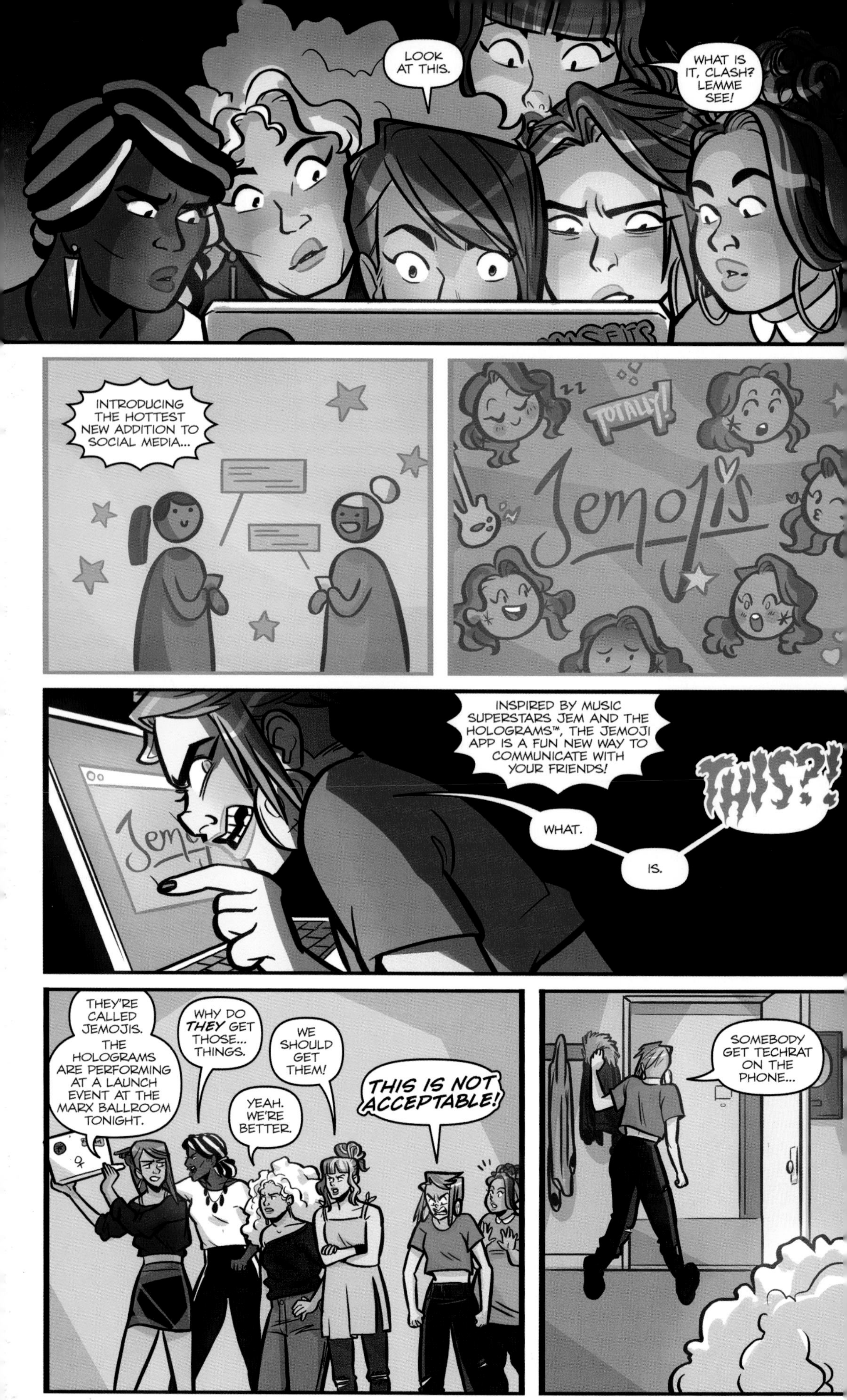
LOOK AT THIS.
WHAT IS IT, CLASH? LEMME SEE!
INTRODUCING THE HOTTEST NEW ADDITION TO SOCIAL MEDIA...
TOTALLY!
Jemojis
INSPIRED BY MUSIC SUPERSTARS JEM AND THE HOLOGRAMS™, THE JEMOJI APP IS A FUN NEW WAY TO COMMUNICATE WITH YOUR FRIENDS!
WHAT.
IS.
THIS?!
THEY'RE CALLED JEMOJIS. THE HOLOGRAMS ARE PERFORMING AT A LAUNCH EVENT AT THE MARX BALLROOM TONIGHT.
WHY DO *THEY* GET THOSE... THINGS.
YEAH. WE'RE BETTER.
WE SHOULD GET THEM!
THIS IS NOT ACCEPTABLE!
SOMEBODY GET TECHRAT ON THE PHONE...

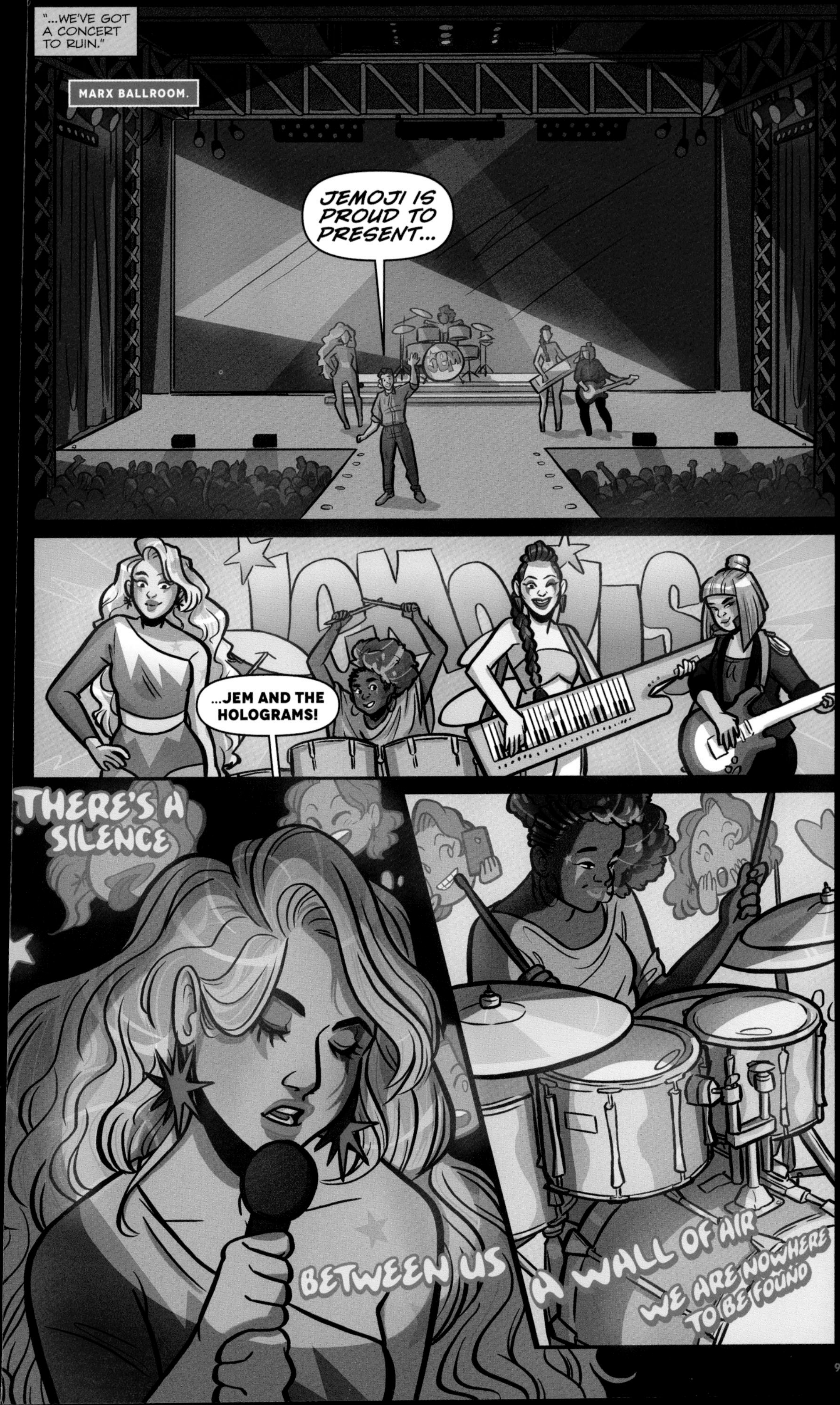

"...WE'VE GOT A CONCERT TO RUIN."
MARX BALLROOM.
JEMOJI IS PROUD TO PRESENT...
...JEM AND THE HOLOGRAMS!
THERE'S A SILENCE
BETWEEN US
A WALL OF AIR
WE ARE NOWHERE TO BE FOUND

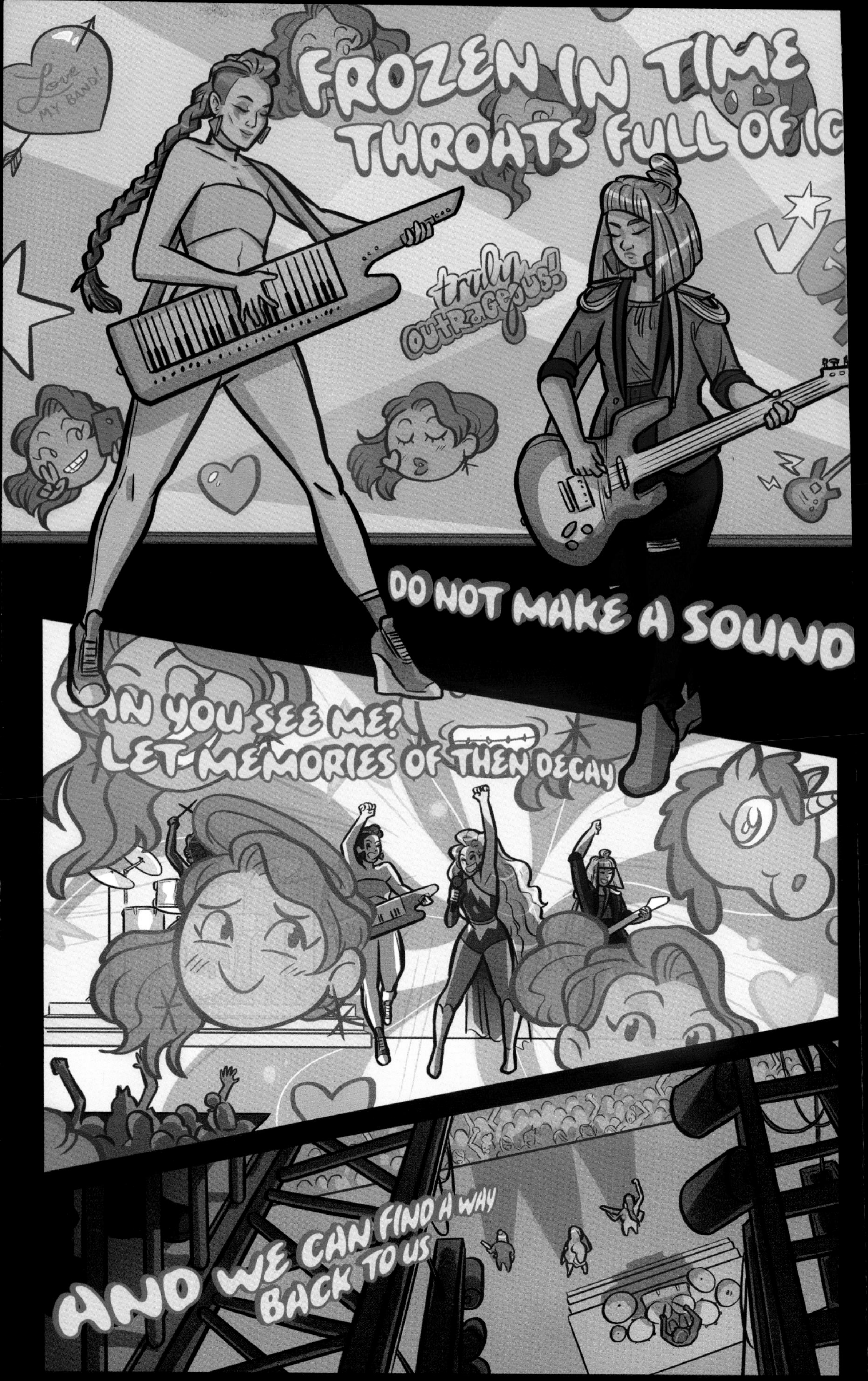

FROZEN IN TIME
THROATS FULL OF IC
Love MY BAND!
truly outrageous!
DO NOT MAKE A SOUND
AN YOU SEE ME?
LET MEMORIES OF THEN DECAY
AND WE CAN FIND A WAY
BACK TO US

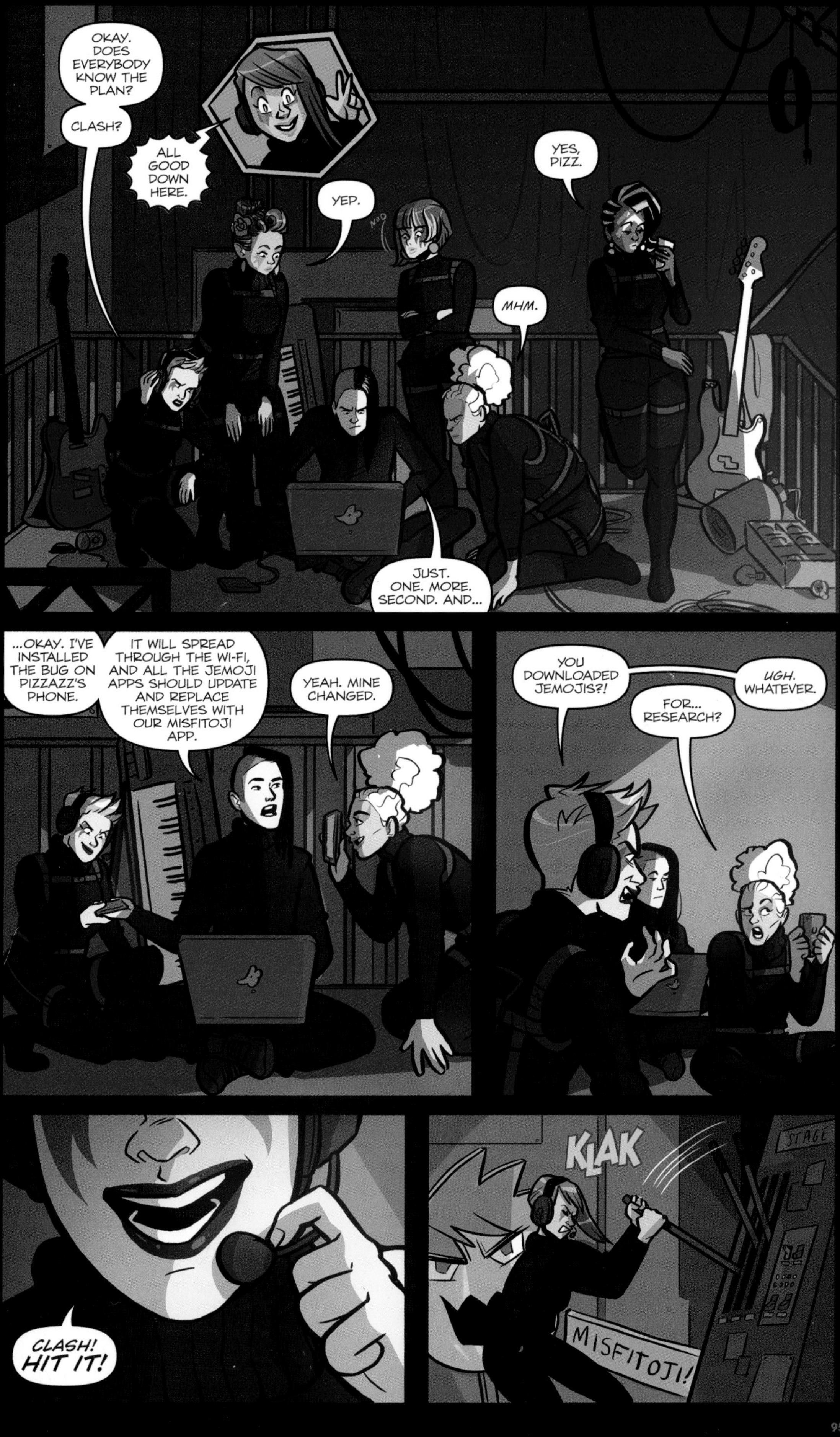
OKAY. DOES EVERYBODY KNOW THE PLAN?
CLASH?
ALL GOOD DOWN HERE.
YEP.
YES, PIZZ.
NOD
MHM.
JUST. ONE. MORE. SECOND. AND...
...OKAY. I'VE INSTALLED THE BUG ON PIZZAZZ'S PHONE.
IT WILL SPREAD THROUGH THE WI-FI, AND ALL THE JEMOJI APPS SHOULD UPDATE AND REPLACE THEMSELVES WITH OUR MISFITOJI APP.
YEAH. MINE CHANGED.
YOU DOWNLOADED JEMOJIS?!
UGH. WHATEVER.
FOR... RESEARCH?
CLASH! HIT IT!
KLAK
STAGE
MISFITOJI!

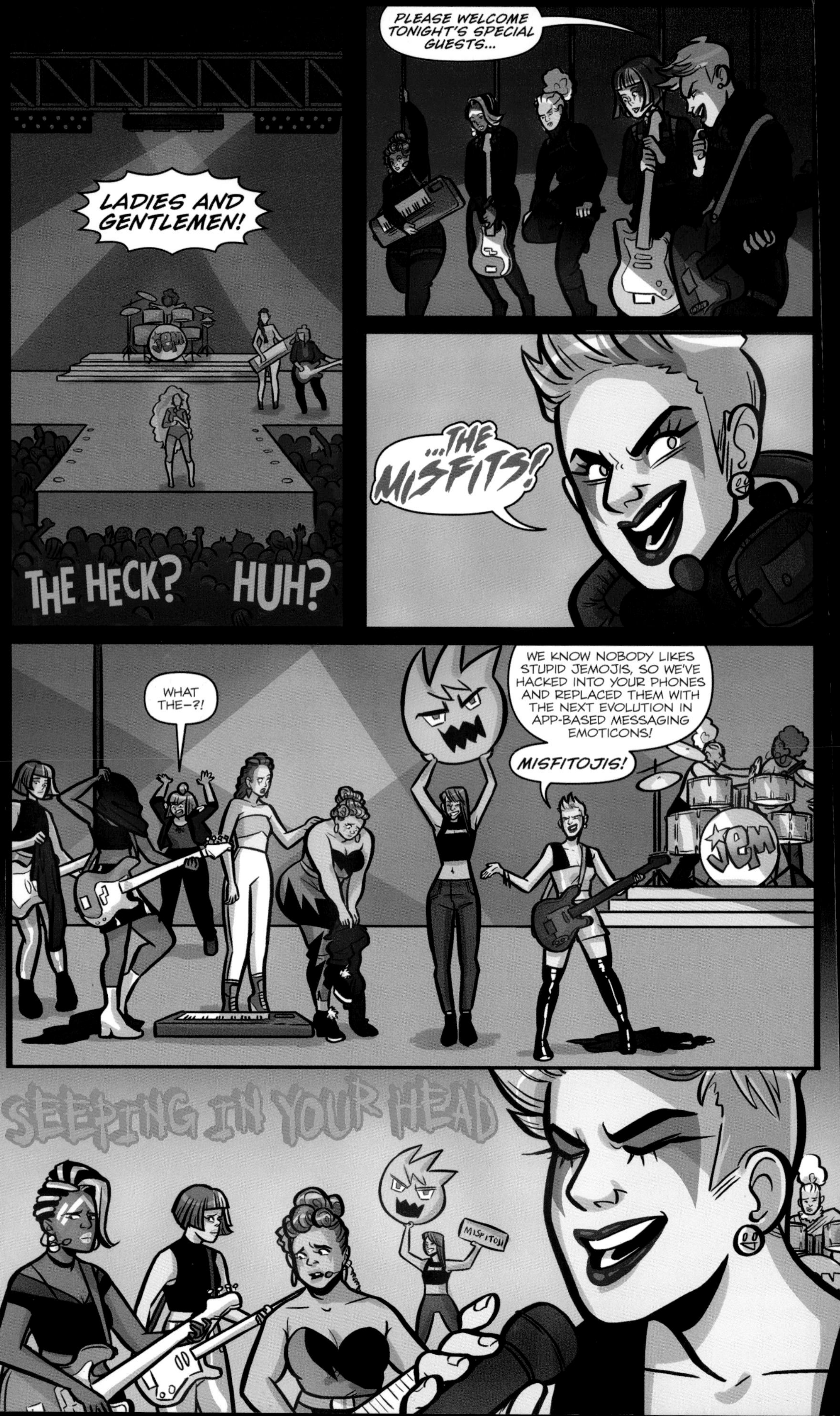
LADIES AND GENTLEMEN!
THE HECK?
HUH?
PLEASE WELCOME TONIGHT'S SPECIAL GUESTS...
...THE MISFITS!
WHAT THE--?!
WE KNOW NOBODY LIKES STUPID JEMOJIS, SO WE'VE HACKED INTO YOUR PHONES AND REPLACED THEM WITH THE NEXT EVOLUTION IN APP-BASED MESSAGING EMOTICONS!
MISFITOJIS!
SEEPING IN YOUR HEAD
MISFITOJI

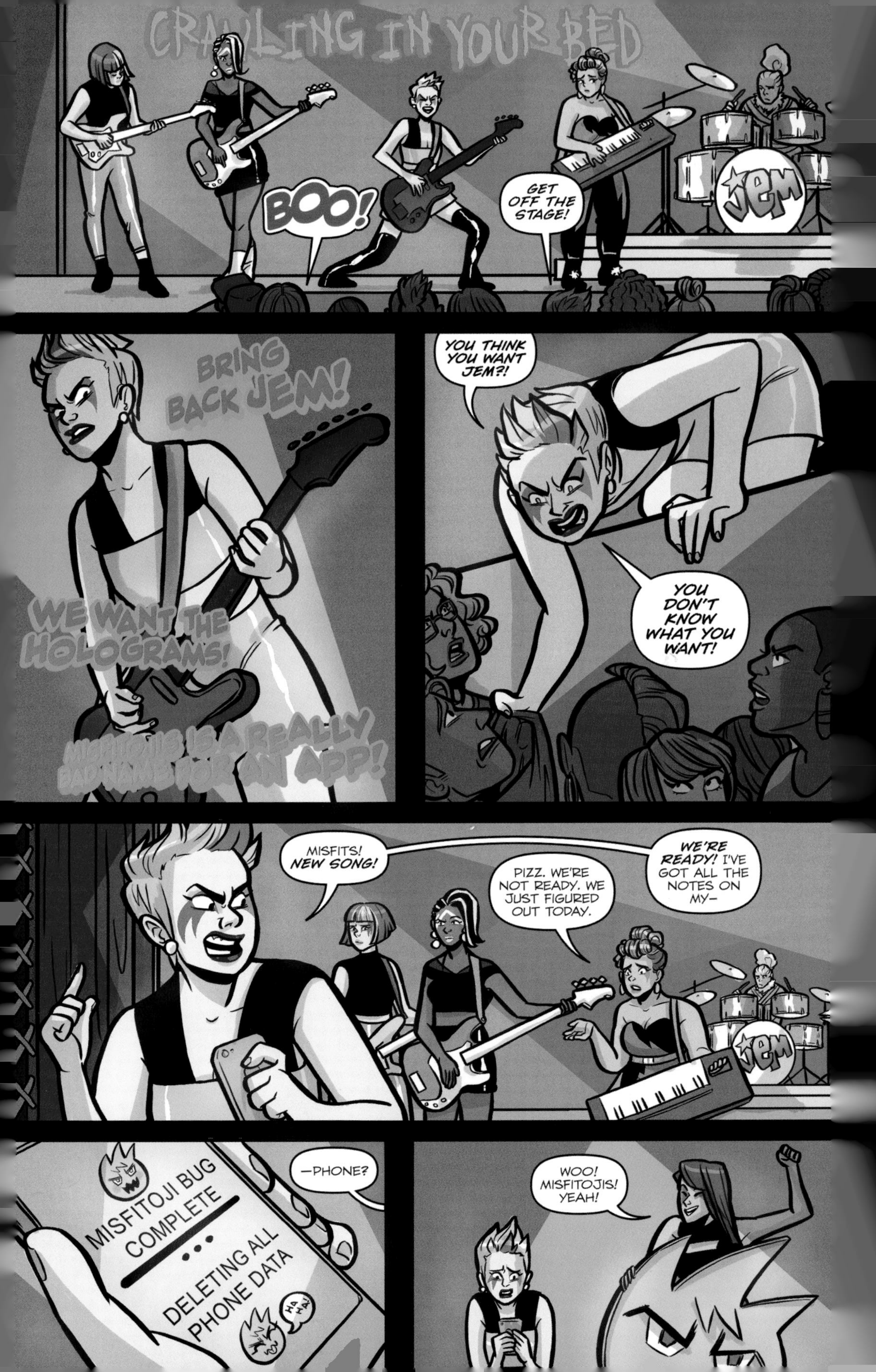
CRAWLING IN YOUR BED
BOO!
GET OFF THE STAGE!
BRING BACK JEM!
WE WANT THE HOLOGRAMS!
MISFITOJIS IS A REALLY BAD NAME FOR AN APP!
YOU THINK YOU WANT JEM?!
YOU DON'T KNOW WHAT YOU WANT!
MISFITS! NEW SONG!
PIZZ. WE'RE NOT READY. WE JUST FIGURED OUT TODAY.
WE'RE READY! I'VE GOT ALL THE NOTES ON MY—
—PHONE?
MISFITOJI BUG COMPLETE
DELETING ALL PHONE DATA
HA HA!
WOO! MISFITOJIS! YEAH!

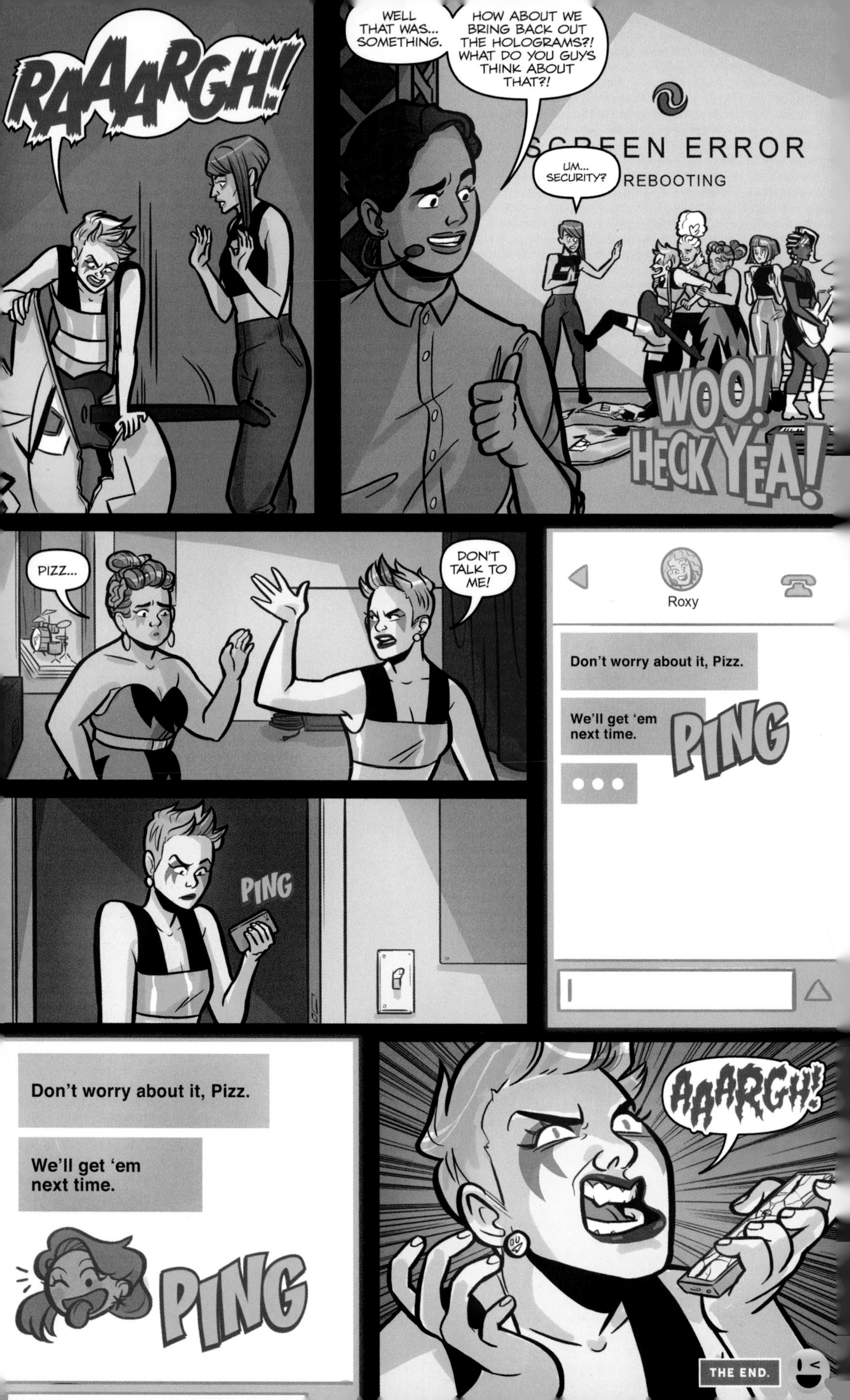
RAAARGH!!
WELL THAT WAS... SOMETHING.
HOW ABOUT WE BRING BACK OUT THE HOLOGRAMS?! WHAT DO YOU GUYS THINK ABOUT THAT?!
SCREEN ERROR
REBOOTING
UM... SECURITY?
WOO! HECK YEA!
PIZZ...
DON'T TALK TO ME!
Roxy
Don't worry about it, Pizz.
We'll get 'em next time.
PING
PING
Don't worry about it, Pizz.
We'll get 'em next time.
PING
AAARGH!
THE END.

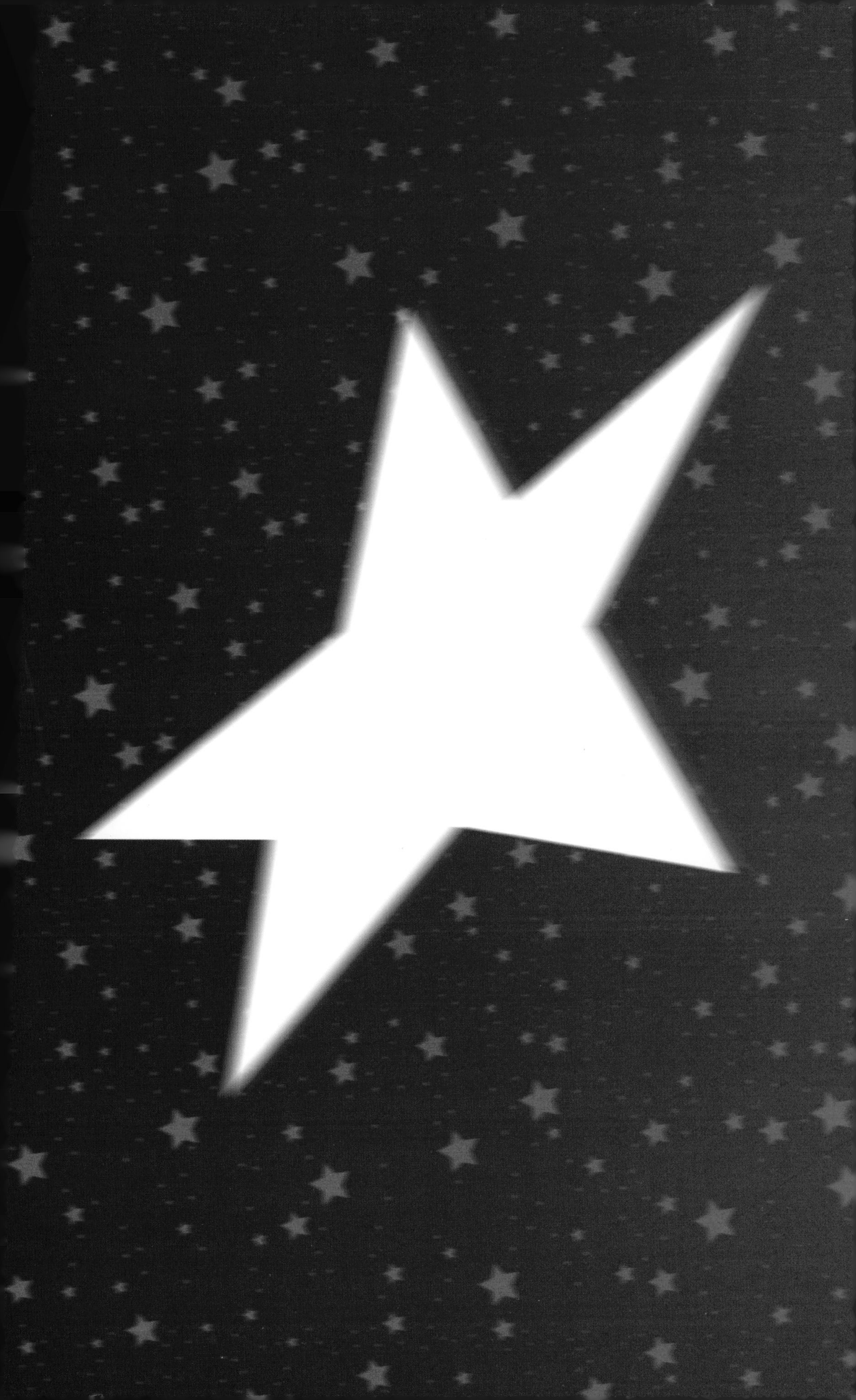

ART BY **DEREK CHARM**

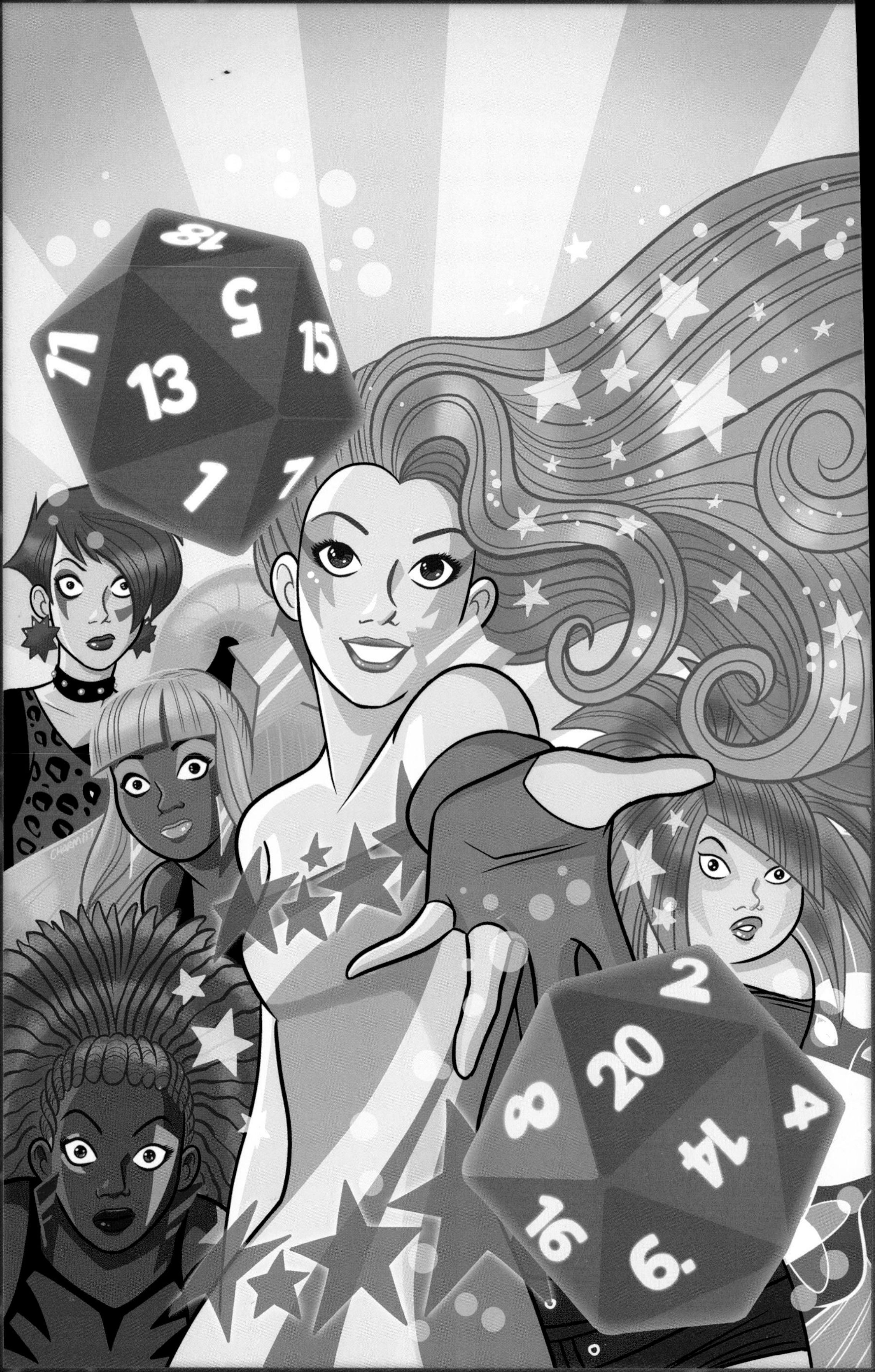

ART BY **M. VICTORIA ROBADO**

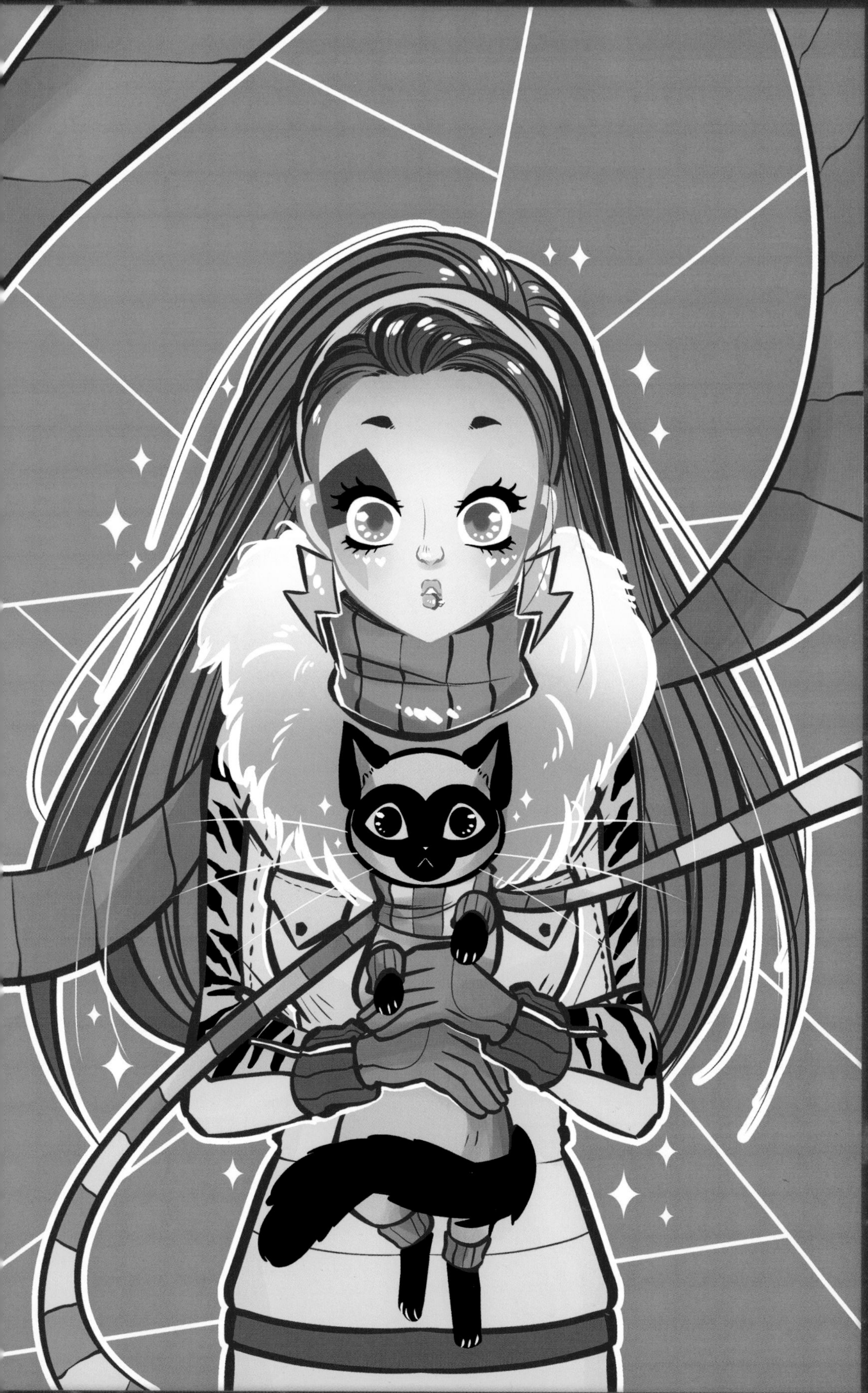

ART BY **KEEZY YOUNG**

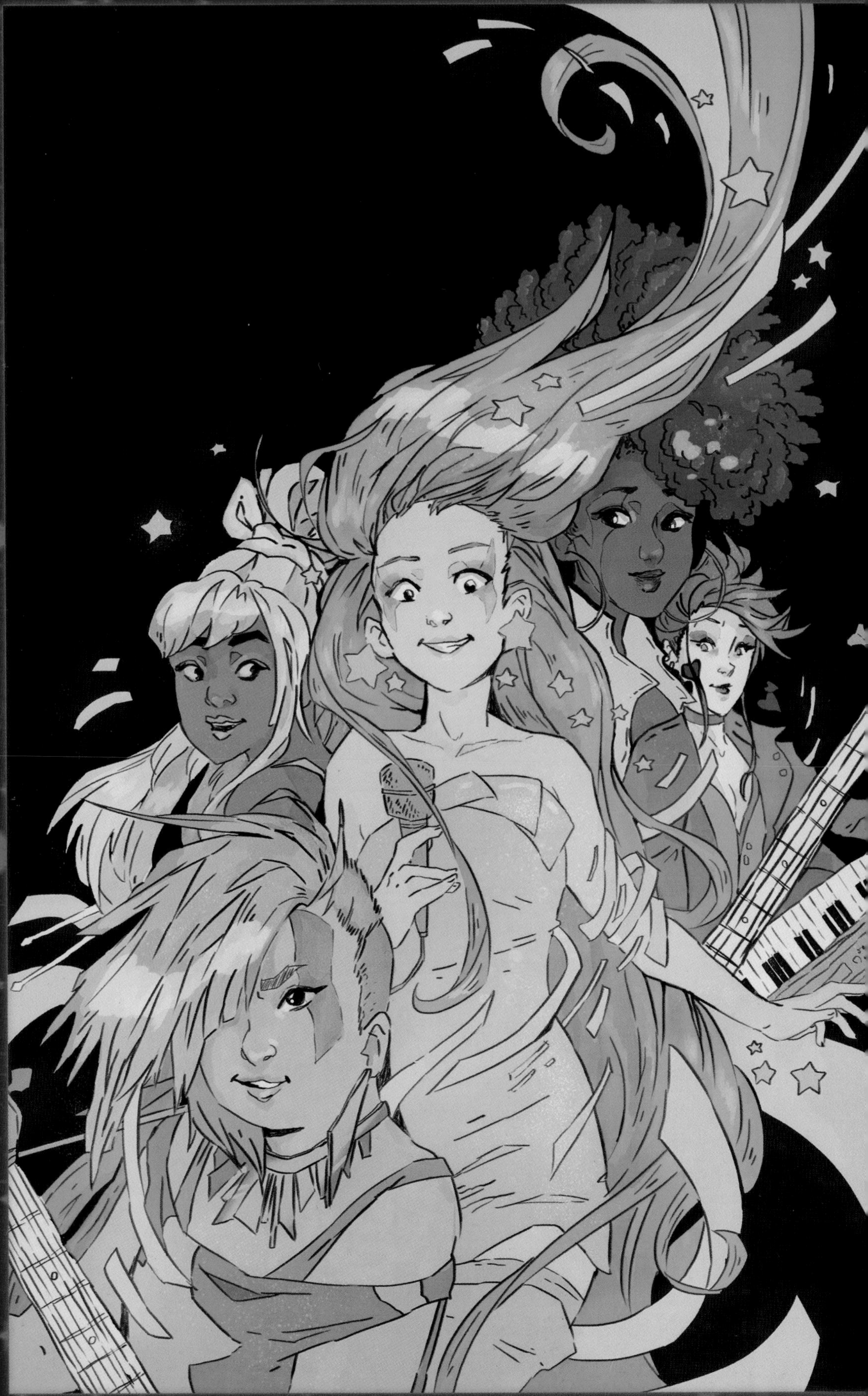